MW01174072

UNITEL   _...KATES YEARBOOK 1999

Editors: Ibrahim Al Abed, Paula Vine
Special contributor: Peter Hellyer

Text copyright ©2000: Trident Press

Photographs ©: Trident Press Ltd
                Gulf News
                Emirates News Agency
                Ministry of Information and Culture
(also see photographer acknowledgements in appendix)

English edition typesetting: Johan Hofsteenge
Cover design: Trident Press

Enquiries may be addressed to:
Ministry of Information and Culture
PO Box 17, Abu Dhabi, UAE.
Tel: (9712) 453000; Fax (9712) 450458
E-mail: mininfex@emirates.net.ae
Web site: www.uaeinteract.com

Published by Trident Press Ltd
175 Piccadilly, Mayfair, London WIV 9DB,
Tel: 0171 491 8770; Fax: 0171 491 8664
E-mail: admin@tridentpress.ie
Web site: www.tridentpress.com

British Library Cataloguing in Publication Data
A CIP catalogue record for this book is available
from the British Library.

ISBN 1-900724-29-4

CONTENTS

FOREWORD

The period under review has been one of continued progress and consolidation in the United Arab Emirates. With most of the major infrastructural developments complete and the process of economic diversification also well under way, the UAE Government has been focusing on how best to ensure that its people are well equipped to face the challenges of a changing world while retaining the values of their heritage. Education plays a key role in this process and there has been significant further development of educational facilities in the UAE, involving federal, regional and private investments. As we move forward, it remains important that our young people should identify with their roots and the Government supports and welcomes the increasing number of interpretative and interactive projects that address this need.

While the UAE continues to offer a high standard of living, the dreadful suffering of people in other countries has been a major concern. The issues at stake are primarily humanitarian ones and much of our focus has been on relieving the plight of victims of both natural and manmade disasters. It is an unfortunate reflection on our times that places such as Kosovo, Iraq and Palestine have become household words, not for their positive attributes, but for the suffering of their populations.

The UAE has always fought against injustice and has sought to alleviate civilian suffering by practical measures. As the pages of this book report, its activities on these fronts during the last 12 months have dominated its foreign policy and its forces continue to play an active role as part of the UN-led peacekeeping force in war-torn Kosovo.

We are witnessing a real revolution and a fast pace of change in both technological and intellectual fields, which will eventually shape the future of humanity. A deep insight into this transformation is an indispensable step towards keeping pace with it. The media plays an increasingly central role this process. Improvements in local and regional broadcasting networks, widespread use of the Internet, together with a surge in foreign travel by UAE residents, have all helped to build a well-informed population that is discerning in its choice of what to read, listen to, or watch. This places a great challenge and responsibility on the media itself, to deliver accurate information presented with integrity and quality as its watchwords. This is a field in which we can play a leading role in the years ahead.

Abdullah bin Zayed Al Nahyan
Minister of Information and Culture

SHEIKH ZAYED PROFILE

On 6 August 1999, His Highness Sheikh Zayed bin Sultan Al Nahyan completed 33 years as Ruler of the Emirate of Abu Dhabi, one of the seven emirates that together comprise the Federation of the United Arab Emirates (UAE), of which he has also been President since its creation in December 1971.

Having first served in government in 1946 as Ruler's Representative in Abu Dhabi's Eastern Region based in the inland oasis of Al Ain, Sheikh Zayed has now provided leadership to the country for well over half a century.

Born around 1918 (the date is uncertain), Sheikh Zayed is the youngest of the four sons of Sheikh Sultan bin Zayed, Ruler of Abu Dhabi from 1922 to 1926. He was named after his grandfather, Sheikh Zayed bin Khalifa, who ruled the emirate from 1855 to 1909, the longest reign in the three centuries since the Al Nahyan family emerged as leaders of the Emirate of Abu Dhabi.

Abu Dhabi, like the other emirates of the southern Arabian Gulf known as the Trucial States, was then in treaty relations with Britain. At the time Sheikh Zayed was born the emirate was poor and undeveloped, with an economy based primarily on fishing and pearl diving along the coast and offshore and on simple agriculture in scattered oases inland.

Life, even for a young member of the ruling family, was simple. Education was primarily confined to the provision of instruction in the principles of Islam from the local preacher, while modern facilities such as roads, communications and health care were conspicuous only by their absence. Transport was by camel or by boat, and the harshness of the arid climate meant that survival itself was often a major concern.

In early 1928, following the death of Sheikh Sultan's successor, a family conclave selected as Ruler Sheikh Shakhbut, Sultan's eldest son, a post he was to hold until August 1966 when he stepped down in favour of his brother Zayed.

During the late 1920s and 1930s, as Sheikh Zayed grew to manhood he displayed an early thirst for knowledge that took him out into the desert with the *bedu* tribesmen to learn all he could about the way of life of the people and the environment in which they lived. He recalls with pleasure his experience of desert life and his initiation into the sport of falconry, which has been a lifelong passion.

In his book, *Falconry: Our Arab Heritage*, published in 1977, Sheikh Zayed noted that the companionship of a hunting party:

...permits each and every member of the expedition to speak freely and express his ideas and viewpoints without inhibition and restraint, and allows the one responsible to acquaint himself with the wishes of his people, to know their problems and perceive their views accurately, and thus to be in a position to help and improve their situation.

From his desert journeys, Sheikh Zayed learned to understand the relationship between man and his environment and in particular, the need to ensure that sustainable use was made of natural resources. Once an avid shot, he abandoned the gun for falconry at the age of 25, aware that hunting with a gun could lead rapidly to extinction of the native wildlife.

His travels in the remoter areas of Abu Dhabi provided Sheikh Zayed with a deep understanding both of the country and of its people. In the early 1930s, when the first oil company teams arrived to carry out preliminary surface geological surveys, he was assigned by his brother the task of guiding them around the desert. At the same time he obtained his first exposure to the industry that was later to have such a great effect upon the country.

In 1946, Sheikh Zayed was chosen to fill a vacancy as the Ruler's Representative in the Eastern Region of Abu Dhabi, centred on the oasis of Al Ain, approximately 160 kilometres east of the island of Abu Dhabi itself. Inhabited continuously for at least 5,000 years, the oasis had nine villages, six of which belonged to Abu Dhabi, and three, including Buraimi, by which name the oasis was also known, belonged to the Sultanate of Oman. The job included the task of not only administering the six villages, but the whole of the adjacent desert region, providing Sheikh Zayed with an opportunity to learn the techniques of government. In the late 1940s and early 1950s when Saudi Arabia put forward territorial claims to Buraimi he also gained experience of politics on a broader scale.

Sheikh Zayed brought to his new task a firm belief in the values of consultation and consensus, in contrast to confrontation. Foreign visitors, such as the British explorer Sir Wilfred Thesiger, who first met him at this time, noted with approbation that his judgements 'were distinguished by their astute insights, wisdom and fairness'.

Sheikh Zayed swiftly established himself not only as someone who had a clear vision of what he wished to achieve for the people of Al Ain, but also as someone who led by example.

A key task in the early years in Al Ain was that of stimulating the local economy, which was largely based on agriculture. To do this, he ensured that the subterranean water channels, or *falajes (aflaj)*, were dredged and personally financed the construction of a new one, taking part in the strenuous labour that was involved.

He also ordered a revision of local water ownership rights to ensure a more equitable distribution, surrendering the rights of his own family as an example to others. The consequent expansion of the area under cultivation in turn generated more income for the residents of Al Ain, helping to re-establish the oasis as a predominant economic centre throughout a wide area.

With development gradually beginning to get under way, Sheikh Zayed commenced the laying out of a visionary city plan, and, in a foretaste of the massive afforestation programme of today, he also ordered the planting of ornamental trees that now, grown to maturity, have made Al Ain one of the greenest cities in Arabia.

In 1953 Sheikh Zayed made his first visit abroad, accompanying his brother Shakhbut to Britain and France. He recalled later how impressed he had been by the schools and hospitals he visited, becoming determined that his own people should have the benefit of similar facilities:

There were a lot of dreams I was dreaming about our land catching up with the modern world, but I was not able to do anything because I did not have the wherewithal in my hands to achieve these dreams. I was sure, however, that one day they would become true.

Despite constraints through lack of government revenues, Sheikh Zayed succeeded in bringing progress to Al Ain, establishing the rudiments of an administrative machinery, personally funding the first modern school in the emirate and coaxing relatives and friends to contribute towards small-scale development programmes.

However, the export of Abu Dhabi's first cargo of crude oil to the world market in 1962 was to provide Sheikh Zayed with the means to fund his dreams. Although prices for crude oil were then far lower than they are today, the rapidly growing volume of exports revolutionised the economy of Abu Dhabi and its people began to look forward eagerly to some of the benefits that were already being enjoyed by their near-neighbours in Qatar, Bahrain, Kuwait and Saudi Arabia. The pearling industry had finx;ally come to an end shortly after the Second World War, and little had emerged to take its place. Indeed, during the late 1950s and early 1960s, many of the people of Abu Dhabi left for other oil-producing Gulf states where there were opportunities for employment.

The economic hardships faced by Abu Dhabi since the 1930s had accustomed the Ruler, Sheikh Shakhbut, to a cautious frugality. Despite the growing aspirations of his people for progress, he was reluctant to invest the new oil revenues in development. Attempts by members of his family, including Sheikh Zayed, and by the leaders of the other tribes in the emirate to persuade him to move with the times were unsuccessful, and eventually the Al Nahyan family decided that the time had come for him to step down. The record of Sheikh Zayed over the previous 20 years in Al Ain and his popularity among the people made him the obvious choice as successor.

On 6 August 1966 Sheikh Zayed became Ruler, with a mandate from his family to press ahead as fast as possible with the development of Abu Dhabi.

He was a man in a hurry. His years in Al Ain had not only given him experience in government, but had also provided him with the time to develop a vision of how the emirate could progress. With revenues growing year by year as oil production increased, he was determined to use them in the service of the people and a massive programme of construction of schools, housing, hospitals and roads got rapidly under way.

Of his first few weeks as Ruler, Sheikh Zayed has said:

All the picture was prepared. It was not a matter of fresh thinking, but of simply putting into effect the thoughts of years and years. First I knew we had to concentrate on Abu Dhabi and public welfare. In short, we had to obey the circumstances: the needs of the people as a whole. Second, I wanted to approach other emirates to work with us. In harmony, in some sort of federation, we could follow the example of other developing countries.

As Abu Dhabi embarked on development, Sheikh Zayed also turned his attention rapidly to the building of closer relations with the other emirates: 'Federation is the way to power, the way to strength, the way to well-being,' he felt. 'Lesser entities have no standing in the world today, and so has it ever been in history.'

One early step was to increase contributions to the Trucial States Development Fund established a few years earlier by the British; Abu Dhabi soon became its largest donor. At the beginning of 1968, when the British announced their intention of withdrawing from the Arabian Gulf by the end of 1971, Sheikh Zayed acted swiftly to initiate moves towards a closer relationship with the other emirates.

Together with the late Ruler of Dubai, Sheikh Rashid bin Saeed Al Maktoum, who was to become Vice-President and Prime Minister of the UAE, Sheikh Zayed took the lead in calling for a federation that would include not only the seven emirates that together made up the Trucial States, but also Qatar and Bahrain. When early hopes of a federation of nine states eventually foundered, with Qatar and Bahrain opting to preserve their separate status, Sheikh Zayed led his fellow Rulers in agreement on the establishment of the UAE, which formally emerged on to the international stage on 2 December 1971.

While his enthusiasm for federation – clearly displayed by his willingness to spend the oil revenues of Abu Dhabi on the development of the other emirates – was a key factor in the formation of the UAE, Sheikh Zayed also won support for the way in which he sought consensus and agreement among his brother Rulers:

I am not imposing unity on anyone. That is tyranny. All of us have our opinions, and these opinions can change. Sometimes we put all opinions together, and then extract from them a single point of view. This is our democracy.

Sheikh Zayed was elected by his fellow Rulers as the first President of the UAE, a post to which he has been successively re-elected at five-yearly intervals.

The new state came into being at a time of political turmoil in the region. A couple of days earlier, on the night of 30 November and early morning of 1 December, Iran had forcibly and unlawfully seized the islands of Abu Musa, part of Sharjah, and Greater and Lesser Tunb (see section on International Relations).

On land, demarcation of the borders between the individual emirates and its neighbours had not been completed, although a preliminary agreement had already been reached between Abu Dhabi and Oman.

Foreign observers, lacking an understanding of the importance of a common history and heritage in bringing together the people of the UAE, predicted that the new state would survive only with difficulty, pointing to disputes with its neighbours and to the wide disparity in the size, population and level of development of the seven emirates.

Better informed about the nature of the country, Sheikh Zayed was naturally more optimistic. Looking back a quarter of a century later, he noted:

> *Our experiment in federation, in the first instance, arose from a desire to increase the ties that bind us, as well as from the conviction of all that they were part of one family, and that they must gather together under one leadership.*
>
> *We had never (previously) had an experiment in federation, but our proximity to each other and the ties of blood relationships between us are factors which led us to believe that we must establish a federation that should compensate for the disunity and fragmentation that earlier prevailed.*
>
> *That which has been accomplished has exceeded all our expectations, and that, with the help of God and a sincere will, confirms that there is nothing that cannot be achieved in the service of the people if determination is firm and intentions are sincere.*

The predictions of the pessimists at the time of the formation of the UAE have indeed been clearly proven to be unfounded. Over the course of the past 28 years, the UAE has not only survived, but has developed at a rate that is almost without parallel. The country has been utterly transformed. Its population has risen from around 250,000 to a 1999 estimate of 2.94 million. Progress, in terms of the provision of social services, health and education, as well as in sectors such as communications and the oil and non-oil economy, has brought a high standard of living that has spread throughout the seven emirates, from the ultra-modern cities to the remotest areas of the desert and mountains. The change has, moreover, taken place against a backdrop of enviable political and social stability, despite the insecurity and conflict that has dogged much of the rest of the Gulf region.

At the same time, the country has also established itself firmly on the international scene, both within the Gulf and Arab region and in the broader community of nations. Its pursuit of dialogue and consensus and its firm adherence to the tenets of the Charter of the United Nations, in particular those dealing with the principle of non-interference in the affairs of other states, have been coupled with a quiet but extensive involvement in the provision of development assistance and humanitarian aid that, in per capita terms, has few parallels.

There is no doubt that the experiment in federation has been a success and the undoubted key to the achievements of the UAE has been the central role played by Sheikh Zayed.

During his years in Al Ain, he was able to develop a vision of how the country should progress, and, since becoming first Ruler of Abu Dhabi, and then President of the UAE, he has devoted more than three decades into making that vision a reality.

One foundation of his philosophy as a leader and statesman is that the resources of the country should be fully utilised to the benefit of the people. The UAE is fortunate to have been blessed with massive reserves of oil and gas and it is through careful utilisation of these, including the decision in 1973 that the Government should take a controlling share of the oil reserves and assume total ownership of associated and non-associated gas, that the financial resources necessary to underpin the development programme have always been available. Indeed, there has been sufficient to permit the Government to set aside large amounts for investment on behalf of future generations and, through the Abu Dhabi Investment Authority created by Sheikh Zayed, the country now has reserves unofficially estimated at around US $200 billion.

The financial resources, however, have always been regarded by Sheikh Zayed not as a means unto themselves, but as a tool to facilitate the development of what he believes to be the real wealth of the country – its people, and in particular the younger generation:

Wealth is not money. Wealth lies in men. That is where true power lies, the power that we value. They are the shield behind which we seek protection. This is what has convinced us to direct all our resources to building the individual, and to using the wealth with which God has provided us in the service of the nation, so that it may grow and prosper.

Unless wealth is used in conjunction with knowledge to plan for its use, and unless there are enlightened intellects to direct it, its fate is to diminish and to disappear. The greatest use that can be made of wealth is to invest it in creating generations of educated and trained people.

Addressing the graduation ceremony of the first class of students from the Emirates University in 1982, Sheikh Zayed said:

The building of mankind is difficult and hard. It represents, however, the real wealth [of the country]. This is not found in material wealth. It is made up of men, of children and of future generations. It is this which constitutes the real treasure.

Within this framework, Sheikh Zayed believes that all of the country's citizens have a role to play in its development. Indeed he defines it not simply as a right, but a duty. Addressing his colleagues in the Federal Supreme Council, he noted:

The most important of our duties as Rulers is to raise the standard of living of our people. To carry out one's duty is a responsibility given by God, and to follow up on work is the responsibility of everyone, both the old and the young.

Both men and women, he believes, should play their part. Recognising that in the past a lack of education and development had prevented women taking a full role in much of the activity of society, he has taken action to ensure that this situation does not continue.

Although women's advocates might argue that there is still much to be done, the achievements have been remarkable and the country's women are now increasingly playing their part in political and economic life by taking up senior positions in the public and private sectors. In so doing, they have enjoyed full support from the President:

Women have the right to work everywhere. Islam affords to women their rightful status, and encourages them to work in all sectors, as long as they are afforded the appropriate respect. The basic role of women is the upbringing of children, but, over and above that, we must offer opportunities to a woman who chooses to perform other functions. What women have achieved in the

Emirates in only a short space of time makes me both happy and content. We sowed our seeds yesterday, and today the fruit has already begun to appear. We praise God for the role that women play in our society. It is clear that this role is beneficial for both present and future generations.

Sheikh Zayed has made it clear that he believes that the younger generation, those who have enjoyed the fruits of the UAE's development programme, must now take up the burden once carried by their parents. Within his immediate family, Sheikh Zayed has ensured that his sons have taken up posts in government at which they are expected to work and not simply enjoy as sinecures. Young UAE men who have complained about the perceived lack of employment opportunities at an unrealistic salary level have been offered positions on farms as agricultural labourers, so that they may learn the dignity of work:

Work is of great importance, and of great value in building both individuals and societies. The size of a salary is not a measure of the worth of an individual. What is important is an individual's sense of dignity and self-respect. It is my duty as the leader of the young people of this country to encourage them to work and to exert themselves in order to raise their own standards and to be of service to the country. The individual who is healthy and of a sound mind and body but who does not work commits a crime against himself and against society. We look forward to seeing in the future our sons and daughters playing a more active role, broadening their participation in the process of development and shouldering their share of the responsibilities, especially in the private sector, so as to lay the foundations for the success of this participation and effectiveness. At the same time, we are greatly concerned to raise the standing and dignity of the work ethic in our society, and to increase the percentage of citizens in the labour force. This can be achieved by following a realistic and well-planned approach that will improve performance and productivity, moving towards the long-term goal of secure and comprehensive development.

In this sphere, as in other areas, Sheikh Zayed has long been concerned about the possible adverse impact upon the younger generation of the easy life they enjoy, so far removed from the resilient, resourceful lifestyle of their parents. One key feature of Sheikh Zayed's strategy of government, therefore, has been the encouragement of initiatives designed to conserve and cherish aspects of the traditional culture of the people, in order to familiarise the younger generation with the ways of their ancestors. In his view, it is of crucial importance that the lessons and heritage of the past are not forgotten. They provide, he believes, an essential foundation upon which real progress can be achieved:

History is a continuous chain of events. The present is only an extension of the past. He who does not know his past cannot make the best of his present and future, for it is from the past that we learn. We gain experience and we take advantage of the lessons and results [of the past]. Then we adopt the best and that which suits our present needs, while avoiding the mistakes made by our fathers and our grandfathers. The new generation should have a proper appreciation of the role played by their forefathers. They should adopt their model, and the supreme ideal of patience, fortitude, hard work and dedication to doing their duty.

Once believed to have been little more than an insignificant backwater in the history of mankind in the Middle East, the UAE has emerged in recent years as a country which has played a crucial role in the development of civilisation in the region for thousands of years.

The first archaeological excavations in the UAE took place 40 years ago, in 1959, with the archaeologists benefiting extensively from the interest shown in their work by Sheikh Zayed. Indeed he himself invited them to visit the Al Ain area to examine remains in and around the oasis that proved to be some of the most important ever found in southeastern Arabia. In the decades that have followed, Sheikh Zayed has continued to support archaeological studies throughout the country, eager to ensure that knowledge of the achievements of the past becomes available to educate and inspire the people of today.

Appropriately, one of the most important archaeological sites has been discovered on Abu Dhabi's western island of Sir Bani Yas, which for more than 20 years has been a private wildlife reserve created by Sheikh Zayed to ensure the survival of some of Arabia's most endangered species.

If the heritage of the people of the UAE is important to Sheikh Zayed, so too is the conservation of its natural environment and wildlife. After all, he believes the strength of character of the Emirati people derives, in part, from the struggle that they were obliged to wage in order to survive in the harsh and arid local environment.

His belief in conservation of the environment owes nothing to modern fashion. Acknowledged by the presentation of the prestigious Gold Panda Award from the Worldwide Fund for Nature, it derives, instead, from his own upbringing, living in harmony with nature. This has led him to ensure that conservation of wildlife and the environment is a key part of government policy, while at the same time he has stimulated and personally supervised a massive programme of afforestation that has now seen over 150 million trees planted.

In a speech on the occasion of the UAE's first Environment Day in February 1998 Sheikh Zayed spelt out his beliefs:

We cherish our environment because it is an integral part of our country, our history and our heritage. On land and in the sea, our forefathers lived and survived in this environment. They were able to do so only because they recognised the need to conserve it, to take from it only what they needed to live, and to preserve it for succeeding generations.

With God's will, we shall continue to work to protect our environment and our wildlife, as did our forefathers before us. It is a duty: and, if we fail, our children, rightly, will reproach us for squandering an essential part of their inheritance, and of our heritage.

Like most conservationists Sheikh Zayed is concerned wherever possible to remedy the damage done by man to wildlife. His programme on the island of Sir Bani Yas for the captive breeding of endangered native animals such as the Arabian oryx and the Arabian gazelle has achieved impressive success, so much so that not only is the survival of both species now assured, but animals are also carefully being reintroduced to the wild.

As in other areas of national life, Sheikh Zayed has made it clear that conservation is not simply the task of government. Despite the existence of official institutions like the Federal Environmental Agency and Abu Dhabi's Environmental Research and Wildlife Development Agency, (empowered by a growing catalogue of legislation), the UAE's President has stressed that there is also a role both for the individual and for non-governmental organisations, both of citizens and expatriates.

He believes that society can only flourish and develop if all of its members acknowledge their responsibilities. This does not only to concerns such as environmental conservation, but also to other areas of national life.

Members of the Al Nahyan family, of which Sheikh Zayed is the current head, have been Rulers of Abu Dhabi since at least the beginning of the eighteenth century, longer than any other ruling dynasty in the Arabian peninsula. In Arabian *bedu* society, however, the legitimacy of a Ruler, and of a ruling family, derives essentially from consensus and from consent. Just as Sheikh Zayed himself was chosen by members of his family to become Ruler of Abu Dhabi in 1966, when his elder brother was no longer able to retain their confidence, so does the legitimacy of the political system today derive from the support it draws from the people of the UAE. The principle of consultation *(shura)* is an essential part of that system.

At an informal level, that principle has long been put into practice through the institution of the *majlis* (council) where a leading member of society holds an 'open-house' discussion forum, at which any individual may put forward views for discussion and consideration. While the *majlis* system – the UAE's form of direct democracy – still continues, it is naturally, best suited to a relatively small community.

In 1970, recognising that Abu Dhabi was embarking upon a process of rapid change and development, Sheikh Zayed created the Emirate's National Consultative Council, bringing together the leaders of each of the main tribes and families which comprised the population. A similar body was created for the UAE as a whole, the Federal National Council, the state's parliament,

Both institutions represent the formalisation of the traditional process of consultation and discussion and their members are frequently urged by Sheikh Zayed to express their views openly, without fear or favour.

At present, members of both the National Consultative Council and the Federal National Council continue to be selected by Sheikh Zayed and the other Rulers, in consultation with leading members of the community in each emirate. However, in the future, Sheikh Zayed has said, a formula for direct elections will be devised. He notes, however, that in this, as in many other fields, it is necessary to move ahead with care to ensure that only such institutions as are appropriate for Emirati society are adopted.

Questioned by the *New York Times* on the topic of the possible introduction of an elected parliamentary democracy, Sheikh Zayed replied:

Why should we abandon a system that satisfies our people in order to introduce a system that seems to engender dissent and confrontation? Our system of government is based upon

our religion, and is what our people want. Should they seek alternatives, we are ready to listen to them. We have always said that our people should voice their demands openly. We are all in the same boat, and they are both captain and crew.

Our doors here are open for any opinion to be expressed, and this is well known by all our citizens. It is our deep conviction that God the Creator has created people free, and has prescribed that each individual must enjoy freedom of choice. No-one should act as if he owns others. Those in a position of leadership should deal with their subjects with compassion and understanding, because this is the duty enjoined upon them by God Almighty, who enjoins us to treat all living creatures with dignity. How can there be anything less for man, created as God's vice-gerent on earth? Our system of government does not derive its authority from man, but is enshrined in our religion, and is based on God's book, the Holy Quran. What need have we of what others have conjured up? Its teachings are eternal and complete, while the systems conjured up by man are transitory and incomplete.

Sheikh Zayed imbibed the principles of Islam in his childhood and it remains the foundation of his beliefs and philosophy today. Indeed, the ability with which he and the people of the UAE have been able to absorb and adjust to the remarkable changes of the past few decades can be ascribed largely to the fact that Islam has provided an unchanging and immutable core of their lives. Today, it provides the inspiration for the UAE judicial system and its place as the ultimate source of legislation is enshrined in the country's constitution.

Islam, like other divinely revealed religions, has those among its claimed adherents who purport to interpret its message as justifying harsh dogmas and intolerance. In Sheikh Zayed's view, however, such an approach is not merely a perversion of the message but is directly contrary to it. Extremism, he believes, has no place in Islam. In contrast, he stresses that:

Islam is a civilising religion that gives mankind dignity. A Muslim is he who does not inflict evil upon others. Islam is the religion of tolerance and forgiveness, and not of war, of dialogue and understanding. It is Islamic social justice which has asked every Muslim to respect the other. To treat every person, no matter what his creed or race, as a special soul is a mark of Islam. It is just that point, embodied in the humanitarian tenets of Islam, that makes us so proud of it.

Within that context, Sheikh Zayed has set his face firmly against those who preach intolerance and hatred:

In these times we see around us violent men who claim to talk on behalf of Islam. Islam is far removed from their talk. If such people really wish for recognition from Muslims and the world, they should themselves first heed the words of God and His Prophet. Regrettably, however, these people have nothing whatsoever that connects them to Islam. They are apostates and criminals. We see them slaughtering children and the innocent. They kill people, spill their blood and destroy their property, and then claim to be Muslims.

Sheikh Zayed is an eager advocate of tolerance, discussion and a better understanding between those of different faiths, recognising that this is essential if mankind is to ever move forward in harmony. His faith is well summed up by a statement explaining the essential basis of his own beliefs: 'My religion is based neither on hope, nor on fear, I worship my God because I love him.'

That faith, with its belief in the brotherhood of man and in the duty incumbent upon the strong to provide assistance to those less fortunate than themselves, is fundamental to Sheikh Zayed's vision of how his country and people should develop. It is, too, a key to the foreign policy of the UAE, which he has devised and guided since the establishment of the state.

The UAE itself has been able to progress only because of the way in which its component parts have successfully been able to come together in a relationship of harmony, working together for common goals.

Within the Arabian Gulf region, and in the broader Arab world, the UAE has sought to enhance cooperation and to resolve disagreement through a calm pursuit of dialogue and consensus. Thus one of the central features of the country's foreign policy has been the development of closer ties with its neighbours in the Arabian peninsula. The Arab Gulf Cooperation Council, (AGCC) grouping the UAE, Kuwait, Saudi Arabia, Bahrain, Qatar and Oman, was founded at a summit conference held in Abu Dhabi in 1981, and has since become, with strong UAE support, an effective and widely-respected grouping.

Intended to facilitate the development of closer ties between its members and to enable them to work together to ensure their security, the AGCC has faced two major external challenges during its short lifetime: first, the long and costly conflict in the 1980s between Iraq and Iran, which itself prompted the Council's formation and second, the August 1990 invasion by Iraq of one of its members, Kuwait.

Following the invasion of Kuwait, President Zayed was one of the first Arab leaders to offer support to its people and units from the UAE armed forces played a significant role in the alliance that liberated the Gulf state in early 1991.

While fully supporting the international condemnation of the policies of the Iraqi regime and the sanctions imposed on Iraq by the United Nations (UN) during and after the conflict, the UAE has, however, expressed its serious concern about the impact that the sanctions have had upon the country's people. In his interview with the *New York Times* in mid-1998, Sheikh Zayed noted:

Moderate states in the Arab world recognise that Saddam [Hussein] *did injustice, and received the appropriate response. He paid the price, and sanctions have now been imposed on Iraq for seven years.*

Now, Iraq is sick, tired, hungry and naked. How can you continue to impose sanctions on it for ever in a situation like this? It [Iraq] *should not continue to receive punishment, and should no longer have sanctions imposed upon it. We believe that the time has come to say that enough is enough.*

Continuing to argue forcefully for a lifting of sanctions, the UAE has, at the same, time, provided an extensive amount of humanitarian assistance to the Iraqi people, ensuring, as far as possible, that the aid reaches those for whom it is intended.

Another key focus of the UAE's foreign policy in an Arab context has been the provision of support to the Palestinian people in their efforts to regain their legitimate rights to self-determination and to the establishment of their own state. As early as 1968, before the formation of the UAE, Sheikh Zayed extended generous assistance to Palestinian organisations, and has done so throughout the last three decades, although he has always believed that it is for the Palestinians themselves to determine their own policies.

Following the establishment of the Palestinian Authority in Gaza and on parts of the occupied West Bank, the UAE has provided substantial help for the building of a national infrastructure, including not only houses, roads, schools and hospitals, but also for the refurbishment of Muslim and Christian sites in the city of Jerusalem. While much of the aid has been bilateral, the UAE has also taken part in development programmes funded by multilateral agencies and groupings and has long been a major contributor to the United Nations Relief Works Agency (UNRWA).

Substantial amounts of aid have also been given to a number of other countries in the Arab world, such as Lebanon, to help it recover from the devastation caused by over a decade of civil war, and to less-developed countries such as Yemen.

Sheikh Zayed has a deeply held belief in the cherished objective of greater political and economic unity within the Arab world. At the same time, however, he has long adopted a realistic approach on the issue, recognising that to be effective any unity must grow slowly and with the support of the people. Arab unity, he believes, is not something that can simply be created through decrees of governments that may be temporary, political phenomena.

That approach has been tried and tested both at the level of the UAE itself, which is the longest-lived experiment in recent times in Arab unity, and at the level of the Arabian Gulf Cooperation Council.

On a broader plane, Sheikh Zayed has sought consistently to promote greater understanding and consensus between Arab countries and to reinvigorate the League of Arab States. Relations between the Arab leaders, he believes, should be based on openness and frankness:

They must make it clear to each other that each one of them needs the other, and they should understand that only through mutual support can they survive in times of need.
A brother should tell his brother: you support me, and I will support you, when you are in the right. But not when you are in the wrong. If I am in the right, you should support and help me, and help to remove the results of any injustice that has been imposed on me.
Wise and mature leaders should listen to sound advice, and should take the necessary action to correct their mistakes. As for those leaders who are unwise or immature, they can be brought to the right path through advice from their sincere friends.

Within that context, and since the Iraqi invasion of Kuwait which split the Arab world asunder, Sheikh Zayed has consistently argued for the holding of a new Arab summit conference at which leaders can honestly and frankly address the disputes between them. Only thus, he believes, can the Arab world as a whole move forward to tackle the challenges that face it, both internally and on the broader international plane:

I believe that an all-inclusive Arab summit must be held, but before attending it, the Arabs must open their hearts to each other and be frank with each other about the rifts between them and their wounds. They should then come to the summit, to make the necessary corrections to their policies, to address the issues, to heal their wounds and to affirm that the destiny of the Arabs is one, both for the weak and the strong. At the same time, they should not concede their rights, or ask for what is not rightfully theirs.

The UAE President acknowledges, however, that unanimity, although desirable, cannot always be achieved. He has, therefore, been the only Arab leader to openly advocate a revision of the Charter of the League of Arab States to permit decisions to be taken on the basis of the will of the majority. Such has been the experience of the society from which he comes, and such has been one of the foundations of the success of the federal experiment in the UAE. It is time, he believes, that a similar approach was adopted within the broader Arab world.

This should not, however, mean that essential rights and principles should be set aside; these include, of course, the principle of the inviolability of the integrity of Arab territories.

This principle has been a matter of major concern to the UAE since its formation, due to the Iranian occupation in 1971 of the UAE islands of Abu Musa and Greater and Lesser Tunb. That occupation was undertaken in contravention of all norms of international law and of the Charter of the United Nations.

Successive governments in Iran have continually consolidated their military hold over the islands and have failed to respond to efforts by the UAE to resolve the issue. The UAE in turn, has never abandoned its attempts to regain its rights over the islands. Iran, however, has rejected the UAE suggestion that the matter be referred to the International Court of Justice and it has also stated that while it is willing to hold bilateral negotiations, these would only deal with what it describes as 'misunderstandings', failing to acknowledge that a question of sovereignty exists.

While Sheikh Zayed wishes to see an improvement in relations with Iran, not only a near-neighbour of the Emirates but also a fellow Muslim state, he has made it clear that a concrete and positive initiative is now required from the Iranian side. 'It is said that [Iranian] President Khatami wants to pursue a policy of openness towards his neighbours and the world, but we are still waiting [for action].'

Here, as on other foreign policy issues, Sheikh Zayed has consistently adopted a firm but calmly worded approach, eschewing rhetoric that could make the search for a solution to problems more difficult.

In recent years, the conflicts ensuing from the disintegration of the former Yugoslavia have been the cause of considerable concern. Prior to the imposition of a peace in Bosnia

19

by the western industrialised powers, Sheikh Zayed's frustration with the continued slaughter of Bosnian Muslims was scarcely concealed.

Commenting to the Emirates News Agency, WAM, at the height of the Serbian campaign of 'ethnic cleansing' against the Muslims, he said that the UN seemed 'enfeebled like a dead machine' in the face of Serbian atrocities:

It is as if the United Nations has been turned into stone, with no feeling or compassion for the agony of the Bosnian people.

We call on all people with a conscience, those who believe in justice and who deplore aggression and unjust wars to stand up against the horrors being perpetrated against the innocent people of Bosnia-Herzegovina.

The world has to move forcefully to put an end to the horrifying tragedy. Governments must move now to enable the people of that besieged country to defend themselves. The right of self-defence is the most basic human and elementary right.

Once the international community had forced the Serbs to cease their campaign of slaughter in Bosnia, Sheikh Zayed promptly moved to ensure that substantial assistance was sent by the UAE to enable the Bosnian Muslims to begin the task of rebuilding their society.

The lessons of the Bosnian tragedy were not, however, lost on Sheikh Zayed. The time had come, he recognised, for the UAE itself to play a more proactive role in international peacekeeping operations.

The UAE's armed forces had already begun to establish a record in such peacekeeping activities, first as part of the joint Arab Deterrent Force that sought for a few years to bring to an end the civil strife in Lebanon, and then through participation in UNISOM TWO, the UN peacekeeping and reconstruction force in Somalia.

In early 1999, as a new campaign of Serbian atrocities began to get under way against the Albanian population of Kosovo, Sheikh Zayed was among the first world leaders to express support for the decision by the North Atlantic Treaty Organisation (NATO) to launch its aerial campaign to force Serbia to halt its genocidal activities.

Recognising early on in the campaign that there would be a need for an international peacekeeping force once the NATO campaign ended, Sheikh Zayed ordered that the UAE's armed forces should be a part of any such force operating under the aegis of the UN. In late 1999, with the UN's KFOR force in place in Kosovo, the contingent from the UAE was the largest taking part from any of the non-NATO states.

While ensuring that the UAE should now increasingly come to shoulder such international responsibilities, however, Sheikh Zayed has also made it clear that the UAE's role is one that is focused on relief and rehabilitation.

In the Balkans and in other countries, the policy adopted by the UAE clearly reflects the desire of Sheikh Zayed to utilise the good fortune of his country to provide assistance to those less fortunate. Through bodies like the Zayed Foundation and the Abu Dhabi Fund for Development, established by Sheikh Zayed before the foundation of the UAE, as well as through institutions like the Red Crescent Society, chaired by his son, Sheikh

Hamdan bin Zayed Al Nahyan, the country now plays a major role in the provision of relief and development assistance worldwide.

In essence, the philosophy of Sheikh Zayed, derived from his deeply held Muslim faith, is that it is the duty of man to seek to improve the lot of his fellow man. His record in over half a century in government, first within the UAE and then concurrently on a broader international plane, is an indication of the dedication and seriousness with which he has sought to carry out that belief.

THE COUNTRY

Established on 2 December 1971, the UAE is a federation of seven emirates: Abu Dhabi, Dubai, Sharjah, Ajman, Umm al-Qaiwain, Ras al-Khaimah and Fujairah. Comprising an area of 83,600 square kilometres (including an archipelago which extends over approximately 5,900 square kilometres), the country lies between latitudes 22°–26.5°N and longitudes 51°–56.5°E. It is bordered to the north by the Arabian Gulf, to the east by the Gulf of Oman and the Sultanate of Oman, to the south by the Sultanate of Oman and Saudi Arabia and to the west by Qatar and Saudi Arabia.

The UAE has some 700 kilometres of coastline, including 100 kilometres on the Gulf of Oman. Along the Arabian Gulf coast are offshore islands, coral reefs and salt marshes. Stretches of gravel plain and barren desert characterise the inland region. To the east lie the Hajar mountains, close to the Gulf of Oman, which reach north into the Musandam peninsula, at the mouth of the Arabian Gulf. The western interior of the Federation, most of which is Abu Dhabi territory, consists mainly of desert interspersed with oases. One of the largest oases is Al Liwa, beyond which is the vast Rub al-Khali desert, or Empty Quarter.

CLIMATIC CONDITIONS

The UAE lies in the arid tropical zone extending across Asia and northern Africa, however the Indian Ocean has a strong influence on the climatic conditions in the area, since the country borders both the Arabian Gulf and the Gulf of Oman. This explains why high temperatures in summer are always accompanied by high humidity along the coast. Noticeable variations in climate occur between the coastal regions, the deserts of the interior and mountainous areas.

Between the months of November and March a moderate, warm climate prevails during the day at an average temperature of 26°C, and a slightly cooler climate prevails throughout the night at an average temperature of 15°C. The humidity tends to rise in the summer months, between June and August.

Prevailing winds, influenced by the monsoons, vary between south or southeast, to west or north to northwest depending upon the season and location.

Average rainfall is low at less than 6.5 centimetres annually and more than half of the average rainfall occurs in December and January.

SEVEN EMIRATES
Abu Dhabi

Abu Dhabi is the largest of all seven emirates with an area of 67,340 square kilometres, equivalent to 86.7 per cent of the country's total area, excluding the islands. It has a coastline extending for more than 400 kilometres and is divided for administrative purposes into three major regions.

The first region encompasses the city of Abu Dhabi which is both the capital of the emirate and the federal capital. Sheikh Zayed, President of the UAE resides here. The parliamentary buildings in which the federal Cabinet meets, most of the federal ministries and institutions, the foreign embassies, state broadcasting facilities, and most of the oil companies are also located in Abu Dhabi, which is also the home of Zayed University and the Higher Colleges of Technology. Major infrastructural facilities include Mina (Port) Zayed and Abu Dhabi International Airport. The city also has extensive cultural, sport and leisure facilities, together with the wonderfully engineered Abu Dhabi Corniche which offers many kilometres of risk-free walking, cycling, jogging and roller-blading along the seashore of Abu Dhabi island. Architecturally speaking the city is also a fascinating place where older buildings such as small mosques have been preserved and sit comfortably in the shade of futuristic modern skyscrapers.

Abu Dhabi's second region, known as the Eastern Region, has as its capital Al Ain city. This fertile area is rich in greenery with plenty of farms, public parks and important archaeological sites. It is also blessed by substantial groundwater resources which feed into numerous artesian wells. Points of particular interest in this region are the Ain Al Faydah Park, Jebel Hafit, the leisure park at Al Hili, Al Ain Zoo and Al Ain Museum. This is also a cultural and educational centre and site of the UAE's first university, the UAE University, which includes among its many faculties a vibrant medical school. Internal transport is facilitated by a superb road network and Al Ain is connected to the outside world through Al Ain International Airport.

The Western Region, the emirate's third administrative sector, comprises 52 villages and has as its capital Bida Zayed, or Zayed City. Extensive afforestation covers at least 100,000 hectares, including more than 20 million evergreens. The country's main onshore oil fields are located here, as is the country's largest oil refinery, at Al Ruwais.

In addition to the three mainland regions of Abu Dhabi there are a number of important islands within the emirate including Das, Mubarraz, Zirku and Arzanah, near where the main offshore oil fields are located. Closer inshore are Dalma, Sir Bani Yas, Merawah, Abu al-Abyadh and Saadiyat, together with many other islands.

Dubai

The Emirate of Dubai extends along the Arabian Gulf coast of the UAE for approximately 72 kilometres. Dubai has an area of *c.* 3,885 square kilometres, which is equivalent to 5 per cent of the country's total area, excluding the islands.

Dubai city is built along the edge of a narrow 10-kilometre long, winding creek which divides the southern section of Bur Dubai, the city's traditional heart, from the northern

area of Deira. The Ruler's office, together with many head offices of major companies, Port Rashid, the Dubai World Trade Centre, customs, broadcasting stations and the postal authority are all situated in Bur Dubai. Deira is a thriving commercial centre containing a huge range of retail outlets, markets, hotels and Dubai International Airport. Bur Dubai and Deira are linked by Al Maktoum and Al Garhoud bridges, as well as Al Shindagha tunnel which passes under the creek.

Jebel Ali, home of a huge man-made port, has the largest free-trade zone in Arabia housing an ever growing list of international corporations which use the zone for both manufacturing and as a redistribution point.

Jumeirah beach is a major tourism area with a number of spectacular award winning hotels and sports facilities.

Inland, the mountain resort town of Hatta is an extremely attractive location. Adjacent to a lake reservoir, the Hatta Fort Hotel is set in extensive parkland and provides a perfect base for exploring the nearby wadis and mountains, which extend into Omani territory.

Sharjah

The Emirate of Sharjah extends along approximately 16 kilometres of the UAE's Gulf coastline and for more than 80 kilometres into the interior. In addition there are three enclaves belonging to Sharjah situated on the east coast, bordering the Gulf of Oman. These are Kalba, Khor Fakkan and Dibba al-Husn. The emirate has an area of 2,590 square kilometres, which is equivalent to 3.3 per cent of the country's total area, excluding the islands.

The capital city of Sharjah, which overlooks the Arabian Gulf, contains the main administrative and commercial centres together with an especially impressive array of cultural and traditional projects, including several museums. Distinctive landmarks are the two major covered souqs, reflecting Islamic design; a number of recreational areas and public parks such as Al Jazeirah Fun Park and Al Buheirah Corniche. The city is also notable for its numerous elegant mosques. Links with the outside world are provided by Sharjah International Airport and Port Khalid.

Sharjah also encompasses some important oasis areas, the most famous of which is Dhaid where a wide range of vegetables and fruits are cultivated on its rich and fertile soil. Khor Fakkan provides Sharjah with a major east coast port. Two offshore islands belong to Sharjah, Abu Musa, which has been under military occupation by Iran since 1971, and Sir Abu Nu'air.

Ajman

Ajman, located a short distance northeast of Sharjah's capital city, has a beautiful 16-kilometre stretch of white sand beach. It is a small emirate in terms of its physical size, covering about 259 square kilometres, which is equivalent to 0.3 per cent of the country's total area, excluding the islands.

The capital city, Ajman, has an historic fort at its centre. This has been recently renovated and now houses a fascinating museum. In addition to the Ruler's office, various companies,

banks and commercial centres, the emirate is also blessed with a natural harbour in which the Port of Ajman is situated.

Masfut is an agricultural village located in the mountains 110 kilometres to the southeast of the city, while the Manama area lies approximately 60 kilometres to the east.

Umm al-Qaiwain

The Emirate of Umm al-Qaiwain, which has a coastline stretching to 24 kilometres, is located on the Arabian Gulf coast of the UAE, between Sharjah to the southwest, and Ras al-Khaimah to the northeast. Its inland border lies about 32 kilometres from the main coastline. The total area of the emirate is about 777 square kilometres, which is equivalent to 1 per cent of the country's total area, excluding the islands.

The city of Umm al-Qaiwain, capital of the emirate, is situated on a narrow peninsula which encircles a large creek 1 kilometre wide by 5 kilometres long. The Ruler's office, administrative and commercial centres, the main port and a Mariculture Research Centre where prawns and fish are reared on an experimental basis, are located here. The city also has the preserved remains of an old fort, its main gate flanked by defensive cannons.

Falaj al-Mualla, an attractive natural oasis, is located 50 kilometres southeast of Umm al-Qaiwain city. Sinayah island, lying a short distance offshore has important mangrove areas together with a breeding colony of Socotra cormorants.

Ras al-Khaimah

Ras al-Khaimah, the most northerly emirate on the UAE's west coast, has a coastline of about 64 kilometres on the Arabian Gulf, backed by a fertile hinterland, with a separate enclave in the heart of the Hajar mountains to the southeast. Both parts of the emirate share borders with the Sultanate of Oman. In addition to its mainland territory, Ras al-Khaimah possesses a number of islands including those of Greater and Lesser Tunb, occupied by Iran since 1971. The area of the emirate is 168 square kilometres, which is equivalent to 2.2 per cent of the country's total area, excluding islands.

The city of Ras al-Khaimah is divided into two sections by Khor Ras al-Khaimah. In the western section, known as Old Ras al-Khaimah, are Ras al-Khaimah National Museum and a number of government departments. The eastern part, known as Al Nakheel, houses the Ruler's office, several government departments and commercial companies. The two sections are connected by a large bridge built across the khor.

Khor Khuwayr is an industrial region situated approximately 25 kilometres to the north of Ras al-Khaimah city. In addition to its major cement, gravel and marble enterprises, it is also the location for Port Saqr, the main export port for the emirate and the traditional fishing district of Rams. Digdagga district, on the other hand, is a well-known agricultural area and houses the Julphar pharmaceutical factory, the largest in the Arabian Gulf.

Other important centres within the emirate include: Al-Hamraniah, an agricultural centre and also the location for Ras al-Khaimah International Airport, Khatt, a tourist resort that is renowned for its thermal springs, Masafi which is well known for its orchards and natural springs and Wadi al-Qawr, an attractive valley in the southern mountains.

Population Projections (Mn)	Population Annual Growth Projections

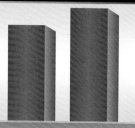 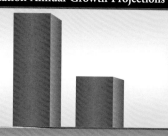

1999	2005		1999	2005
2.94	3.48		6.5%	2.9%

Population by Emirate 1997	Population by Emirate 1975

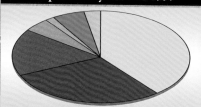 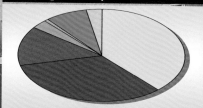

Abu Dhabi	39%		Abu Dhabi	38%
Dubai	29%		Dubai	33%
Sharjah	16.5%		Sharjah	14%
Ajman	5%		Ajman	3%
Umm al-Qaiwain	1.5%		Umm al-Qaiwain	1%
Ras al-Khaimah	6%		Ras al-Khaimah	8%
Fujairah	3%		Fujairah	3%

Population by Age Groups 1997	Population by Age Groups 1975

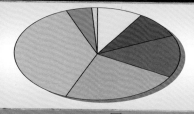 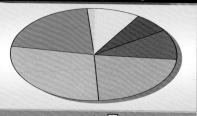

0-4	9%		0-4	12%
5-9	9%		5-9	9%
10-19	15%		10-19	14%
20-29	23%		20-29	30%
30-49	38%		30-49	28%
50-64	5%		50-64	5%
65+	1%		65+	2%

Source: *Development Indicators in the UAE 1999*, Crown Prince Court – Research and Studies Dept., Abu Dhabi.

Fujairah

With the exception of some small enclaves belonging to Sharjah, Fujairah is the only emirate situated along the Gulf of Oman. Its coast is more than 90 kilometres in length and its strategic location has played a key role in its development. The area of the emirate is 1165 square kilometres, which is equivalent to 1.5 per cent of the country's total area, excluding islands.

Fujairah city, the capital of the emirate, is a rapidly developing centre which contains the Ruler's office, government departments, many commercial companies and a number of hotels, as well as an airport and the Port of Fujairah, one of the world's top oil bunkering ports.

The physical features of the emirate are characterised by the jagged Hajar mountains which border the fertile coastal plain where most of the settlement has taken place. Blessed with dramatic scenery, Fujairah is well placed to continue building upon its tourism trade. Attractions include some excellent diving sites, the natural beauty of the mountains and coastline, cultural and historic attractions and, of course, reliable winter sunshine.

The historic town of Dibba al-Fujairah, at the northern end of the emirate, is an important centre for both agriculture and fishing, while the village of Bidiya has a unique four-domed mosque that is the oldest in the country.

POPULATION

The population of the UAE is estimated to be 2.94 million. Growth at present is 6.5 per cent per year. This is expected however to slow to 2.9 per cent by the year 2005, when the population will number approximately 3.48 million.

Arabic is the country's official language, although English is widely spoken, and Islam is the state religion.

A GLIMPSE OF HISTORY

Man probably arrived in the area now known as the UAE at the beginning of the Late Stone Age, around 8,000 years ago. Some of the earliest sites have been found on offshore islands like Merawah and Ghagha', where fine flint arrowheads have been discovered. Evidence from these islands, as well as other important sites, notably Dalma, Akab and Jebel Buhays, indicate that by the late sixth or early fifth millennium BC the people had begun to settle in permanent or semi-permanent communities, capable of organising extensive fishing and even herding domestic animals. Finds of pottery sherds at some of these sites of a type known from the 'Ubaid culture in Mesopotamia show that they had extensive trading links to the northern Gulf – evidence of the early beginnings of the country's continuing tradition of maritime commerce. Pearls were already being harvested and could have been an important export commodity.

EMERGING COPPER TRADE

The earliest large-scale architecture dates back to the period from c. 3,200 BC to 2,800 BC, about 5,000 years ago. On the foothills and slopes of Jebel Hafit and Qarn bint Saud, near Al Ain, as well as on the neighbouring Hajar mountains, hundreds of stone tombs from this period have been discovered, showing a sophisticated pattern of construction that could only have been undertaken by a well-organised and settled society. These people, too, traded with Mesopotamia and Baluchistan. The reason for that trade is clear: copper implements and nearby mines show the people were mining and smelting copper. The Jebel Hafit people also grew a variety of crops such as wheat, barley, melons, sorghum and dates, evidence of a fertile climate at this time.

UMM AL-NAR

Umm al-Nar, a port-town and complex of collective graves on a small island adjacent to Abu Dhabi, which appears to have been a focal point of the copper trade, has lent its name to the Umm al-Nar Period (c. 2,500 BC to 2,000 BC). This was the peak of local Bronze Age civilisation with extensive trading links to Mesopotamia and the Harappan culture of the Indus Valley, as is evidenced by a staggering array of foreign goods found at archaeological sites from this era. Cuneiform tablets from Mesopotamia, written during the last few centuries of the third millennium BC, refer to the import of copper from

'Magan', now understood to have been an area which included the present-day UAE and the Hajar mountains.

Excavations at Tell Abraq, on the border between Sharjah and Umm al-Qaiwain, have revealed a massive structure with several layers of construction dating from around 2,200 BC. Faced with stone and with a massive mudbrick foundation, the fortress would have towered over the nearby shoreline like the original Martello tower on the coast of Corsica. It is the largest Bronze Age building discovered anywhere in the Arabian peninsula and was probably the seat of a local lord in the land of Magan.

Evidence of the Umm al-Nar period has been found all over the country, as at Bidiya and Bithna in Fujairah, at Shimal and Ghalilah in Ras al-Khaimah, at Ras Ghanadha and Qattarah in Abu Dhabi and at Umm Suqeim in Dubai. Finds show that the people in that long-off past enjoyed a sophisticated lifestyle, trading along desert and marine routes with other civilisations hundreds or thousands of kilometres away. It is perhaps no coincidence that at Umm al-Nar the earliest evidence has yet been found of the domestication of that 'ship of the desert', the camel, dating back over 4,000 years.

WADI SUQ

Excavated sites from the Wadi Suq Period (2,000 BC to 1,300 BC) reveal a different pattern of external trade, influenced by changes in the civilisations of Mesopotamia and the Indus Valley. Finds from this period include some of the finest early gold and silver jewellery to be found in the UAE.

NEW IRRIGATION TECHNIQUES

Iron Age (1,300 BC to *c.* 300 BC) villages from around 1,000 BC have been uncovered at Hili, near Al Ain and on Sharjah's Al Madam plain, revealing evidence of the *falaj* undergound water system, an ingenious innovation which permitted agriculture to continue in a climate that was becoming progressively drier. Excavations at a fortified settlement near Sharjah airport from this period yielded the first evidence of the use of iron and writing in the UAE.

GREEK AND ROMAN INFLUENCES

Evidence from the settlement at Mileiha, near Dhaid, where pottery from the island of Rhodes has been found show that it was heavily influenced by the ancient Greeks from around 300 BC. At al-Dur, near Umm al-Qaiwain, an ancient temple dating to around 100 BC to 100 AD has been uncovered, as well as more evidence of substantial international trade – pottery from India and Mesopotamia, glass and coins from the Roman Empire.

LATE PRE-ISLAMIC

Trading continued to characterise the lifestyle of the people. Settlements at Kush in Ras al-Khaimah, show evidence of Sasanian links in the fifth and sixth centuries AD, while on Sir Bani Yas island, a major pre-Islamic Christian religious complex has been found. Over on the east coast at Dibba, a great port existed for several hundred years until the

early days of Islam, at the beginning of the seventh century. Scattered across the plains behind Dibba are gravestones from a battle in 632 AD, when the forces of Islam finally established their control over the area.

INDIAN OCEAN TRADE

From the beginning of the Christian era to the seventeenth century, the people of the emirates, drawing upon the maritime skill of their forefathers, ranged far and wide across the Indian Ocean, trading as far away as Mombasa in Kenya, Sri Lanka, Vietnam and even China, in great wooden dhows, similar to those that can still be seen under construction in boatyards around the country today.

Evidence of that trading tradition can be viewed on the surface at the site of Julfar, in Ras al-Khaimah, where fine Chinese and Vietnamese potsherds mingle with pottery from nearer at hand. According to one Portuguese author, Duarte Barbosa, writing in 1517, the people of Julfar were 'persons of worth, great navigators and wholesale dealers. Here is a very great fishery as well, of seed pearls as well as large pearls'.

One of those navigators was Ahmed bin Majid, the 'Lion of the Sea', and one of the greatest figures in the UAE's history, some of whose manuals of navigation still survive. When the Portuguese opened up the area to contact with Europe, they did so in a wave of battles and bloodshed, levelling cities like Julfar and Khor Fakkan, on the east coast. By the early eighteenth century, Julfar was abandoned and the great trading tradition of the region went into decline.

QAWASIM CHALLENGE THE BRITISH

While European powers like Portugal, Holland, France and Britain competed for regional supremacy, however, a new power grew almost unnoticed in the emirates, the State of the Qawasim (or Qasimis), whose descendants today still rule Sharjah and Ras al-Khaimah. Drawing on centuries of maritime experience, the Qawasim by the beginning of the nineteenth century had built up a fleet of over 60 large vessels, and could put nearly 20,000 sailors to sea. Their strength posed a serious challenge to the British, then emerging as the dominant power in the Indian Ocean, and in the first two decades of the nineteenth century a series of clashes between the two sides ended in the virtual destruction of the Qasimi fleet and the consolidation of British influence in the Gulf.

The British claimed that the Qasimi vessels had engaged in piracy, and from that the area gained the name 'The Pirate Coast'. In a masterful debunking of this claim, however, the Ruler of Sharjah, HH Dr Sheikh Sultan bin Mohammed Al Qasimi, in his book, *The Myth of Arab Piracy in the Gulf*, has shown that behind the British offensive lay the desire to control the maritime trade routes between the Gulf and India.

TRUCIAL STATES

The British established themselves in the Gulf at the beginning of 1820, signing a series of agreements with the sheikhs of the individual emirates that later, augmented with treaties on preserving a maritime truce, resulted in the area becoming known as 'The Trucial States'.

Peace at sea meant that the 7,000-year-old pearl fisheries of the lower Gulf could be exploited without interruption, and fine pearls from the emirates were exported, not only to India, but also to the growing market in Europe. The pearling industry thrived during the nineteenth and early twentieth centuries, providing both income and employment to the people of the Arabian Gulf coast. The First World War, however, dealt it a heavy blow, while the world economic depression of the late 1920s and early 1930s, coupled with the invention by the Japanese of the cultured pearl, virtually finished it off.

On land, freed from the damaging effects of warfare at sea, but lacking any real economic resources, the region developed only slowly during the nineteenth and early twentieth centuries. One of the greatest figures of the period was Sheikh Zayed bin Khalifa of Abu Dhabi, who ruled for over 50 years, from 1855 to 1909, earning the title 'Zayed the Great'. His son, Sheikh Sultan, father of the present Ruler, Sheikh Zayed, was Ruler between 1922 and 1926, and then, after a brief reign by a brother, one of Sheikh Sultan's sons, Sheikh Shakhbut, came to the throne at the beginning of 1928.

Times were hard following the collapse of the pearl trade, however, relief was on its way. Following extensive exploration in the 1950s, both offshore and onshore, the first cargo of Abu Dhabi crude oil was exported to the world market in 1962. By the time Sheikh Zayed was elected as Ruler of Abu Dhabi (in 1966) and as President of the UAE once the federation was established (in 1971), the tide had begun to turn. (For more information on this period see section on Sheikh Zayed Profile.)

In 1971 the country's population was only around 200,000 and there were substantial differences between the individual emirates, in terms of size, population, economic resources and degree of development

The larger emirates of Abu Dhabi and Dubai were already oil exporters and the process of their economic development was well under way. At the other end of the scale, Ajman, the smallest emirate, had an area of only 259 square kilometres, while the east coast emirate of Fujairah, with only a few tens of thousands of inhabitants, was not even connected by a proper road through the mountains to the rest of the country.

Twenty-eight years later the judicious use of oil revenues has brought economic prosperity and massive development to all of the seven emirates and the country's unique level of political stability stands as a testimony to the wisdom of federation.

ARCHAEOLOGY UPDATE

Each year the UAE Yearbook endeavours to summarise results of recent research in the field of archaeology. The following brief account focuses on some of the main discoveries that have taken place over the past 12 months.

HILI TOMB

The Department of Antiquities and Tourism in Abu Dhabi's Eastern Region commenced excavations early in November 1998 at Al Ain's Hili garden in conjunction with the French archaeological mission in Abu Dhabi. A team comprising French scientists and a British anthropologist have excavated Tomb N, a subterranean grave dating to the Bronze Age (Umm al-Nar period, around 2,300 BC). The scientific objective is to document local funerary practices that have not been identified before in Abu Dhabi. Originally discovered in 1983, this grave was first excavated by a local team led by Dr Walid Yasin Al Tikriti. However, the methodology of field anthropology has dramatically improved in the past 15 years and this new development prompted the decision to excavate the remaining part of Hili's Tomb N.

The shape, techniques of construction and internal organisation of the deposits of Tomb N strongly differ from those of the nearby well-known circular and monumental Umm al-Nar graves. Tomb N is an 8-metre long oval pit with two parts, an original section and a later addition. It adjoins a circular Umm al-Nar grave Tomb E, an older structure. Like other graves dating from the third millennium BC, Tomb N is a collective grave, meaning that more than two bodies were buried in the same place but at different times.

The number of people buried in Tomb N was very high: the remains of more than 250 skeletons have been found. Men, women and children were buried together. Most of the adults died before they were 45 years old. It is believed the bodies were buried over a period not exceeding 200 years.

The great variety and number of local and imported objects buried with the bodies is another striking characteristic that differentiates the tomb from most of the others of the Umm al-Nar period. The objects include about 400 complete and semi-complete pottery vessels, soft-stone vases, copper rings and other metal artefacts, as well as large quantities of beads, most of which are made of carnelian. One objective of the archaeologists is to analyse the evolution of commercial exchanges within the Arabian Gulf and the Indian

Ocean in the Early Bronze Age during a period corresponding to an increase in long-distance trade. Many of the objects found in the grave originate from the Indus valley and from the Makran/Baluchistan area. Only a single pottery vessel from southern Mesopotamia has been discovered in Tomb N.

EARLY DATE CONSUMPTION

The earliest evidence ever recovered in the Arabian peninsula for the consumption of dates has been found on the island of Dalma, in Abu Dhabi's Western Region. Radiocarbon dating of two burnt stones from a site on the island have produced results suggesting that one date stone can be dated to 4670 (+/-130) BC, and the other to 5110 (+/-160) BC, about 6,500 to 7,000 years ago, late sixth to early fifth millennia BC. Although it cannot be determined if the stones are from wild or cultivated dates, they certainly confirm that dates were being consumed at this early time.

Both date stones, together with impressions of date stones on fragments of mudbrick, were recovered during excavations on the site in the compound of the Abu Dhabi Women's Association branch on Dalma, where the Abu Dhabi Islands Archaeological Survey (ADIAS) has been working for several years.

The age of the Dalma date stones is of great interest as the previous earliest evidence for date palm remains in the UAE was date palm imprints excavated from Hili site 8 in Al Ain, which have been dated to around 3,000 BC, the fourth millennium BC. The significance of the Dalma date stones lies in the fact that they are at least 1,500 years, and perhaps even 2,000 years older.

Other finds from the 7,000-year-old site include at least two round house-like structures with surviving post-holes and floors, one of which is at least 7 metres in diameter. There are also small quantities of imported painted pottery from the 'Ubaid culture of southern Mesopotamia. Large quantities of what appear to be locally-made gypsum plaster vessels were also found, of a type not known anywhere else in the Middle East, along with many thousands of flint flakes and a good number of stone tools (including awls, arrowheads and tile knives); other finds included ornamental beads and huge quantities of food debris in the form of marine shells and animal and fish bones.

The new discovery further underlines the importance of the Dalma site – the oldest settlement yet identified in the Emirates. The archaeological evidence from Dalma shows that 7,000 years ago the people of Dalma were already importing pottery by sea from Mesopotamia, the earliest confirmed evidence of the maritime traditions of the people of the UAE. They were making vessels of gypsum of a type not known anywhere else in the region and were already keeping domestic animals.

ADIAS was established on Sheikh Zayed's instructions to undertake comprehensive archaeological investigations on the numerous islands and coast of Abu Dhabi. Operating under the patronage of Lt-General Sheikh Mohammed bin Zayed Al Nahyan, ADIAS has carried out extensive surveys and identified many major archaeological sites on a number of islands besides Dalma, including Sir Bani Yas, north and south Yasat and Merawah.

ANCIENT SULPHUR MINES

An archaeological survey carried out by ADIAS in November 1998 with the support of the Abu Dhabi Company for Onshore Oil Operations (ADCO) has identified the first ever evidence of ancient sulphur mining to be found in the UAE. The evidence of sulphur mining was located on the slopes of Jebel Dhanna in western Abu Dhabi, where ADCO has its oil export terminal from which export of Abu Dhabi's onshore oil production first began 35 years ago. Around 100 circular shafts dug into the slopes of Jebel Dhanna to a depth of roughly 5 metres, together with a number of deep trenches, some up to 50 metres long, were found by the team. Also discovered were underground galleries dug by miners seeking deposits of pure sulphur crystals.

According to ADIAS, the date of the mines is still to be determined. However, some of the mines appear to have been in use until relatively recent times. Pottery found in some other mines suggests that they may have been in use several hundred years ago, perhaps from the sixteenth century to the early eighteenth century.

Historical records from the early nineteenth century do not mention sulphur mining in Jebel Dhanna, suggesting that major mining operations had ceased by that time. There is a possibility that the mines were used to supply sulphur for making gunpowder. The number of mine shafts and trenches suggests that the sulphur mining must have been on an industrial scale for export as well as for local use. Gunpowder was probably introduced in the Arabian Gulf by the Ottoman emperors, and might have become widespread after the arrival of the Portuguese in the early sixteenth century. Evidence of copper mining in the mountains of the Emirates dates back several thousand years, but the discovery of the Jebel Dhanna sulphur mines adds a previously-unknown element to the knowledge of ancient exploitation of the country's natural resources. Further study of the mines is being undertaken by ADCO and ADIAS.

EXTENSIVE TRADING LINKS

Pottery collected by ADIAS on the islands of Ghagha', in the far west of Abu Dhabi, and Merawah, 100 kilometres west of Abu Dhabi, has shown that the trading links between this region and the civilisation centred in the ancient city of 'Ubaid in southern Iraq, over 7,000 years ago, were more extensive than previously realised.

The existence of trading links between the UAE and the 'Ubaid civilisation has been known for a number of years and distinctive black painted pottery from 'Ubaid has been identified on the northern UAE coastline as well as on the island of Dalma and in Qatar and eastern Saudi Arabia. The new evidence found in the far west of Abu Dhabi indicates that these links were extensive. Pieces of pottery found during survey work on the two islands were examined by Professor Dan Potts of Sydney University, Australia, a leading expert on Gulf archaeology. He concluded that several pieces from each island were probably of the 'Ubaid type. They were also examined by Dr Sophie Mery of the French Centre Nationale pour les Recherches Scientifiques (CNRS) an expert on the early pottery of the Gulf, who confirmed that they were of types manufactured in the city of 'Ubaid. The Ghagha' and Merawah potsherds were sent to the CNRS facility at Nanterre, Paris,

where their chemical composition is being studied as part of a programme run by Dr Mery to determine the place of manufacture of the 'Ubaid type shards.

The discovery on the UAE islands of the Mesopotamian pottery is an indication that their inhabitants, like those of Dalma and the northern UAE, were part of an extensive commercial network. Many of the most significant sites discovered by ADIAS have been on the islands of western Abu Dhabi and this underlines their important role in the country's history as the focus of settlements for thousands of years.

EXCAVATIONS IN SHARJAH

The archaeological team of the Sharjah Department of Culture and Information recommenced excavations in November 1998 of a Bronze Age circular collective tomb from the Umm al-Nar period at Mileiha, on the inland plain south of Dhaid. Dating to around 2,000 BC, the end of the Umm al-Nar period, the tomb is the first of its type to be found in the Mileiha area where the bulk of the sites so far discovered date from the Iron Age, (1,300–300 BC) and the succeeding late Pre-Islamic Period until around 350 AD.

Excavations also continued for the fourth successive year in the Jebel Buhays area, south of Mileiha, both on Iron Age tombs and, with the participation of a team from Germany's University of Tubingen, on a mass cemetery from the Late Stone Age.

A resistivity survey was carried out by the University of Sydney on the important Iron Age fortified village at Muwailah, near Sharjah International Airport, which has yielded the earliest writing ever found in the UAE. The survey was designed to delineate the full extent of the village.

THIRD MILLENNIUM SITE AT KALBA

Further work was also undertaken in Sharjah's enclaves on the UAE's east coast, from Khatmat Milaha, in the south, to Dibba, in the north. This included further excavations by a team from London University's Institute of Archaeology on a *tell* in the date-palm groves of the southern town of Kalba.

With over 10 metres of archaeological deposits, the tell contains evidence of occupation from the early third millennium BC until around 500 BC. During several seasons of work, archaeologists have found the walls of a fortified settlement from the third millennium, overlain with further buildings from the Wadi Suq period (2,000–1,300 BC) and from the succeeding Iron Age.

Artefacts recovered from the Kalba site have included extensive amounts of imported pottery from Mesopotamia, Bahrain, Iran and the Indus Valley, as well as faunal remains which have provided useful insight into the way of life of Kalba's inhabitants over a period of more than 2,000 years.

PORTUGUESE FORT

A team from Australia's University of Sydney, working in association with Fujairah's Department of Antiquities, conducted a first season of study of a small fort, believed to have been built by the Portuguese, in the coastal town of Bidiya. Carbon-14 dating of charcoal from the foundations of the fort suggests that it was constructed in the sixteenth century, while other finds confirm occupation during this period.

The site is the first to be excavated in the UAE to provide evidence of the short-lived Portuguese presence along the country's coastline, although other forts, yet to be discovered, are known to have been built at Kalba, Khor Fakkan, Dibba and Julfar (Ras al-Khaimah).

Other work in Fujairah included a detailed survey of an extensive Late Islamic settlement site and hilltop fort in the Wadi Safad, conducted by a team from Trinity College, Carmathen, in Britain.

COLLECTIVE GRAVE AT SHIMAL

Archaeologists continued study of a collective grave from the Bronze Age at Shimal, in Ras al-Khaimah. Circular in shape, it has been dated to around 2,200 BC, during what is known as the Umm al-Nar period.

Although extensively robbed, the grave produced jewellery and pottery, as well as skeletal material. As many as 300 people may have been originally buried in the grave, which would have been in use for a period of over 100 years. The age of death appears to have ranged between 18 and 40 years. Of particular interest was the discovery of the skeleton of a young woman who was buried with her pet dog, the first time that such a burial has been found in the UAE.

The tomb probably stood when it was built to a height of around 3 metres and is one of the largest Umm al-Nar tombs ever located in the UAE.

Archaeologists working with the National Museum of Ras al-Khaimah, which was responsible for the excavations, believe that other Umm al-Nar tombs may be discovered in the vicinity, as well as a number of other sites.

A few kilometres north of the city of Ras al-Khaimah, on the plain between the coastline and the nearby mountains, Shimal has produced a large number of archaeological sites, ranging in date from the early Bronze Age, at the beginning of the third millennium BC.

SEMINAR ON ARABIAN STUDIES

Recent archaeological discoveries in the UAE figured prominently in the annual three-day Seminar on Arabian Studies held in London from 14–17 July 1999. Five papers on UAE archaeology were presented: Mark Beech of ADIAS and Britain's York University examined recent discoveries at the 7,000-year-old site on Abu Dhabi's western island of Dalma. Henrike Kiesewetter dealt with the neolithic jewellery found during excavations at Jebel Buhays in Sharjah. Dr Walid Al Tikriti, of the Department of Antiquities and Tourism in Al Ain, and Dr Sophie Mery from Paris, reported on the burial customs from the Umm al-Nar period, utilising data from the Hili Tomb N. Dr Jose-Maria Cordoba of Madrid University, reported on findings at an Iron Age settlement at Madam, in Sharjah. The UAE mountains' rock art was examined by the University of Sydney's Michele Ziolkowski.

TRADITIONAL LIFE

The people of the UAE, like those of the rest of the peninsula, are of Arab stock. Their forefathers formed part of successive waves of migration 2,000–3,000 years ago that spread eastwards across Arabia, bringing with them their culture, their language and their skills at surviving in what was becoming an increasingly harsh climate.

As they arrived, they mingled and then merged with the people already living in the region now known as the UAE, people who, like them, were of Semitic stock. Inscriptions in now-extinct Semitic languages found on archaeological sites at Mileiha, in Sharjah, and at al-Dur, in Umm al-Qaiwain, testify to the presence of these early inhabitants, but in the centuries that followed, the population coalesced into a homogeneous whole, united by a common heritage, and, since the coming of Islam in the seventh century AD, by a common faith.

SETTLED TRIBES

Popular accounts from such explorers as the British writer, Sir Wilfred Thesiger, who crossed the Empty Quarter by camel to arrive in the emirates 50 years ago, have created an impression in the outside world that the people of the region were traditionally nomadic herdsmen, the bedu, moving with their camels and goats across the desert from one pasture to another. There is, of course, some truth in that impression, but it is far from the whole picture.

Of the many different tribes that make up the country's population, very few were ever wholly nomadic. The bulk of them were settled, at least for much of the year, engaged in simple agriculture, or in the age-old practice of harvesting the pearl banks and fishery stocks of the Arabian Gulf and the Gulf of Oman coast in the east of the country.

The real desert, with its great sand dunes, is confined to the south and southwest of the country, bordering the Empty Quarter or Rub al-Khali. Across these impressive sand dunes and the gravel plains that fringe them the nomadic tribesmen migrated, like the Awamir, one of the four tribes that together comprise the bulk of the indigenous population of the Emirate of Abu Dhabi. For these resourceful wanderers, a journey across the desert from waterhole to waterhole was a normal part of a harsh life to be endured with equanimity.

Yet even in the desert, as at Liwa, in the south of Abu Dhabi, there are little oases that have been used for hundreds of years by tribes such as the Manasir and the Bani Yas (the confederation headed today by Sheikh Zayed) to cultivate a few palm trees and to grow some vegetables.

CENTRAL ROLE OF THE CAMEL

A legendary capacity for survival in the sandy wastes rendered the camel an ideal beast of burden and winding camel caravans carrying goods for hundreds of kilometres were a familiar feature of this southeastern corner of Arabia right throughout history. Before the discovery of oil, large convoys of camels regularly crossed the desert to Abu Dhabi, Al Ain and Dubai, carrying firewood, charcoal, agricultural products and livestock, returning with much-needed supplies to the desert camp or small villages. Camels transported whole families and their belongings from the humid coast to summer activities in the cooler oases. Camels were also the main means of transport for pilgrims visiting Mecca.

But the camel was much more than a useful pack animal. Not only did it provide milk, meat, wool, skin for water containers, belts, sandals and dung for fuel, it was also a marketable resource used to acquire certain essentials such as rifles, clothes, rice, coffee, sugar or even jewellery.

Today, modern transport is available to everyone and well-stocked, readily accessible supermarkets provide the necessities of life. However, many local families still own a few camels for meat and for milk and they are encouraged to do so by the offer of generous government subsidies.

Camels are also bred for racing, an ancient sport which has been revived with much enthusiasm in recent years. During the great camel races held in the winter months, owners from the Emirates and the rest of Arabia pit their fastest steeds one against the other.

PEARLING

Along the coast, groups like the Qubeisat, the Rumaithat and the Sudan, all part of the Bani Yas, engaged in pearl diving or fishing. Indeed, many of the men spent part of the year in the oases and the remainder at sea, following a lifestyle far different from the romantic image of the nomadic *bedu*.

The women of the family stayed at home, looking after the date-palm gardens and the children, obliged to develop a tough and resilient independence far removed from the false perceptions held in much of the world about the women of Arabia.

In the heyday of the pearling industry, over 1,200 pearling boats operated out of the area now known as the UAE, each carrying an average crew of about 18 men. All the boats from the same port under the authority of one sheikh departed for the main summer harvest at the beginning of June in one great picturesque swoop of sail and returned to port together, approximately 120 days later, towards the end of September.

Life was hard for the individual diver, but pearling was not merely a trade or a means of subsistence, it was an entirely integrated social system, which left behind a rich heritage following the collapse of the industry in the 1930s.

Although the days of large numbers of pearling dhows heading off at the start of the pearling season are long past, efforts are being made to revive the pearl fishery to ensure that this traditional way of life will be preserved in some way.

TRADING

Along the whole of the coast in the Northern Emirates, small towns sprang up around sheltered creeks that provided havens from the often tempestuous waters of the Arabian Gulf and the Gulf of Oman. Here the people derived their living not only from fishing, but also from overseas trade, while the more successful ports, like Dubai, Sharjah or Julfar (later Ras al-Khaimah), the focal point of the Qawasim, looked for their livelihood outwards to the sea, rather than inland, to the desert. The wooden dhows that still can be seen carrying goods to and fro across the Gulf, apart from their diesel engines, are almost identical to the vessels that have been used for centuries.

BOAT-BUILDING

When pearling was at its height, the most important manufacturing industry of the southern Gulf was boat-building. Today in many of the UAE cities and towns, in particular in the Bateen area of Abu Dhabi and along the creek at Ajman, boat-builders can still be seen hard at work constructing dhows with few tools and no blueprints, practising the skills that have been handed down for centuries.

Shell construction, involving the fitting of planks first and ribs later, is the traditional mode of dhow construction, contrasting with the European method of forming a skeleton of ribs prior to planking. Boats are carvel-built with planks laid edge to edge: hundreds, sometimes thousands, of holes are hand-drilled to avoid splitting the wood and long thin nails, wrapped in oiled fibre, are driven through to secure the planks to the frames. Measurements are made solely by eye and experience; templates are, however, used to shape the hull planking. Although it appears that accuracy depends solely on the instinct of the boat-builder, in reality a highly experienced master-craftsman usually oversees the calculations. The tools used in building traditional boats are very basic: hammer, saw, adze, bow-drill, chisel, plane and caulking iron are all that is required to produce such a sophisticated and graceful end-product.

Nowadays, traditional dhows are used as short-haul cargo vessels while specially adapted craft take part in traditional sailing races.

In fact, two kinds of boats are used in traditional boat-racing. The first is powered by a single sail that catches the wind to drive the wooden boats of shallow draught. A couple of dozen such sailing boats scudding across the waves, their sails shining in the sun, is one of the most romantic sights to be seen anywhere in this often-romantic country. Other craft are powered by man, not the wind, great rowing boats of 20 metres or more in length, rowed by up to 100 oarsmen straining every muscle to reach the finishing line.

At the present time, boat races are held on special occasions throughout the year, to commemorate events such as the annual National Day holiday, serving to keep alive the maritime traditions of the region.

FARMING

In areas along the edge of the Hajar mountains, where subterranean water supplies were much more plentiful, such as at Al Ain, the inland oasis-city 160 kilometres from Abu Dhabi, tribes like the Dhawahir spent the whole year tending their palm groves and farms irrigated by tapping the underground water through *falajes* tunnelled through the earth. The earliest *falaj* so far discovered dates back to around 1,000 BC, evidence that agriculture has long been a part of the local way of life.

In the Northern Emirates where the gravel plains are more fertile than the sand dunes, and where there is generally more rainfall, it was also possible to cultivate crops throughout the year, while in the Hajar mountains, tribes like the Shariqiyin, whose centre is the east coast town of Fujairah, and the Shihuh from Musandam, delved deep for the water flowing under the gravel beds of the wadis (valleys) to irrigate small terraces carved out of the mountainsides.

FALCONRY

Falconry, an integral part of desert life for many centuries, was practised originally for purely practical reasons, i.e. the necessity to supplement a meagre diet of dates, milk and bread with a tasty hare or well-fed bustard. In time it developed into a major sport enjoyed by rich and poor alike.

The saker *(Falco cherrug)* and the peregrine *(Falco peregrinus)* are the two main species of falcon used for hunting in the UAE, the former being the most popular since it is well-suited to desert hawking. The female saker *(al hurr)*, larger and more powerful, is utilised more frequently than the male *(garmoush)*. Sakers, brave, patient hunters with keen eyesight, take easily to houbara as their primary quarry. They are less fussy feeders and more able to cope with the stress and rigours of camp life than the temperamental peregrine whose brittle feathers tend to get damaged when struggling with houbara.

Like other hunters, the people of the UAE are concerned with the need to understand and protect the environment and the quarry which they hunt, lest it disappear. With government support, there are now a number of programmes designed to study ways of breeding in captivity the most popular quarry, the houbara bustard and a full programme of research into the country's birdlife is now well under way.

BULL-FIGHTING

Camels were always a beast of burden in the desert areas and are rarely seen on the east coast, a narrow agricultural strip hemmed in by the Hajar mountains. Here, a rather different traditional sport still survives; that of bullfighting. No Spanish-style corrida, however, but a contest that pits bull against bull, with the massive animals locking their horns and wrestling until one turns tail and flees. These bulls are descendants of animals from the Indian subcontinent that were brought in to turn the waterwheels lifting water from shallow wells. Today, their traditional function has been taken over by the pipe or the diesel pump, but the east coast's bulls survive and thrive as the popularity of bullfighting among both expatriates and UAE citizens grows.

The people of the UAE have seen dramatic change in the few short years since the state was established, change that has provided them with all the benefits of a modern, developed society. At the same time, however, both government and people are determined that their heritage shall be preserved, in line with Sheikh Zayed's belief that 'a people that knows not its past can have neither a present nor a future'.

In the past, life in the UAE was hard and it took extraordinary skill to be able to survive in the harsh terrain and arid climate. Today, things are easier, but by holding on to their heritage the people are able to draw upon their confidence in their past to tackle and overcome the challenges of the present and future.

POLITICAL SYSTEM

Since the establishment of the Federation in 1971, the seven emirates comprising the UAE have forged a distinct national identity through consolidation of their federal status and now enjoy an enviable degree of political stability. The UAE's political system, which is a unique combination of the traditional and the modern, has underpinned this political success, enabling the country to develop a modern administrative structure while at the same time ensuring that the best of the traditions of the past are maintained, adapted and preserved.

FORMATION OF THE FEDERATION

Following the British termination of their agreements with the Trucial States (the name by which the area was formally known), the rulers of the seven emirates established a federal state officially entitled *Dawlat al Imarat al Arabiyya al Muttahida* (State of the United Arab Emirates).

The philosophy behind the state was explained in a statement which was released on 2 December 1971 when the new state was formally established:

The United Arab Emirates has been established as an independent state, possessing sovereignty. It is part of the greater Arab nation. Its aim is to maintain its independence, its sovereignty, its security and its stability, in defence against any attack on its entity or on the entity of any of its member Emirates. It also seeks to protect the freedoms and rights of its people and to achieve trustworthy cooperation between the Emirates for the common good. Among its aims, in addition to the purposes above described, is to work for the sake of the progress of the country in all fields, for the sake of providing a better life for its citizens, to give assistance and support to Arab causes and interests, and to support the Charter of the United Nations and international morals.

FEDERAL CONSTITUTION

Each of the component emirates of the Federation already had its own existing institutions of government and to provide for the effective governing of the new state, the Rulers agreed to draw up a provisional Constitution specifying those powers which were to be allocated to new federal institutions, all others remaining the prerogative of the individual emirates.

Assigned to the federal authorities, under Articles 120 and 121 of the Constitution, were the areas of responsibility for foreign affairs, security and defence, nationality and immigration issues, education, public health, currency, postal, telephone and other communications services, air traffic control and licensing of aircraft, as well as a number of other topics specifically prescribed, including labour relations, banking, delimitation of territorial waters and extradition of criminals.

In parallel, the Constitution also stated in Article 116 that: 'the Emirates shall exercise all powers not assigned to the federation by this Constitution'. This was reaffirmed in Article 122, which stated that 'the Emirates shall have jurisdiction in all matters not assigned to the exclusive jurisdiction of the federation, in accordance with the provision of the preceding two Articles'.

The new federal system of government included a Supreme Council, a Cabinet or Council of Ministers, a parliamentary body, the Federal National Council and an independent judiciary, at the peak of which is the Federal Supreme Court.

SUPREME COUNCIL OF THE FEDERATION

In a spirit of consensus and collaboration, the Rulers of the seven emirates agreed during the process of federation that each of them would be a member of a Supreme Council, the top policy-making body in the new state. They agreed also that they would elect a President and a Vice-President from amongst their number, to serve for a five-year term of office. The Ruler of Abu Dhabi, Sheikh Zayed bin Sultan Al Nahyan, was elected as the first President, a post to which he has been re-elected at successive five-yearly intervals, while the Ruler of Dubai, Sheikh Rashid bin Saeed Al Maktoum, was elected as first Vice-President, a post he continued to hold until his death in 1990, at which point his eldest son and heir, Sheikh Maktoum bin Rashid Al Maktoum, was elected to succeed him.

Current members of the Supreme Council

HH President Sheikh Zayed bin Sultan Al Nahyan, Ruler of Abu Dhabi

HH Vice-President and Prime Minister Sheikh Maktoum bin Rashid Al Maktoum, Ruler of Dubai

HH Dr Sheikh Sultan bin Mohammed Al Qasimi, Ruler of Sharjah

HH Sheikh Saqr bin Mohammed Al Qasimi, Ruler of Ras al-Khaimah

HH Sheikh Rashid bin Ahmed Al Mu'alla, Ruler of Umm al-Qaiwain

HH Sheikh Humaid bin Rashid Al Nuaimi, Ruler of Ajman

HH Sheikh Hamad bin Mohammed Al Sharqi, Ruler of Fujairah

Crown Princes and Deputy Rulers

HH Sheikh Khalifa bin Zayed Al Nahyan, Crown Prince of Abu Dhabi and Deputy Supreme Commander of the UAE Armed Forces, Chairman of the Executive Council of the Emirate of Abu Dhabi

HE Sheikh Hamdan bin Rashid Al Maktoum, Deputy Ruler of Dubai, Minister of Finance and Industry

General HE Sheikh Mohammed bin Rashid Al Maktoum, Crown Prince of Dubai and
 Minister of Defence

HE Sheikh Sultan bin Mohammed Al Qasimi, Crown Prince and Deputy Ruler of
 Sharjah

HE Sheikh Khalid bin Saqr Al Qasimi, Crown Prince and Deputy Ruler
 of Ras al-Khaimah

HE Sheikh Saud bin Rashid Al Mu'alla, Crown Prince of Umm al-Qaiwain

HE Sheikh Ammar bin Humaid Al Nuaimi, Crown Prince of Ajman

HE Sheikh Ahmed bin Sultan Al Qasimi, Deputy Ruler of Sharjah

HE Sheikh Hamad bin Saif Al Sharqi, Deputy Ruler of Fujairah

HE Sheikh Sultan bin Saqr Al Qasimi, Deputy Ruler of Ras al-Khaimah

The Federal Supreme Council is vested with legislative as well as executive powers. It ratifies
federal laws and decrees, plans general policy, approves the nomination of the Prime
Minister and accepts his resignation. It also relieves him from his post upon the
recommendation of the President. The Supreme Council elects the President and his
deputy for five-year terms; both may be re-elected.

At an historic meeting on 20 May 1996 the Federal Supreme Council approved a draft
amendment to the country's provisional Constitution, making it the permanent Constitution
of the UAE. The amendment also named Abu Dhabi as the capital of the state.

THE COUNCIL OF MINISTERS

The Council of Ministers or Cabinet, described in the Constitution as 'the executive
authority' for the Federation, includes the usual complement of ministerial portfolios and
is headed by a Prime Minister chosen by the President in consultation with his colleagues

on the Supreme Council. The Prime Minister, currently the Vice-President, although this has not always been the case, then selects the ministers who may be drawn from any of the Federation's component emirates although, naturally, the more populous emirates have generally provided more members of each Cabinet.

The current 21-member Cabinet, comprising 17 ministers and four ministers of state, was appojnted on 25 March 1997 under the terms of Decree No. 67 of 1997 and according to the proposal of Vice-President HH Sheikh Maktoum bin Rashid Al Maktoum, who was requested by the President to form a new government.

Members of the Cabinet

Prime Minister: Vice-President HH Sheikh Maktoum bin Rashid Al Maktoum
Deputy Prime Minister: Sheikh Sultan bin Zayed Al Nahyan
Minister of Finance and Industry: Sheikh Hamdan bin Rashid Al Maktoum
Minister of Defence: Gen. Sheikh Mohammed bin Rashid Al Maktoum
Minister of State for Foreign Affairs: Sheikh Hamdan bin Zayed Al Nahyan
Minister of Information and Culture: Sheikh Abdullah bin Zayed Al Nahyan
Minister of Planning: Sheikh Humaid bin Ahmed Al Mu'alla
Minister of Higher Education and Scientific Research: Sheikh Nahyan bin Mubarak Al Nahyan
Minister of Economy and Commerce: Sheikh Fahim bin Sultan Al Qasimi
Minister of State for Supreme Council Affairs: Sheikh Majed bin Saeed Al Nuaimi
Minister of Foreign Affairs: Rashid Abdullah Al Nuaimi
Minister of Interior: Lt Gen. Dr Mohammed Saeed Al Badi
Minister of Health: Hamad Abdul Rahman Al Madfa
Minister of Electricity and Water: Humaid bin Nasir Al Owais
Minister of State for Cabinet Affairs: Saeed Khalfan Al Ghaith
Minister of Agriculture and Fisheries: Saeed Mohammed Al Ragabani
Minister of Communications: Ahmed Humaid Al Tayer
Minister of Public Works and Housing: Rakad bin Salem Al Rakad
Minister of Petroleum and Mineral Resources: Obeid bin Saif Al Nassiri
Minister of Education and Youth: Dr Abdul Aziz Al Sharhan
Minister of Justice, Islamic Affairs and Awqaf: Mohammed Nukhaira Al Dhahiri
Minister of Labour and Social Affairs: Mattar Humaid Al Tayer
Minister of State for Financial and Industrial Affairs: Dr Mohammed Khalfan bin Kharbash.
The Director General of the President's Office, Sheikh Mansour bin Zayed Al Nahyan, also has ministerial status.

FEDERAL NATIONAL COUNCIL

The Federal National Council (FNC) has 40 members drawn from the emirates on the basis of their population, with eight for each of Abu Dhabi and Dubai, six each for Sharjah and Ras al-Khaimah, and four each for Fujairah, Umm al-Qaiwain and Ajman. The selection of representative members is left to the discretion of each emirate and the members' legislative term is deemed to be two calendar years.

Day-to-day operation of the FNC is governed by standing orders based on the provisions of Article 85 of the Constitution. These orders were first issued in 1972 and subsequently amended by Federal Decree No. 97 of 1977.

The FNC plays an important role in serving the people and the nation and consolidating the principles of *shura* (consultation) in the country. Presided over by a speaker, or either of two deputy speakers, elected from amongst its members, the FNC has both a legislative and supervisory role under the Constitution. This means that it is responsible for examining and, if it wishes, amending all proposed federal legislation, and is empowered to summon and to question any federal minister regarding ministry performance. One of the main duties of the FNC is to discuss the annual budget. Specialised sub-committees and a Research and Studies Unit have been formed to assist FNC members to cope with the increasing demands of modern government.

Since its inception the council has been successively chaired by the following Speakers:
Thani bin Abdulla
Taryam bin Omran Taryam
Hilal bin Ahmed bin Lootah
Al-Haj bin Abdullah Al Muhairbi
Mohammed Khalifa Al Habtoor

During a meeting with Speaker Mohammed Khalifa Al Habtoor at the conclusion of the eleventh legislative chapter of the FNC, Sheikh Zayed said that the establishment of the FNC, which coincided with the creation of the UAE Federation, was intended to provide a means to assess the needs of the country's citizens so that a decent standard of living could be provided for them. Sheikh Zayed urged the FNC chairman and members to live up to their responsibilities and serve the country and its people to the best of their abilities. 'We have high hope of your loyalty and integrity, as these two traits are invaluable,' he said. The President added that, although many people thought that politics was solely a government concern, in fact it is an integral part of everyday life.

The President praised the achievements of the FNC during its last session, saying: 'This is not a courtesy because your tribute to us is also directed at you, and what you are doing in the service of your country. Its people will hold you in greater esteem, as they may do us.' Mr Habtoor thanked Sheikh Zayed for his continuous support for the FNC and for taking a personal interest in solving problems facing the UAE, especially in the housing sector. He also thanked the President for his efforts to secure a decent life for all citizens.

At an international level, the FNC is a member of the International Parliamentary Union (IPU), as well as the Arab Parliamentary Union (APU) and participates actively in these bodies.

FEDERAL JUDICIARY

The federal judiciary, whose independence is guaranteed under the Constitution, includes the Federal Supreme Court and Courts of First Instance. The Federal Supreme Court consists of five judges appointed by the Supreme Council of Rulers. The judges decide on the constitutionality of federal laws and arbitrate on intra-emirate disputes and disputes between the federal government and the emirates.

LOCAL GOVERNMENT

Parallel to and, on occasion interlocking with the federal institutions, each of the seven emirates also has its own local government. Although all have expanded significantly as a result of the country's growth over the last 28 years, these differ in size and complexity from emirate to emirate, depending on a variety of factors such as population, area and degree of development. Thus the largest and most populous emirate, Abu Dhabi, has its own central governing organ, the Executive Council, chaired by the Crown Prince Sheikh Khalifa bin Zayed Al Nahyan. The Eastern and Western Regions are headed by an official with the title of Ruler's Representative. There is also a Ruler's Representative on the important oil terminal island of Das.

The main cities, Abu Dhabi and Al Ain, the latter also the capital of the Eastern Region, are administered by municipalities, each of which has a nominated municipal council, while the National Consultative Council, chaired by a Speaker and with 60 members drawn from among the emirate's main tribes and families, undertakes a role similar to that of the FNC on a country-wide level, questioning officials and examining and endorsing local legislation. It is also a source of vocal suggestion for the introduction or revision of federal legislation.

Administration in the emirate is implemented by a number of local departments, covering topics such as public works, water and electricity, finance, customs and management. Some have a responsibility for the whole of the emirate although in certain spheres, such as water and electricity, there are also departments covering only the Eastern Region.

A similar pattern of municipalities and departments can be found in each of the other emirates, while Sharjah, with its three enclaves on the country's east coast, has also adopted the practice of devolving some authority on a local basis with branches headed by deputy chairmen in both Kalba and Khor Fakkan of the Sharjah Emiri Diwan (Court).

In smaller or remoter settlements, the Ruler and government of each emirate may choose a local representative, (known as an emir or wali) to act as a conduit through which the concerns of inhabitants may be directed to government. In most cases these are the leading local tribal figures whose influence and authority derives both from their fellow tribesmen and from the confidence placed in them by the Ruler. This is an example of the way in which local leaders within the traditional system have become involved with, and lend legitimacy to, the new structures of government.

FEDERAL AND LOCAL GOVERNMENT

The powers of the various federal institutions and their relationship with the separate institutions in each emirate, as laid down in the Constitution, have evolved and changed since the establishment of the state. Under the terms of the Constitution Rulers may, if they wish, relinquish certain areas of authority, prescribed as being the responsibility of individual emirates, to the federal government, one significant such decision being that to unify the armed forces in the mid-1970s. The 1971 Constitution also permitted each emirate to retain, or to take up, membership in the Organisation of Petroleum Exporting Countries (OPEC) and the Organisation of Arab Petroleum Exporting Countries

(OAPEC), although none have done so; the only emirate to be a member in 1971, Abu Dhabi, having chosen to relinquish its memberships in favour of the Federation.

In line with the dramatic social and economic development that has taken place since the foundation of the state the organs of government, both federal and local, have also developed impressively and their influence now affect almost all aspects of life for both UAE citizens and expatriates. As with other relatively young states, new institutions that were created for the first time have derived their legitimacy and status from the extent of their activities and achievements and from acknowledgement and appreciation of their role by the people.

The relationship between the new systems of government, federal and local, has itself evolved in a constructive manner. As the smaller emirates have benefited from development in terms of, for example, education, so they have been able to find the personnel to extend the variety of services provided by their own local governments which had once been handled on their behalf by federal institutions, such as tourism. At the same time, in other areas such as the judiciary, there has been an evolving trend towards a further voluntary relinquishment of local authority to the federal institutions. These new systems of government have not, however, replaced the traditional forms which coexist and evolve alongside them.

TRADITIONAL GOVERNMENT

Traditionally the Ruler of an emirate, the sheikh, was the leader of the most powerful, though not necessarily the most populous, tribe, while each individual tribe and often its various sub-sections also generally had a chief or sheikh. Such Rulers and chiefs maintained their authority only insofar as they were able to retain the loyalty and support of their people, in essence a form of direct democracy, though without the paraphernalia of western forms of suffrage. Part of that democracy was the unwritten but strong principle that the people should have free access to their sheikh and that he should hold a frequent and open *majlis*, or council, in which his fellow tribesmen could voice their opinions.

Such a direct democracy, of course, may be ideally suited to small and relatively uncomplicated societies but becomes steadily more difficult to maintain as populations grow, while the increasing sophistication of government administration means that on a day-to-day basis many of the inhabitants of the emirates now find it more appropriate to deal directly with these institutions on most matters, rather than to seek to meet directly with their Ruler or sheikh.

The role of the *majlis*

One fascinating aspect of life in the UAE today and one that is essential to an understanding of its political system, is the way in which the institution of the *majlis* has continued to maintain its relevance. In larger emirates, not only the Ruler, but also a number of other senior members of his family continue to hold open *majlises* (or *majalis*), in which participants may raise a wide range of topics, from a request for a piece of land or for a scholarship for a son or daughter to go abroad, to more weighty subjects such as the impact of large-scale foreign immigration upon society or complaints about perceived flaws in the practices of various ministries and departments.

In smaller emirates, the *majlis* of the Ruler himself, or of the crown prince or deputy Ruler, remain the main focus. In Fujairah, for example, the Ruler holds an open *majlis* at least once a week (daily during the Muslim holy fasting month of Ramadan), which may be attended by both citizens and expatriates. To these *majlises* come traditionally-minded tribesmen who may have waited several months for the opportunity to discuss with their Ruler directly, rather than choose to pursue their requests or complaints through a modern governmental structure. In modern society, of course, as President Sheikh Zayed himself has commented, it is naturally easier for a Ruler to go to meet his people than for them to come to meet him. Sheikh Zayed frequently travels within the UAE, providing opportunities for him to meet with citizens away from the formal surroundings of an office or palace. During his regular inspection tours of projects he also takes pains to ensure that citizens living nearby are guaranteed easy access to him.

EVOLVING TRADITIONS

Just as the modern institutions have developed in response to public need and demand, so have the traditional forms of tribal administration adapted. With many relatively routine matters now being dealt with by the modern institutions, the traditional ones, like the *majlis*, have been able to focus on more complex issues rather than on the routine matters with which they were once heavily involved.

In the *majlises*, for example, it is possible to hear detailed, and often heated, discussions between sheikhs and other citizens on questions such as the policy that should be adopted towards the evolution of the machinery of government, or the nature of relations with neighbouring countries. On matters more directly affecting the individual, such as the topic of unemployment among young UAE graduates, debates often tend to begin in the *majlises*, where discussion can be fast and furious, before a consensus approach is evolved that is subsequently reflected in changes in government policy.

Through such means the traditional methods of government in the UAE have been able to retain both their relevance and vitality and they continue to play an important, although often unpublicised, role in the evolution of the state today.

A BALANCED APPROACH

When the Rulers of the seven emirates met 28 years ago to agree on the forms of government for their new federal state, they chose deliberately not simply to copy from others. They chose instead to work towards a society that would offer the best of modern administration while at the same time retaining the traditional forms of government that with their inherent commitment to consensus, discussion and direct democracy, offered the best features of the past.

With the benefit of hindsight, it is evident that they made the correct choice for despite the massive economic growth and the social dislocation caused by a population explosion, the state has enjoyed political stability. During the course of the last few decades there have been numerous attempts to create federal states, both in the Arab world and elsewhere. The UAE is the only one in the Arab world to have stood the test of time.

INTERNATIONAL RELATIONS

The basic guidelines of foreign policy, still followed today, first began to emerge clearly in the mid-1960s when Sheikh Zayed became the Ruler of Abu Dhabi, not long after its commencement of oil exports gave it both the need to extend its international ties and also the economic weight to play a regional and then an international role.

Those guidelines, like those of many other small states in the community of nations, are based upon the principles enunciated in the Charter of the United Nations, notably those of non-interference in the internal affairs of others, respect for the sovereignty and territorial integrity of nations, as well as inadmissibility of the acquisition of territory by force. The UAE also faithfully adheres to the principles outlined in the Charter of the Organisation of the Islamic Conference (OIC).

Some of the basic foci of policy have been constant over the years. In particular, from the earliest days of the state the UAE has upheld a desire for close relations with other Arab states and, therefore, Arab unity, Arab solidarity and reconciliation within the Arab League have been constant themes. To this end the UAE presses for regular summit meetings of the Arab League and stresses that Arabs and Muslims must learn to resolve their differences through dialogue based on truth, justice and forgiveness.

Cooperation and neighbourliness are particularly evident in the UAE's relations with other Gulf states. Indeed the Arab Gulf Cooperation Council (AGCC), founded in Abu Dhabi in 1981, is a central component of UAE foreign policy, especially its continuous efforts, through collective action, to encourage regional stability.

The nineteenth annual AGCC summit, which was hosted in Abu Dhabi on 7 December 1998, marked a milestone in the Council's 18-year history. For the first time an AGCC summit was addressed by a foreign head of state, South African President Nelson Mandela. The leading role of the AGCC on the global stage was also underlined by the presence of the UN Secretary-General Kofi Annan who attended the opening session along with the Organisation of Islamic Conference Secretary-General Dr Izzedin Al Iraqi and Arab League Secretary-General Dr Esmat Abdel-Meguid.

The following brief summary of international relations during the year under review underlines the fact that the UAE, in accordance with the convictions outlined above, continues to play a positive role as a significant influence for rapprochement and peace, as a firm voice for justice and human rights and as a generous aid donor.

THREE ISLANDS ISSUE

During 1999 the Government of the UAE has sought, with considerable success, to consolidate international support for its continuing diplomatic efforts to resolve the Iranian occupation in 1971 of the three islands of Greater and Lesser Tunb and Abu Musa.

While the UAE, like other member states of the AGCC, seeks to develop bilateral economic and political links with Iran, there is a clearly defined and agreed policy, both in the UAE and at the AGCC level, that such development will not take place at the expense of the UAE's sovereignty over the islands.

It is now 28 years since Iran forcibly seized Greater and Lesser Tunb on the night of 30 November 1971. At that time, a Memorandum of Understanding was signed between Iran and Sharjah, to allow for both to administer part of the island of Abu Musa, without prejudice to their continuing claims of sovereignty. Since then and most particularly since 1994, Iran has continually been in breach of the terms of the Memorandum of Understanding, interfering with free access, building military installations and placing military equipment on the island and moving in settlers whose presence has demonstrably and significantly altered the demographic structure of the population of Abu Musa. It has also, in contravention of the Memorandum of Understanding, imposed its control over areas of Abu Musa which were reserved under the agreement to Sharjah.

UAE suggestions for resolution

The Government of the UAE has consistently reaffirmed its right to sovereignty over the islands, protesting at the military occupation and subsequent fortification of the Tunbs and at the overt breach of the terms of the Memorandum of Understanding on Abu Musa. At the same time, while continuing to assert its sovereignty over the islands, the UAE has offered two suggestions to Iran as ways of seeking to find a solution to the political impasse.

The first is for the two parties to engage in direct bilateral discussions on the resolution of issues arising out of the Iranian occupation of the three islands, including both the proper implementation of the terms of the Memorandum of Understanding on Abu Musa and the broader, but related, question of sovereignty. The UAE has set no preconditions on the offer to hold such discussions, apart from stating the necessity of laying down a fixed time limit for their conclusion. The second option is for the issue of sovereignty to be submitted to international arbitration or referred to the International Court of Justice (ICJ) in The Hague, the UAE agreeing to be bound in advance to accept any ruling made by the Court.

The Government of Iran has rejected both options. Since the ICJ can only exercise its jurisdiction if both parties agree to referral of a dispute, this effectively means that Iran has rejected the good offices of the world's primary legal body, which would examine in detail any documentation put forward by the parties. The refusal of Iran to agree to a process which would require the submission of legal documentation must, inevitably, cast doubt on the legal validity of its claims.

The Government of Iran has agreed to enter into bilateral discussions and has said that these would be without preconditions. At the same time, Iranian officials have refused to discuss the question of sovereignty over the three islands, referring only to the need to resolve 'misunderstandings'. Frequent Iranian statements have reaffirmed claim to sovereignty over the islands, refusing in particular to enter into any discussion with relation to Greater and Lesser Tunb.

While, in the opinion of the Government of the UAE, its claim to sovereignty over the islands is fully justified, it is willing to allow the issue to be settled through bilateral discussions, through international arbitration, or by the ICJ, and is prepared to submit documentation to be evaluated within the framework of international law.

Legal issues

International law states clearly that sovereignty cannot be acquired by invasion, military force or coercion. In the case of Greater and Lesser Tunb, the Iranian invasion in 1971 in which a number of Ras al-Khaimah policemen were killed, is a matter of historical fact. In the case of the Memorandum of Understanding on Abu Musa, the Government of Sharjah specifically reserved its rights to sovereignty. Quite apart from the fact that the Memorandum was signed only under the threat of invasion, amounting to coercion, it has subsequently been breached substantially and consistently in such a way as to indicate that the Government of Iran has no intention of abiding by its terms.

Arab rulers since 1330

Aside from the legal issues outlined above there is a wealth of historical documentation to support the UAE's claim to sovereignty over the islands. Apart from short and interrupted periods in the seventeenth and eighteenth centuries the three islands have been governed by Arab rulers since 1330. From then until 1622 they were part of the Arab-ruled Kingdom of Hormuz, based on the island of the same name, which also included much of what is now the UAE and Oman.

From the middle of the eighteenth century the islands were ruled by the Al Qawasim dynasty which today provides the sheikhs of Ras al-Khaimah and Sharjah. At that time the State of the Al Qawasim included not only much of the northern UAE and the three islands but also extended along the southern coast of Iran to include the port of Bandar Lingeh. Treaties signed with the British in the early nineteenth century acknowledged that the Al Qasimi dominions extended to both sides of the Arabian Gulf and, at the same time, represented an acknowledgement of their sovereignty under prevailing international law.

Bandar Lingeh remained under the rule of an Al Qasimi sheikh until 1886, at which time it was absorbed by Iran, regardless of the fact that it had by then been part of the Al Qasimi state for over a century. In 1887 Iran occupied a fourth island, Sirri, also part of the Al Qasimi dominions although administered by the Bandar Lingeh branch of the family. In a protest to Tehran, the British Government, which had been in treaty relations with the Emirates since 1820, noted that Sirri, as well as the other islands, 'formed part of the hereditary estates of the Jowasimi (Qasimi) Arab Sheikhs'. Many of Sirri's inhabitants, rejecting the occupation, then moved to Abu Musa, which remained uncontested as part of the Al Qasimi state.

As late as 1903 the British Political Resident in the Gulf was able to state that, as far as he was aware, Iran had made no claim to the Tunbs. The next year, however, Iranian customs officials landed on both Abu Musa and Greater Tunb, although, after protests from the Ruler of Sharjah (which then included Ras al-Khaimah) and from Britain, they withdrew. At the time the Government of Iran failed to respond to a request from Britain that it should produce documentation in support of its claim to the islands.

Al Qasimi state divided

In 1920 the Al Qasimi state divided into two, with Abu Musa becoming part of Sharjah, and Greater and Lesser Tunb becoming part of Ras al-Khaimah. Shortly afterwards in 1923, Iran once again put forward a claim to sovereignty over the three islands, but following protests from Sharjah, Ras al-Khaimah and Britain, the claim was dropped. Further incidents of Iranian interference took place, prompting more protests. In 1926 the Iranian customs were instructed by Tehran 'not to take any steps in Abu Musa or Tamb (the Tunbs), pending reply from the Ministry of Foreign Affairs regarding status of these islands', a clear indication that Iran was unsure of the legal validity of its claims.

The weakness of the Iranian position, in terms of international law, was underlined during negotiations between Iran and Britain in the late 1920s. Iran first offered to withdraw its claim to Abu Musa if its title over the Tunbs was recognised. Failing in that objective, in itself an acknowledgement that its claim to Abu Musa had no validity, Iran then offered to buy the Tunbs. The offer was rejected in 1930 by the Ruler of Ras al-Khaimah with the support of his colleague, the Ruler of Sharjah, following which Iran then offered to lease the Tunbs for a period of 50 years. Once again no agreement was reached. Sharjah and Ras al-Khaimah continued to exercise their sovereignty over the three islands unchallenged until the late 1960s.

British withdrawal prompts renewed claims

Following the announcement in 1968 by Britain of its intention to withdraw from the Arabian Gulf by the end of 1971 the Government of Iran put forward a claim to the whole of the island of Bahrain. In the wake of a referendum conducted on Bahrain under UN supervision, Iran was obliged to abandon its claim which had no legal basis. It promptly revived its then-dormant claim to Abu Musa and Greater and Lesser Tunb. It is significant, in terms of international law, that it did so not on the basis of providing historical evidence of its claim to sovereignty but through threat of coercion.

On 28 September 1971 the Shah of Iran stated in an interview with the London *Guardian* that: 'we need them [the islands]; we shall have them; no power on earth shall stop us'.

Attempts by Britain to resolve the problem had mixed results. Sharjah, reserving its claim to sovereignty over Abu Musa but concerned about the obvious coercion from Iran, agreed to sign a Memorandum of Understanding. In the case of Greater and Lesser Tunb, Ras al-Khaimah declined to agree to any form of Iranian presence, with the result that Iran invaded and occupied them.

The Iranian presence on the three islands today is based in the case of the Tunbs on military occupation undertaken in contravention of international law. In the case of Abu Musa, threats and coercion, which are themselves illegal under international law, were used by Iran to obtain agreement on a Memorandum of Understanding which has then been constantly breached in such a manner and to such an extent as to render open to question the continuing validity of the Memorandum itself. In effect, therefore, particularly in the light of Iran's militarisation of those areas of Abu Musa in which it is present, Abu Musa too is under Iranian military occupation.

UAE keen to pursue peaceful option

Notwithstanding the illegal nature of the Iranian presence on the three islands the Government of the UAE is keen to pursue any peaceful option that may lead to a resolution of the issue. The UAE's offer to submit the case to the ICJ or to international arbitration having been rejected by Iran the UAE has suggested once again, with the support of its AGCC partners and with backing from resolutions passed by a number of regional and international organisations, that the two states should engage in bilateral negotiations without preconditions, apart from the setting of a timetable for their completion.

That offer remains on the table. During the past year the Iranian Government has stated, as it has done before, that it wishes to improve relations with the Arab states of the Gulf. The view of the UAE and of its AGCC colleagues is that such talk from Iran cannot be taken seriously until such time as it is supported by concrete and positive steps to deal with the issue of the islands. Their future remains a key factor in intra-Gulf relations.

OMAN

An historic border demarcation pact was signed with Oman during Sheikh Zayed's three-day official visit (1–3 May 1999) to the Sultanate. The pact covers a section of the UAE–Oman border from Umm al-Zumul to the east of Aqeedat. The three-way border between the UAE, Oman and Saudi Arabia is at Umm al-Zumul. The agreement, which is destined to strengthen relations between the countries, marked the culmination of nearly three decades of quiet diplomacy. Arab League Secretary-General Dr Esmat Abdel-Meguid welcomed the border demarcation accord describing it as a major achievement and urging other Arab countries to follow suit.

Sheikh Zayed's visit to Oman was his second official trip to the neighbouring AGCC state. His first, in 1991, culminated in the setting up of a joint UAE–Oman Higher Committee which has convened a number of times. Following the establishment of the committee the UAE and Oman, to facilitate movement between the two countries, have agreed that their citizens may use ID cards for cross-border travel. A joint venture company with a capital of US $100 million has also been set up to promote commercial development.

In June 1999, in a further move to foster ties with the UAE, the Omani Government granted UAE citizens the right to own real estate in Oman. A joint visa for access to both countries is also being prepared in order to promote trade and tourism.

QATAR

The UAE and Qatar signed an agreement in December 1998 on the formation of a Higher UAE–Qatar Cooperation Committee reflecting the desire of the two leaders, Sheikh Zayed and Sheikh Hamad bin Khalifa Al Thani, the Emir of Qatar, to consolidate bilateral relations. The Higher UAE–Qatar Joint Committee held its first meeting in Abu Dhabi on 3 May 1999. Members of the committee include ministers of defence, interior, finance, industry, economy and commerce, communications, petroleum and resources, as well as information and culture. The recommendation by the Higher Joint Committee that specialised ministerial committees should be set up to discuss ways of enhancing cooperation in various fields has been fully implemented, several such meetings having been convened.

BAHRAIN

A three-day closure of offices and 40-day official mourning was declared in the UAE on 8 March following the death of the Emir of Bahrain, HH Sheikh Isa bin Salman Al Khalifa. While offering his condolences on this great loss, Sheikh Zayed pledged the full support of the UAE for the new Emir, HH Shekih Hamad bin Isa Al Khalifa.

A visit by HH Sheikh Hamad to Abu Dhabi in May, which included a meeting with Sheikh Zayed on the island of Sîr Banî Yâs, helped to strengthen cooperation between the two states.

YEMEN

Sheikh Zayed received President Ali Abdullah Saleh of Yemen at the end of May 1999. The meeting formed part of ongoing consultations between the two leaders on Arab and international issues and ways of reinforcing bilateral cooperation. The two leaders also stressed the need for Arab unity and solidarity. President Saleh paid tribute to Sheikh Zayed for his dedication to Arab and Islamic causes and pointed to the financing by the UAE President of the reconstruction of the historic Marib dam as testimony to his unstinting support for Yemen.

As a further indication of the close relationship between the two nations a cultural cooperation agreement was signed at the beginning of June 1999 by Minister of Information and Culture Sheikh Abdullah bin Zayed Al Nahyan, who was visiting Yemen, and the Yemeni Minister of Culture and Tourism Abdel Malik Mansour.

The agreement, which is valid for five years and is subject to automatic renewal by mutual consent, envisages the setting up of a joint committee to supervise its implementation.

IRAQ

The UAE has continuously demanded that Iraq abide by UN Security Council resolutions imposed following its invasion of Kuwait, at the same time expressing its sympathy for the hardships which the Iraqi people are forced to endure as a result of economic sanctions, In this context, Foreign Minister Rashid Abdullah, in his opening speech to the fifty-fourth session of the UN General Assembly on 21 September 1999, emphasised that the security of the Arab Gulf is the collective and joint responsibility of the states of the region, and called upon the Government of Iraq:

> ... to complete its implementation of the relevant resolutions of the Security Council, in particular those relating to revealing the whereabouts and to the release of the Kuwaitis and nationals of other countries who are detained or held prisoners of war by Iraq, and the restitution of Kuwaiti property and documents, which would contribute to the restoration of the normal role of Iraq at the regional and international levels.

> The inhuman conditions visited upon the Iraqi people make it incumbent upon all of us to seek an early end to their suffering. We, therefore, call upon the Security Council, and in particular its permanent members, to reach consensus on the drafts before it, leading to the implementation of its resolutions in full in order to lift the international economic embargo imposed on Iraq, and emphasizing the importance of respect for the integrity and unity of its territory.

JORDAN

Sheikh Zayed expressed his deep sadness and pain over the passing of King Hussein of Jordan:

> The death of King Hussein is a great loss not only for the Hashemite family and Jordan, but also for the UAE leadership, government and people. His Majesty King Hussein was a great leader who devoted his life to the service of the Arab and Islamic nation and the defence of right and justice. His Majesty was a faithful and intimate friend of the UAE. The UAE has lost a dear brother, a person faithful to his people and nation and a wise and courageous leader who dedicated his life to serving his nation and people.

Sheikh Zayed also expressed his confidence in King Hussein's chosen successor, His Majesty King Abdullah and stressed that the UAE would support the Government and people of Jordan and would provide them with all possible assistance.

A 40-day period of official mourning was declared and federal ministries, and local government departments were closed for three days.

King Abdullah paid a three-day visit to the UAE in April 1999 and was warmly received at Abu Dhabi International Airport by Sheikh Zayed and Vice-President, Prime Minister Sheikh Maktoum bin Rashid Al Maktoum and other dignitaries. Sheikh Zayed held talks with King Abdullah and decorated him with the Order of Zayed the First.

PALESTINE

Proceeding from its belief in the necessity of achieving a just and comprehensive peace in the Middle East based on the principle of land for peace and the relevant UN Security Council resolutions, the UAE welcomed the Palestinian–Israeli peace agreement signed by the new Israeli Government at Sharm El-Sheikh on 5 September 1999, and the preliminary contacts between Palestine and Israel regarding the final phase negotiations which are to deal with the issues of Jerusalem, settlements, refugees and borders. At the same time the UAE called upon the Israeli Government to implement, fully and scrupulously, without further delay or obstruction, all the undertakings and commitments it had assumed within the framework of the accords, in particular, those relating to halting settlement activities in various parts of occupied Palestine and other Arab territories, including Jerusalem, and the return of Palestinian refugees in accordance with .the relevant resolutions of the international community and the Fourth Geneva Convention

The UAE also applauded the positive role played by the United States of America in reviving the peace process and expressed the hope that the co-sponsors of the process, members of the European Union (EU) and other states, would continue with their efforts to persuade the Israeli Government to fulfil its historical, political and legal obligations, thus restoring to the Palestinian people their legitimate right to self-determination, including the right to establish an independent state in Palestine, with Jerusalem as its capital.

The UAE also demanded that the Government of Israel implement Security Council resolution 425 which calls for the withdrawal of Israeli forces without any preconditions, from the south of Lebanon and from the western Beqaa valley, and that it resume negotiation on the Syrian and Lebanese tracks from the point where they were cut off, with a view to ensuring a complete Israeli withdrawal from the Syrian Arab Golan to the line existing on 4 June 1967, in accordance with Security Council resolutions 242 and 338 and the principle of land for peace.

At the donors conference held in Washington in November 1998 the UAE pledged US $50 million in aid to the Palestinian economy. This sum is additional to the UAE's undertaking to finance a US $350 million low-income housing project. The UAE had met its previous pledge of US $25 million and called on donor countries to increase their contributions, at the same time stressing the need to pursue a just, comprehensive and permanent settlement on the basis of Israeli withdrawal from the occupied territories and in accordance with UN Security Council resolutions 242, 338 and 425 and the land-for-peace formula.

A Memorandum of Understanding for construction of the housing project in Gaza, to be named Sheikh Zayed City, was signed at the end of July by the Director of the Abu Dhabi Fund for Development (ADFD) and the Palestinian Housing Minister. The latter indicated that the project, which will contain 3,574 low-income housing units, would help ease the housing problem, create new job opportunities and have a positive impact on the Palestinian economy.

EGYPT

A meeting was held in Abu Dhabi on 14 April 1999 between Sheikh Zayed, the visiting Egyptian President Hosni Mubarak and King Abdullah of Jordan as part of continuous consultations and contacts between the three leaders on matters relating to the Arab nation. During President Mubarak's visit it was announced that ADFD would contribute US $100 million to the Toshka land reclamation project in southern Egypt. The money will be used to finance the construction of the third phase of the Sheikh Zayed Canal, a 320-kilometre waterway named after the UAE President, its main contributor.

MOROCCO

Sheikh Zayed expressed his grief at the passing of His Majesty King Hassan of Morocco:

King Hassan was a great leader who dedicated his life to the service of the Arab and Muslim nation and championed the cause of truth and justice . . . In the death of King Hassan, the UAE has lost a sincere and close brother and his people a brave and wise leader who dedicated his life to their service.

Sheikh Zayed also commented that he was fully confident that Crown Prince Sidi Mohammed, now King, would uphold the great cause his father stood for and follow in his footsteps. The President pledged full support for and solidarity with Morocco.

Sheikh Khalifa bin Zayed Al Nahyan attended the late King's funeral to convey the country's heartfelt condolences to the royal family and people of Morocco. The UAE also declared a period of 40 days' official mourning for King Hassan with federal ministries and local government departments remaining closed for three days.

PAKISTAN

In line with the UAE's constant belief in the peaceful settlement of disputes, the UAE Cabinet called on India and Pakistan to exercise restraint in the crisis over Kashmir, requesting the two states 'to show restraint and remove the source of tension and improve communication and bilateral negotiations'. The Cabinet statement also stressed 'the right of the Muslim people of Kashmir to self-determination . . . in accordance with UN Security Council resolutions'.

In May 1999 Sheikh Abdullah bin Zayed Al Nahyan, on behalf of the UAE, presented Pakistan with a cheque for 15 million rupees towards the Government's efforts to provide relief to thousands of victims of the cyclone that wreaked havoc on Pakistan's coastal area of Sindh. Sheikh Abdullah expressed the hope that his visit to Pakistan would help promote cooperation between the two countries in various fields, especially information, culture and information technology.

Pakistan's Prime Minister visited the UAE several times in 1999, further consolidating the good relations between the two states.

TURKEY

The UAE responded immediately to the plight of earthquake victims following the overwhelming disaster which hit western Anatolia at the end of August 1999. Plane loads of relief supplies, including much-needed medical aid, food and tents, were despatched at once. On the instructions of the President and General Sheikh Mohammed bin Rashid Al Maktoum, Crown Prince of Dubai and UAE Defence Minister, government and non-governmental organisations such as the RCS, headed by Minister of State for Foreign Affairs Sheikh Hamdan bin Zayed Al Nahyan, continued to send emergency aid to the earthquake victims and worked closely together to ensure that relief supplies were despatched as swiftly as possible. Dr Kamal Demirel, Chairman of the Turkish Red Crescent Society, emphasising the deep-rooted relationship between the UAE and Turkey, also praised the UAE's continuous assistance to earthquake victims saying, 'UAE is always at the forefront of humanitarian assistance'.

UNITED KINGDOM

Lt-General Sheikh Mohammed bin Zayed Al Nahyan, Chief of Staff of the UAE armed forces, met with British Defence Secretary George Robertson and other senior British officials at the UAE Defence Ministry on 3 June 1999 under the auspices of the Joint Defence Committee, which was formed following the signing of a defence cooperation agreement between the two countries.

Additional security agreements were concluded between the two parties and discussions focused on a number of pertinent issues, including security in the Arabian Gulf, joint training programmes, the Iraqi situation and developments in the Kosovo crisis. In a statement following the meeting, Lt-General Sheikh Mohammed reviewed relations between the UAE and Britain and other issues of mutual concern, while the British Defence Secretary reiterated his country's commitment to strengthen ties with the UAE.

The UAE held naval exercises with US and British forces in the Gulf at the beginning of April 1999 and again with US forces in August, in order to improve the UAE defence forces' combat readiness.

UNITED STATES

A major conference on Sheikh Zayed's leadership and the social, political and economic development of the UAE since 1971 was held in Washington at the end of April 1999. The conference, entitled 'A Century in 30 Years . . . Sheikh Zayed and the United Arab Emirates', was attended by senior policy figures from the US Congress, White House, armed forces, Departments of State, Commerce and Treasury, business, non-government organisations, media and academia.

In the opening session, a letter from US President Bill Clinton praised Sheikh Zayed's role in the UAE's development:

I am pleased and proud to have this opportunity to recognise the enormous role His Highness Sheikh Zayed bin Sultan Al Nahyan has played in the UAE's founding and development . . . The UAE today is a symbol of wise and thoughtful leadership . . . a tribute to Sheikh Zayed and his vision. All Emiratis can be proud of the UAE's successful efforts to address the concerns of its people and of the importance and positive role your country plays in the region.

He added that the UAE had always been a close friend and partner: 'As our two countries work together towards peace and security in the region, I look forward to the continued strengthening of our relationship.'

NUCLEAR NON-PROLIFERATION

Recognising that the acquisition and possession of weapons of mass destruction, especially nuclear weapons, not only contributes to the spiralling of the arms race and the escalation of tensions, but also disrupts the security balance at regional and international levels, the UAE called upon the international community to find ways to implement the 1995 Nuclear Non-Proliferation Treaty (NPT) which stipulates that the Middle East should be free of nuclear weapons. Speaking at the third preparatory meeting for the NPT conference in the year 2000, the UAE's Permanent Representative to the UN said that Israel should be forced to join the treaty and open its nuclear facilities for international inspection. He added that the UAE supported initiatives to form a supervisory sub-committee for implementation of the NPT in the region.

DEVELOPMENT AID

Development aid has been an important aspect of UAE foreign policy since the establishment of the state. Nearly 50 countries have benefited from the Abu Dhabi Fund for Development (ADFD) assistance programme from its inception in 1971 up to the end of 1998. To date Dh 13.8 billion has been used to finance 223 projects in African and Asian countries. The ADFD is also involved in supporting development in the UAE.

In line with the policy adopted by ADFD to facilitate sustainable development in underdeveloped countries, its emphasis has been on projects that upgrade infrastructure, improve health and education facilities and generate employment opportunities. Infrastructure projects such as roads, seaports, airports, energy generation and telecommunications services, as well as agricultural, social, health, education and housing projects amounted to 36.7 per cent of the total aid offered by the ADFD by the end of 1998.

Low-interest, long-term loans used to finance 119 projects in 45 countries, increased from Dh 1 billion in 1977 to Dh 4 billion in 1987 and to Dh 6.8 billion by the end of 1998. Non-repayable grants amounted to Dh 526 million by the end of 1998. The fund also offered another 16 grants to five countries.

In addition to financial grants and easy-term loans the ADFD has expanded its activities to include direct investment in private enterprises to improve private sector participation in the economic development of recipient countries. At the end of 1998 such direct investment amounted to Dh 464 million. Tourism and the hotel industry accounted for 62 per cent of the direct investment deployed by the fund to provide hard currency and jobs for nationals of recipient countries.

Arab countries received 85 per cent of the total grants offered by the fund, the South-Sahara countries received 9 per cent and Asian and European countries received 4 per cent and 2 per cent respectively. In Southeast Asia 75 projects amounting to 83 per cent of ADFD's total financial commitment were financed. South of the Sahara desert, 29 countries have benefited from ADFD loans and grants. These countries are classified as the poorest worldwide and burdened with debts hindering their economic development.

The ADFD is also managing, on behalf of the Abu Dhabi Government, an assistance programme valued at Dh 5.9 billion at the end of 1998, of which 52 per cent or Dh 3.1 billion was offered as non-repayable grants. The balance of Dh 2.8 billion was offered as

long-term easy repayment loans. The Abu Dhabi government grants were used, to cite some examples, to finance the reconstruction of the Marib dam in Yemen, the Sheikh Zayed hospital in Rabat, Morocco, Zayed City in Egypt, a social services centre in Dhaka, Bangladesh, a housing complex in Yemen and Sheikh Zayed's orphanage in Mombasa, Kenya. A total of Dh 5.1 billion, or 87 per cent of the Abu Dhabi government grants, were directed to finance 57 projects in Arab countries. African countries south of the Sahara were granted Dh 639 million, of which Dh 53.8 million went to finance projects undertaken by the Gulf countries programme, set up in 1981 by the AGCC countries, to finance aid projects administered by 15 UN agencies.

On 18 August 1999 a Dh 73.4 million loan agreement was signed between ADFD and the Algerian Gas Company for the financing of Al Hamama power generation project which will supply the capital and central Algeria with electricity through a gas-fired station. The 15-year loan was granted with an interest rate of 4 per cent and a grace period of 4 years.

Zayed Foundation

The Zayed Charitable and Humanitarian Foundation, which was established in 1992 with a capital of Dh 3.761 billion, has also financed numerous projects across the globe. More than Dh 6.8 million was allocated for charity work worldwide during the twelfth meeting of the Council of Trustees in May 1999. In excess of Dh 2.2 million was designated for Kosovo refugees. Fifteen ambulances donated by the Foundation were handed over by UNHCR to the people of Bosnia. Funds totalling Dh 568,850 were also set aside for projects in Ghana, Burundi, Togo, Burkina Faso, Tanzania, Senegal, Uganda, Somalia, Mali and Kenya. The Zayed Foundation also recently completed the biggest mosque in East Africa – the Sheikh Zayed Grand Mosque in Nairobi which cost Dh 14.68 million – and restored Zanzibar's main hospital at a cost of Dh 4.77 million.

UN agencies

At the end of 1998, the UAE donated US $1.48 million to the development funds of a number of the United Nations agencies. The UAE donation covered US $500,000 for the United Nations Relief and Works Agency for Palestinian Refugees (UNRWA), US $554,000 for UNHCR, US $324,000 for UNDP and US $100,000 for UNICEF.

Islamic Fund

Sheikh Zayed donated US $3 million to the Islamic Solidarity Fund in July 1999. The chairman of the fund's permanent council said Sheikh Zayed's generous gesture showed his keenness to maintain and enhance Islamic solidarity and his appreciation of the educational, health and social assistance offered by the fund to Muslim and non-Muslim communities worldwide. The chairman, thanking Sheikh Zayed on behalf of the Jeddah-based fund which was established in 1974, added that Sheikh Zayed also makes an annual donation to the fund to enable it to offer aid to Muslims in a number of countries.

RED CRESCENT SOCIETY

The UAE Red Crescent Society (RCS) has been an active part of the UAE's efforts to assist countries in need, especially in terms of providing humanitarian assistance following natural and man-made disasters. Like other Red Crescent and Red Cross societies, UAE RCS also provides assistance at a national level. In recognition of the active role played by the UAE society in disaster relief, the UAE and the International Federation of Red Cross and Red Crescent Societies reached an agreement in January 1999 to set up a logistics centre in the UAE to coordinate the activities of the Federation in the Middle East. The national society, which will help the Federation to set up the logistics centre, will receive training in crisis and disaster management.

One of the most important activities of the UAE RCS in 1999 was the provision of relief to Kosovar refugees during the recent conflict, details of which are outlined in the section on Kosovo. The RCS sent 55 planeloads of relief material worth Dh 30 million and was praised for its significant role in this and other international humanitarian activities during an executive meeting of the International Federation of the Red Cross and Red Crescent Societies held in Geneva from 11–13 May 1999.

Having sent a delegation to Kosovo to evaluate conditions and determine the needs of returning refugees, the UAE RCS has undertaken reconstruction and maintenance work on damaged houses and mosques in Kosovo as part of its plan to help rebuild the region and facilitate the return of displaced Kosovars. The first phase of the programme included rebuilding 50 houses at a cost of Dh 16,000 each.

During the period under review, RCS officials also went to Bosnia where they visited refugee camps, rehabilitation and educational institutes and orphanages. The society sponsors approximately 2,250 orphans and 1,500 Kosovar refugees in Bosnia. The UAE team attended a graduation ceremony at a school which the society had helped to build. The RCS also financed a computer laboratory and built a mosque for the students.

Emirates airline handed over a substantial cheque to the UAE Red Crescent Society to pay for reconstruction work in the Balkan province. The money, amounting to Dh 1,498,340 (US $408,267), was collected as loose change which Emirates Airlines passengers donated in 1998 as part of the airline's 'Care for Life' project. This is the second time that passengers' donations have been allocated to a specific project since Emirates Airlines launched its onboard donation scheme in 1997. The scheme is also funding the construction of an orphanage in southern Thailand.

The UAE Red Crescent played a pivotal role in the organisation of disaster relief for Turkey and Greece in the aftermath of the massive earthquakes which affected the region in August and September 1999.

The RCS sent a delegation to the stricken area to assess at first hand the victims' requirements and assist in providing aid and the facilities necessary to alleviate the difficult conditions under which they were attempting to survive. Distribution of goods purchased locally was overseen by RCS Board member Mohammed Atiq Habroush and the Director of the Society, Tariq Ali Ghalib, under the supervision of the Turkish Red Crescent Society and the ICRC. The Turkish Red Crescent Society also distributed the consignments of relief aid sent by the UAE.

KOSOVO

The Kosovo crisis, which came to a head in April-May 1999, was the result of a massive repression of Muslims of Albanian extraction living in the province of Kosovo. The province had been in a state of unrest since its autonomous status was abolished by the Republic of Serbia in 1989. However, the situation deteriorated early in 1998 when Serb forces launched major offensives against the ethnic Albanian population. It was at this point that the UAE Red Crescent Society commenced its campaign to relieve the suffering of the civilian population in Kosovo. By September 1998 as many as 200,000 civilians had fled from the ongoing terror prompting UN Secretary General Kofi Annan to comment in his report to the UN Security Council that:

The desperate situation of the civilian population remains the most disturbing aspect of the hostilities in Kosovo. I am particularly concerned that civilians increasingly have become the main target in the conflict. Fighting in Kosovo has resulted in a mass displacement of civilian populations, the extensive destruction of villages and means of livelihood and the deep trauma and despair of displaced populations. Many villages have been destroyed by shelling and burning following operations conducted by federal and Serbian government forces.

By the end of May 1999 approximately 740,000 Kosovo Albanians, about one-third of the entire Kosovo Albanian population, had been expelled from Kosovo by forced removal from, and subsequent looting and destruction of, their homes, or by the shelling of villages. Surviving residents were sent to the borders of neighbouring countries. En route many were killed or abused and had their possessions and identification papers stolen. Thousands more civilians were internally displaced.

The true horror of the events that had taken place only fully unfolded after the Serbian forces retreated and peace keepers entered the territory. This followed a coordinated international response, involving a bombing campaign aimed at persuading Yugoslav President, Slobodan Milosevic to cease the aggression against his fellow countrymen.

Readers will be familiar with the scenes of mass exodus as petrified people fled Serbian terror. The UAE, like many other countries around the world, was completely horrified by what was happening and it took a number of positive steps to play a solid role in bringing the area back to normality and in alleviating the pain and suffering of the ethnic Albanians who had been forced to leave their homes.

As soon as the crisis broke, the UAE Red Crescent Society, in consultation with the International Committee of the Red Cross and the International Federation of Red Cross and Red Crescent Societies, immediately moved to set up a well-provisioned and highly organised refugee camp at Kukes, Albania. The UAE camp became a model for other refugee camps and received widespread international acclaim.

The UAE-managed refugee camp included a field hospital with an operating room, an intensive care unit, a laboratory and an X-ray unit. It treated between 450 and 500 patients daily, most for illnesses such as dehydration and diarrhoea, but patients also sought treatment for bullet wounds, beatings and rape. Almost 70 per cent of the patients were women.

In addition to the urgent medical needs of these displaced people, many of whom had lost close relatives, considerable efforts were also made to lift their spirits and to help them work their way back to psychological, as well as physical, good health. The UAE 'White Hand' force played a key role in this process, opening a host of entertainment facilities at the UAE camp and establishing areas for playing football, basketball and handball to help occupy young refugees. Other projects in the camp included the establishment of a primary school for some 200 children.

Kukes itself was unprepared for such a massive influx of people and the need to care for these refugees placed great strains on Albanian infrastructure and resources. What was needed was a means to fly large transport planes directly into Kukes, but when the crisis broke the only landing strip was an inadequate Second World War airfield whose runway was in a state of disrepair and which lacked proper air-traffic control equipment. The UAE, recognising this as being of pivotal importance to the success of the international mission to assist refugees, undertook an emergency reconstruction programme carried out by the UAE armed forces, which was completed in a record ten days. In addition to resurfacing and extension to the runway, a technologically advanced air-traffic control tower, costing some Dh 4 million, was brought in from Germany. The new aviation centre, renamed Zayed Airport, was opened in Kukes on 8 May 1999, to expressions of relief and gratitude from all concerned.

Kukes airport, with its new 3-kilometre long runway, played a crucial role in facilitating transport between Tirana airport and Kukes, bringing much needed supplies to the thousands of Kosovar refugees in the area. Four Puma helicopters belonging to the UAE armed forces were stationed at Tirana to carry goods to the refugee camp on a regular basis. Following the opening of the airstrip C-130 transport aircraft from the UAE Air Force ferried supplies directly to Kukes. During the key emergency period a total of 1,800 tonnes of aid was distributed in this way.

The Kosovo crisis was so overwhelmingly tragic it touched the hearts and souls of people all over the world. The people of the Emirates were anxious to do as much as possible to help and a number of different groups became involved in the aid programme. One of the first to arrive in the area was a group of women coordinated by the UAE Women's Federation, of which Sheikha Fatima bint Mubarak, wife of Sheikh Zayed, is Chairwoman. The women's delegation distributed food, clothes, blankets and other relief

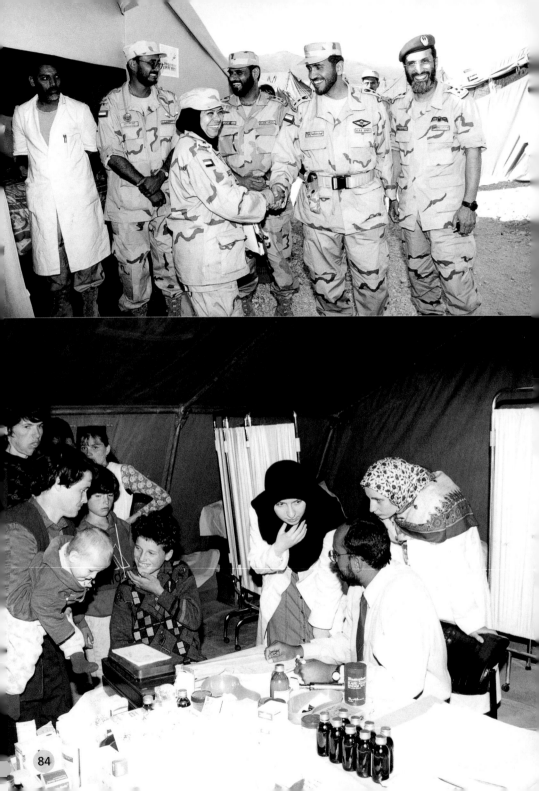

goods among women and children. In all, seven planeloads of relief were sent by the Women's Federation and in one small cameo of life played out at the camps a baby girl born at the UAE field hospital was named Fatima in recognition of Sheikha Fatima's efforts. In a further demonstration of its commitment to reaching a permanent solution to the crisis, the UAE women's delegation was among the first to enter Kosovo following withdrawal of the Serbian troops.

Not all of the refugees ended up in border area camps. A large number were housed in homes of ordinary Albanian citizens leading to inevitable strains on local resources. In order to help tackle this situation the UAE Red Crescent Society expanded the scope of its relief efforts by launching a campaign for distributing relief material to some of the 1.5 million Kosovar refugees residing in a number of Albanian cities, including Tirana. A large team of RCS officials and volunteers distributed warm clothes, blankets and money to these refugees. Meanwhile, back in the UAE, numerous fund raising events took place, providing the funding needed for the sustained efforts of the RCS and other organisations who were engaged in helping the Kosovar people. Just one of these, under the patronage of Minister of State for Foreign Affairs Sheikh Hamdan bin Zayed Al Nahyan, who is also chairman of the RCS, raised Dh 3.5 million.

The UAE's proactive and practical involvement in the Kosovo crisis did not go unnoticed by the international community. In particular, the International Federation of the Red Cross and Red Crescent Societies paid special tribute to the UAE's efforts in humanitarian aid. While the international press reported that the UAE camp at Kukes was the best-run refugee camp in the region and the UAE's programme was widely quoted as being a model for the international community to follow, the UN High Commissioner for Refugees (UNHCR) complimented the leading role played by the UAE in providing humanitarian assistance in the Kosovo crisis. She also praised the Zayed Charitable and Humanitarian Foundation (ZCHF) for donating US $500,000 to UNHCR, which had been allocated for the purchase of ambulances.

In the arena of international relations, the UAE's efforts also elicited high praise from many diplomats and political leader. The new US Ambassador to the UAE Theodore H. Kettouf said: 'It is hard to find a state which is more generous to Kosovars than the UAE. The UAE was the first state that offered political support [to the people of Kosovo]. Their camp in Kukes is well provisioned and well organised'. The ambassador also alluded to the fact that the UAE was the first non-NATO state to express willingness to take part in any peacekeeping force in Yugoslavia.

Once the bombing campaign ended and the Serbian forces had withdrawn from Kosovo, there was an urgent need to provide troops that would help to re-establish stability and security in the devastated region. The UN played a central role in this effort and it welcomed the UAE's offer to join the peacekeeping force (UN KFOR) to be stationed in Kosovo. The fact that the UAE was the first non-NATO state to express willingness to take part in the peacekeeping force should not have surprised informed observers since the UAE has an excellent record of participation in other international peacekeeping missions, including involvement in both the Lebanon and Somalia crises.

In order to prepare for its new mission, a contingent of 1,500 UAE soldiers was sent to southern France for military training to enable them to adapt to the European climate before they were deployed in the French sector at the end of July. On a lighter note, reports of their early days at the orientation camp in June described snowball fights in the French Alps. 'They did what anyone would do when they saw snow for the first time in their lives, they lobbed snowballs at each other,' said a French colonel attached to the UAE's 1,200-strong, 32nd mechanised infantry battalion. 'Many of our officers had been abroad before, but most of the troops had never seen snow except on TV,' unit commander Colonel Yussuf Al Ahmad commented.

The UAE unit, equipped with 15 French-made Leclerc heavy tanks and eight South African 155mm field guns, is the second largest contingent in the 12,000-strong, French-led force responsible for northern Kosovo. Another 250 soldiers backed by Apache helicopters are deployed in the US sector in Kosovo.

It is clear that a sustained effort will be required to bring Kosovo back to normality and the UAE has therefore pledged troops for the KFOR peacekeeping mission for a period of two years. The units will be rotated, each battalion remaining on duty for six months.

In late June 1999 the Albanian Deputy Prime Minister Albert Mitta visited the UAE where he was received by Sheikh Zayed. The UAE President said during the meeting that helping the people of Kosovo is a duty for all those concerned with human rights. 'God Almighty has created people to be brothers and to help each other [in times of trial]. He who is deprived of human traits cannot be considered a human being,' he said. 'The Creator,' Sheikh Zayed added, 'has urged those able to do so, to help the oppressed and to prevail over the oppressor. He does not forget the oppressor but grants him time so he may repent.' Referring to the situation in Kosovo and the steps taken to rebuild the areas destroyed by the war, Sheikh Zayed expressed the UAE's keenness to help both Kosovo and Albania to overcome their difficulties. Mr Mitta, for his part, expressed thanks and appreciation for the role played by Sheikh Zayed and by the Government and people of the UAE in alleviating the sufferings of the Kosovar people.

The task of caring for returning refugees is also one that has engaged the attentions of the UAE's government and aid agencies. The decision to set up an integrated hospital at Petrovitsa forms part of its strategy in this regard. The medical centre, which offers the latest in medical technology, receives between 100 to 120 patients daily and treats Serbs and ethnic Albanians alike. The centre's out-patients department operates for six hours daily. Treatment is handled by 14 medical specialists and 45 nurses and is facilitated by a fleet of 10 ambulances. After the peacekeeping mission is accomplished, the hospital will be handed over to the people of Kosovo.

The UAE is proud of its record in helping to bring peace and security to Kosovo. Not only did it act with conviction and commitment but it also did so without delay. It continues to build on these efforts by studying the needs of the area and attempting to play its role in helping to fulfil these needs in the most appropriate manner.

THE ECONOMY

The unprecedented economic transformation which has taken place in the UAE since the formation of the state has been largely funded by the judicious use of oil revenues. However, although oil and gas production remain the primary source of public revenue, the secret of the country's current economic success has been a determined government strategy of economic diversification, leading to the creation of new productive sectors. This, combined with revenue from foreign investment, has meant that the UAE economy has been relatively immune to the effects of plummeting oil prices: the weighted average of oil per barrel dropped from US $18.8 in 1997 to US $12.4 (-34 per cent) in 1998. During the 1970s and 1980s such a decline would have triggered a major setback.

GENERAL ECONOMIC TRENDS 1998

According to the Central Bank Annual Report for 1998, UAE gross domestic product at current prices (GDP) decreased from Dh 180.6 billion in 1997 to Dh 170.1 billion in 1998 (-5.8 per cent), despite substantial growth in most economic sectors. This drop was largely attributable to a 31 per cent decline in the value of the oil sector output, from Dh 53.5 billion in 1997 to Dh 37 billion in 1998, due to low oil prices. In addition, because of the close link between oil and gas prices and petroleum products, which constitute the bulk of the manufacturing sector's output, values decreased in this sector, albeit very slightly, from Dh 20.23 billion in 1997 to Dh 20.19 billion in 1998, despite increases in production volume. However, overall, the non-oil sector contribution to GDP rose from Dh 127.1 billion in 1997 to Dh 133.1 billion in 1998, achieving a growth rate of 4.7 per cent, partially alleviating the negative impact of the decline in the oil sector.

The relative significance of the wholesale, retail trade and maintenance services sector increased to 12 per cent in 1998, (up from 10.8 per cent in 1997), following an increase in domestic trade activity and the decline in manufacturing output mentioned above. Accordingly, this sector was ranked second after the oil sector which had a 21.7 per cent share of total GDP.

Government services retained its third place position in 1998, accounting for 11.6 per cent of GDP, nearly half the oil sector's contribution. This is mainly attributed to continued investment in education, health and cultural services to keep pace with population growth.

The real estate and business services sector, at 10.7 per cent, recorded a sizeable growth of 5 per cent in 1998, compared with 1997, while the construction sector increased by 1 per cent over its 1997 value to reach 9.6 per cent. Efforts made to promote tourism and trade reflected positively on the hotel and restaurant sector which grew by 7.2 per cent in 1998, compared with 1997. This sector, according to the Central Bank, has recently been one of the most attractive for investment.

Advances in air, sea and land transportation and storage, as indicated in foreign trade data, in addition to continual development of communications, led to a 5.7 per cent increase in the value added to this sector in 1998. Financial institutions and insurance grew by 6 per cent in 1998 as a result of increased activity in the banking and financial sector. Significant increases were also recorded in the electricity, gas and water sector which grew by 11 per cent in 1998, to become the fastest growing sector. This was mainly attributed to major capital investment directed at improving and expanding services in response to burgeoning domestic consumption.

Abu Dhabi emirate's share of GDP continued to account for more than half of total GDP, though it dropped from 59 per cent in 1997 to 55.3 per cent in 1998. In contrast, Dubai and Sharjah's shares rose slightly in 1998 to reach 27.9 per cent and 9.9 per cent respectively, while the remaining emirates ranged between 0.6 per cent and 2.8 per cent.

The decline in GDP, on the one hand, and the increase in population on the other, caused GDP per capita to drop to Dh 61,600 in 1998, a 10.5 per cent fall when compared with 1997 per capita GDP.

Available data on GDP by major expenditure categories show that final consumption reached Dh 119.3 billion in 1998, a 4.3 per cent increase compared with 1997. The ratio of final consumption to GDP also rose from 63.3 per cent in 1997 to 70.2 per cent in 1998. This increase was mainly concentrated in private consumption which rose by 5.1 per cent to reach Dh 90.7 billion in 1998, against Dh 86.2 billion in 1997. This was due, in part, to the rise in population, increased demand for re-exports and increased levels of individual expenditure. On the other hand, despite an expansion in government services, public consumption rose only slightly to reach Dh 28.6 billion in 1998, up from Dh 28.1 billion in 1997, an indication of the success of fiscal policy in rationalising expenditure.

The UAE dirham continued to strengthen during 1998, benefiting from its fixed rate against the US dollar which, in turn, witnessed marked improvement in its exchange rate against other major currencies.

With regard to monetary and banking developments at the end of 1998, compared with 1997, money supply rose by 9.5 per cent to reach Dh 27.8 billion. This increase was distributed between monetary deposits, which grew by 1.59 billion (8.8 per cent), and currency with the public, which rose by Dh 829 billion (2.2 per cent) to Dh 71.04 billion. As increased private sector demand for money and quasi-money continued, private domestic liquidity expanded by 4.2 per cent to reach Dh 98.83 billion.

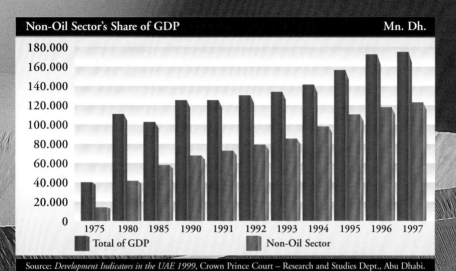

Non-Oil Sector's Share of GDP   **Mn. Dh.**

Legend:
- Total of GDP
- Non-Oil Sector

Source: *Development Indicators in the UAE 1999*, Crown Prince Court – Research and Studies Dept., Abu Dhabi.

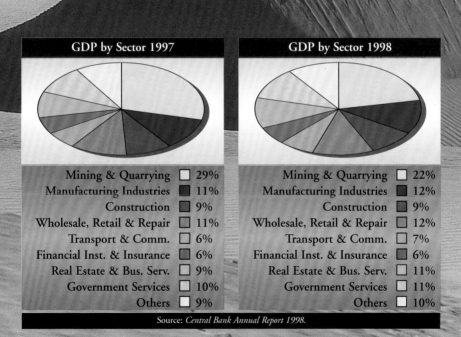

GDP by Sector 1997		GDP by Sector 1998	
Mining & Quarrying	29%	Mining & Quarrying	22%
Manufacturing Industries	11%	Manufacturing Industries	12%
Construction	9%	Construction	9%
Wholesale, Retail & Repair	11%	Wholesale, Retail & Repair	12%
Transport & Comm.	6%	Transport & Comm.	7%
Financial Inst. & Insurance	6%	Financial Inst. & Insurance	6%
Real Estate & Bus. Serv.	9%	Real Estate & Bus. Serv.	11%
Government Services	10%	Government Services	11%
Others	9%	Others	10%

Source: *Central Bank Annual Report 1998.*

PUBLIC FINANCE 1998

The Central Bank reported that the consolidated government account revenues (the consolidated accounts group the federal budget and the budgets of the larger emirates) dropped by 24 per cent in 1998 to Dh 42.7 billion, as opposed to Dh 56.2 billion in 1997. This was mainly due to a decline in earnings from exports resulting from the fall in oil prices. Tax revenues (customs duties, fees and other revenues) decreased by 4.8 per cent to Dh 7.9 billion, accounting for 18.4 per cent of total revenues. Nevertheless, during this period customs revenues actually increased by 8.7 per cent to Dh 1.8 billion, the decline occurring in other tax revenues.

Non-tax revenues decreased by 27.3 per cent in 1998 to reach Dh 34.8 billion, against Dh 47.9 billion in 1997, forming 81.6 per cent of total revenues. The drop was mainly attributed to lower receipts for oil and gas exports as joint-stock corporations actually rose by Dh 899 million (41.8 per cent) over the period to reach Dh 3.1 billion. Likewise other non-tax revenues increased by Dh 1.6 billion (35.2 per cent) to reach Dh 6.3 billion.

Expenditures recorded a substantial increase in 1998, reaching Dh 71.6 billion, against Dh 64.4 billion in 1997 (11.2 per cent). In particular development expenditures rose by 28.2 per cent to reach Dh 13.9 billion in contrast to 10.8 billion in 1997. Loan and equity participation increased by 30.6 per cent in 1998 compared with their 1997 level, reaching Dh 7.2 billion, of which 41.2 per cent was spent locally.

The substantial decline in oil and gas revenues, which resulted from the fall of oil prices and the country's adherence to its production quota as set by OPEC, coupled with the increase in development expenditure and in the amount of loans and equity participation, had an effect on the deficit which reached Dh 28.9 billion in 1998, in comparison to an adjusted deficit of Dh 8.2 billion in 1997. The entire deficit was financed by returns on government investments. The total deficit constituted 17 per cent of GDP in 1998, compared with 5.1 per cent in 1997 and 13 per cent in 1996.

BALANCE OF PAYMENTS 1998

The Central Bank reported that the UAE balance of payments (trade of goods and services, transfers and capital flow) achieved an overall surplus of Dh 2.8 billion in 1998, compared with 1.2 billion in 1997, despite a drop in the surpluses of both the trade balance and the current account. Preliminary data on foreign trade indicated a decrease, for the second consecutive year, in the trade balance surplus which reached Dh 11.6 billion in 1998, against Dh 27.2 billion in 1997 (-57.5 per cent). Exports and re-exports totalled Dh 111.49 billion in 1998 from around Dh 124.8 billion in 1997, while imports were recorded at Dh 99.92 billion slightly higher than the 97.7 billion figure for 1997. The current account surplus of around Dh 6.5 billion was well below the 1997 surplus of Dh 23.1 billion.

The report showed that the balance of payment recorded a surplus mainly due to a sharp decline in capital outflow, which shrank to Dh 6.3 billion from Dh 24.3 billion. Net services also dropped to Dh 7.8 billion from Dh 8.5 billion and investment income to around Dh 17 billion from Dh 17.5 billion.

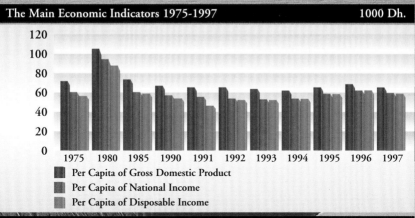

The Main Economic Indicators 1975-1997   1000 Dh.

- Per Capita of Gross Domestic Product
- Per Capita of National Income
- Per Capita of Disposable Income

Source: *Development Indicators in the UAE 1999*, Crown Prince Court – Research and Studies Dept., Abu Dhabi.

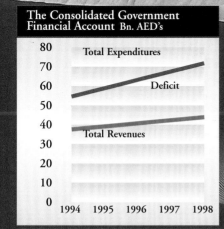

The Consolidated Government Financial Account Bn. AED's

Total Expenditures

Deficit

Total Revenues

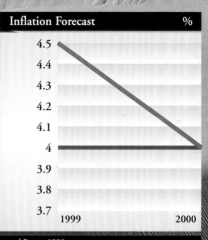

Inflation Forecast   %

Source: *Central Bank Annual Report 1998.*

ECONOMIC TRENDS 1999–2000

GDP at current prices is expected to grow by about 5.2 per cent in 1999 to Dh 185.08 billion, according to a study by the Research and Studies Department of the Abu Dhabi Crown Prince's Court released in mid-July 1999. This is significantly higher than earlier forecasts due to improved oil prices and more sustained growth in non-oil sectors. The study also estimated a 2.6 per cent increase in 1999 GDP at fixed prices to Dh 160.94 billion.

Average per capita income at current prices was estimated by the study at Dh 62,957 in 1999 and forecast to be Dh 63,471 in the year 2000. Government revenues were projected to reach Dh 53.06 billion in 1999, of which Dh 35.31 billion were estimated to be revenues from oil exports. Expenditure is expected to reach Dh 77.35 billion, resulting in a budget deficit of Dh 25.6 billion, or 13.8 per cent of GDP.

Other forecasts for 1999 predict that import growth is likely to slow, but public spending on both current and capital items will push the import bill up to over Dh 128.49 billion by the year 2000 despite lower import prices from Asian suppliers. However, strong growth in other exports and re-exports will boost export values by 8 per cent a year in 1999 and 2000. The trade surplus is expected to rise to nearly Dh 25.70 billion by 2000 and investment income continue to grow. The current account balance is projected to increase to Dh 25.32 billion in the year 2000 and its ratio to GDP to rise to 13.2 per cent.

At the time of writing the continued strength of oil prices would suggest that oil exports could well exceed Dh 40 billion despite the UAE's decision to cut oil output by more than 300,000 barrels per day in line with an OPEC agreement to trim production to stabilise supplies and support prices. The agreement has already pushed prices up by nearly 100 per cent and the price of UAE crude oil is projected to average more than US $15 in 1999.

INTO THE NEW MILLENNIUM

The UAE is expected to increase its industrial diversification drive in the new millennium. Emphasis on development of the finance, trade and services sectors will also be accelerated. Globalisation will encourage the formation of larger banking units through mergers while the move towards emiratisation will also gain momentum.

Having invested heavily in infrastructure since the establishment of the state, the Government is actively encouraging the private sector to participate in further infrastructure development in transport, communications, telecommunications, energy and ports. Private sector investment in industry, involving public shareholding, inflow of foreign capital and technology transfer is expected to increase. New corporate, stock market and banking legislation, a review of the laws governing economic activity and the development of additional legislative and administrative frameworks that promote efficiency and transparency will be key factors in economic development.

BUSINESS ENVIRONMENT

UAE government policy recognises that the private sector is of major importance in the drive for diversified economic growth and full employment for nationals. The creation of a facilitative business environment, which encourages local investors to put their wealth to productive use, as well as attracting foreign investment, has been an important aspect of this policy. Key elements in the UAE's incentive strategy have been the provision of first-class industrial facilities and business support services, the reduction of red tape and streamlining of administrative procedures, as well as the updating of commercial laws and regulations to meet international obligations, increase transparency and ensure effective protection for investors. Favourable tax laws and political stability also assist in making the UAE a prime business location.

WORLD TRADE ORGANISATION

The UAE joined the World Trade Organisation (WTO) in 1995 in the knowledge that developing countries, including Arab states, cannot ignore WTO-sponsored agreements and their impact on the global economy. At the time, the Ministry of Economy and Commerce argued that joining WTO would provide an opportunity for the country to contribute to future commercial decisions and policies and that, as a country aspiring to become a regional trade hub, adherence to the General Agreement on Tariffs and Trade (GATT), a WTO-sponsored multilateral trade treaty, would help boost the UAE's industries and exports. Other relevant WTO treaties are the General Agreement on Trade in Services (GATS) and the Agreement on Trade-Related Aspects of Intellectual Property (TRIPS).

Although the WTO prohibits discrimination in investments or shareholding between nationals and non-nationals, the UAE has been granted certain exemptions for its financial services sector. Nevertheless, WTO agreements will have a direct impact on domestic services such as insurance, banking, transport, tourism, property, brokerage, investment, construction, communications and information, all of which will be required to improve performance to be able to compete globally.

ABU DHABI CHAMBER OF COMMERCE AND INDUSTRY

A bridge between the private sector and government has been provided by the Abu Dhabi Chamber of Commerce and Industry (ADCCI) for over 30 years. Since its inception in

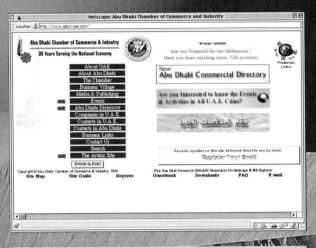

April 1969, operating from a two-room apartment in the capital, the ADCCI has grown in stature to become the largest chamber of commerce in the AGCC states, with a membership of 51,399 at the end of 1998, increased from 27 in 1969. It is now housed in an imposing building on the Corniche.

Private sector partnership

Policies pursued by ADCCI have enhanced the private sector's partnership in local enterprise. In addition to developing economic regulations and offering advice to the government in this field, ADCCI provides a wide range of services, including setting up the Sheikh Khalifa Fund to provide technical and financial support for small and medium enterprises initiated by national youth; establishing a database to furnish businessmen and investors with up-to-date commercial information; organising trade fairs in Abu Dhabi; sending delegations abroad to promote Abu Dhabi as a commercial centre; as well as initiating training programmes such as 'Passport for Work', which trains nationals to join the private sector.

Trade fairs

To mark its thirtieth anniversary, in 1998 the chamber opened a new hall for membership registration and the processing of official documents. It also established a new centre for businessmen and another for businesswomen, issued 6,118 certificates of origin and organised 37 trade fairs. The chamber participated in the Cairo International Fair, the Lisbon International Expo Fair, the Second UAE Exhibition in Beirut and the Baghdad International Exhibition.

In addition, during 1998 the chamber received 39 international trade delegations and official delegations from the ADCCI visited Oman, India, Taiwan, Britain, Thailand, Malaysia, Singapore, Australia, Finland, Sweden, Norway and Denmark, to promote Abu Dhabi as an investment opportunity.

One-stop shop

ADCCI has also been concerned with setting up a one-stop shop at Abu Dhabi Municipality to facilitate the issue of trade licences in the capital. The measure, initiated by the Higher Consultative Committee of Abu Dhabi Emirate, is aimed at simplifying and expediting procedures for issue of trade licences. By the end of 1999 applications for commercial licences sent by e-mail were due to be processed within four hours, instead of three to four months.

The multi-departmental section comprises representative offices of the Ministries of Labour and Social Affairs, Economy and Commerce, Information and Culture, the ADCCI, Civil Defence and Abu Dhabi Police. The project is the first phase of a comprehensive development of the municipality's infrastructure.

NEW BUSINESS SUPPORT SERVICES IN DUBAI

Dubai has also been streamlining its administrative procedures to provide an efficient service for investors. A telephone and fax hotline has been installed at the Dubai

Naturalisation and Residency Department. The 24-hour computerised system, operating in Arabic and English, can handle enquiries about documents needed for all types of visas, including visit, transit, investor, work and domestic servant visas. Callers can access information about documents needed to open a company file at the department, documents for stamping and cancelling visas, court appointments, changing visas and departure certificates.

A 50 per cent reduction in municipality fees levied on business in Dubai, which was announced during 1999, should also assist business development in that emirate. The municipal levy, originally set at 10 per cent of the lease rental, is a major establishment cost for any company. Dubai Municipality, the Department of Economic Development and the Dubai Chamber of Commerce and Industry are working together to ensure that the new system operates efficiently.

Intelak

In an effort to ensure that the smallest investor is not forgotten, Dubai has also launched an innovative programme in which 'individual establishment' trade licences are granted to UAE nationals to set up businesses at home once they have satisfied home ownership requirements. The experimental programme aims to encourage housewives, nationals with spare time, and those who have low-budget projects to establish businesses without facing the competitive risks of the open marketplace. Introductory seminars and technical and economic advice will be provided. Products from such businesses will be marketed through promotional shows and on the Internet.

OFFSETS

The UAE has made it a condition that foreign firms bidding for lucrative defence contracts should invest a portion of the value of the deals in joint venture projects with local partners. The UAE Offsets Group (UOG), which manages this offset programme, has developed its role to become a pioneering institution playing a vital part in the establishment of joint ventures.

Under the offsets programme, foreign defence firms are entitled to hold up to a 49 per cent stake in the joint ventures with the rest being held by local private investors. Projects must generate added value to the UAE within a period of seven years. Since 1992 the offsets programme has announced 31 projects, 17 of which are in operation, with a total investment of around Dh 2 billion. The projects range from a ship-building company to a health care centre. Abu Dhabi Shipbuilding Company, a Dh 178 million venture, was one of the first public shareholding firms to be set up under the scheme. The two biggest ventures are The Oasis International Leasing Company, an aircraft leasing firm, and TABREED, which has developed innovative cooling systems, each capitalised at Dh 500 million. Dassault, with which the UAE signed a US $3.2 billion defence deal, has contributed to five separate offset projects, including a horticulture project, a plant for manufacturing fire-fighting materials, a business services company, as well as fish processing and fish farming companies.

Dolphin Gas Network

UOG's participation in the Dolphin Regional Gas Network, a US $8–10 billion project to build a regional gas network from Qatar to UAE and Oman was announced in early 1999 (See section on Oil and Gas). The Dolphin project represents a strategic initiative to attract investment in industrial sectors in the UAE and other regional countries by modernising the gas supply infrastructure and is intended to provide a framework to stimulate investment in a variety of related industries throughout the value-added gas chain. It will provide employment and wide investment opportunities in financial and other industrial fields.

Key potential regional customers for gas from Dolphin will include the offset programme's own initiatives, especially Sina'at which has been set up with a capital of Dh 550 million to develop basic industries and petrochemical facilities. Other customers will include independent power producers, aluminium smelters, iron and steel plants and gas trading operations.

FREE ZONES

The increased number of free zones operating in the country is serving to offer a wider range of options to potential investors, including 100 per cent ownership of investments. The massive Jebel Ali Free Zone (JAFZ) has become one of the largest industrial complexes worldwide which, together with the adjacent port, the world's largest manmade harbour, has continued to attract investors.

Fujairah Free Trade Zone (FTZ), which was awarded an ISO 9002 certificate in 1999, offers businessmen the locational advantage of an east coast port as well as the benefits of partnership with the Fujairah Government. FTZ has been growing at a rate of 20–22 per cent annually and currently has over 125 projects registered at the zone, representing sector investment worth Dh 750 million. Trade value out of the zone by the end of 1999 should top Dh 1 billion.

Arab, Gulf and international capital investment in Sharjah's Hamriyyah Free Zone had exceeded Dh 2.5 billion by the end of 1999, with local investment accounting for 50 per cent. The Sharjah Government has invested Dh 600 million in infrastructure projects in the zone.

Saadiyat Free Zone Authority

The US $3.3 billion Emirates Global Capital Corporation (EGCC), which was incorporated in April 1999, has been granted a 50-year concession by Saadiyat Free Zone Authority (SFZA) to establish a major new commodities market and free zone on Saadiyat island near Abu Dhabi. The concession covers an area of 26 square kilometres. EGCC will develop a 50,000 square metre trading centre with a stock exchange, futures exchange and clearing house and warehouses, the requisite commercial and residential real estate and physical infrastructure, including a port with storage facilities and a freight airport. Construction of the necessary infrastructure is scheduled to take three years to complete.

Planned facilities on the island, which will have a six-lane bridge to link it with Abu Dhabi, will include a marina, an extensive exhibition centre, a luxury hotel, a golf course,

an equestrian club, a motor racing circuit, water and power plants, a telecommunications network and other utilities.

The Basic Law for the Authority imposes no restrictions on foreign ownership of companies and assets and allows full repatriation of capital and profits as well as exemption from all taxes. Companies and residents will be offered land on lease for periods of 50 years or more and leases will be fully transferable.

Since the announcement of its creation in July 1996, the Saadiyat project has attracted considerable attention from regional and global investment and banking circles. The project will have a major impact on many economic sectors including trade, industry, agriculture, real estate, building contracting and engineering, banking, brokerage, insurance, tourism, hotel, entertainment and services, as well as providing employment for nationals.

Saadiyat Free Zone, shares in which will be offered on domestic and international markets, will give a major boost to the UAE's investment policy and is intended to complement the Jebel Ali Free Zone and other zones in the country and the AGCC.

Dubai Airport Free Zone Authority

Dubai Airport Free Zone Authority (DAFZA), one of the most recently established free zones in the UAE, grants licences to companies with an international reputation who intend to invest properly in environment-friendly projects that are not labour-intensive. The emphasis is on long-term gains within the context of a five-year business plan. By mid-1999, 54 per cent of the 50 companies operating out of DAFZ were European, 32 per cent American, 4 per cent each from the Far East, Middle East and GCC states and 2 per cent from Africa. Applicants to date include global dealers in the jewellery, diamonds, crystal, cosmetics, electronics and computer industries. The free zone has been allocated an area of 1.2 million square metres, including 473,000 square metres of apron space, which will be developed in stages over the coming years.

Ajman Information Technology Park

Ajman Free Zone (AFZ) commenced work in July 1999 on the region's first information technology park. The park will be developed in two phases, the first of which, a pilot project of 10 offices, is under way. A further Dh 5 million will be invested in a purpose-built block that will house 100 offices. The IT park will offer a 'move in and plug in' facility in which a company can start operating as soon as it occupies designated premises. The park offers all the facilities needed for an effective business operation – PCs, ISDN, phone and fax lines, Internet access and related services – to attract IT developers and IT support centres, besides emerging Internet retailing, wholesale and e-commerce business.

AFZ already has a wide cross-section of companies involved in textiles, medical equipment, furniture, foodstuffs, tobacco derivatives, watches, electrical appliances, paper, metal and plastic products. In 1998 the number of companies operating out of AFZ quadrupled and in the first six months of 1999 the zone grew by 7.5 per cent from 400 to 430 companies. Total capitalisation of companies now stands at Dh 1.1 billion (US $300 million).

INTELLECTUAL PROPERTY

Recognition of the close link between the protection of intellectual property rights and foreign investment has acted as an incentive for vigorous action against intellectual property violations in the Emirates.

International obligations

The UAE is a member of the Paris Convention for the Protection of Industrial Property, the World Intellectual Property Organisation (WIPO), and a signatory of the WTO Agreement on Trade-Related Aspects of Intellectual Property (TRIPS) with which it must comply by the year 2000. The latter deals with such issues as copyright, trademarks, patents, industrial designs and trade secrets. The country also acceded to the International Patent Cooperation Treaty in 1998, which protects inventions registered with the International Bureau at WIPO and local patent offices.

Domestic law

Federal Law No. 40/92, Protection of Intellectual Works and Copyright, was issued on 28 September 1992, embracing all aspects of intellectual property such as trademarks, patents, industrial design and copyright. After an extended grace period, the law was implemented in the second half of 1993. In June 1999 the UAE National Committee for Industrial Property Protection discussed amending the federal law within the context of TRIPS, including regulations governing the protection of patents on pharmaceuticals. The initiative to amend the law in line with WTO obligations was announced by the Ministry of Finance and Industry in mid-1997 and work has been under way ever since. All articles of the legislation as well as subsequent by-laws are being reviewed.

Enforcement

Enforcement of trade marks comes under the purview of the Ministry of Economy and Commerce, the copyright law under the Ministry of Information and Culture and the patent and design law under the Ministry of Finance and Industry. Enforcement is also assisted by the Ministry of Interior, particularly the police and the Criminal Investigations Department, Dubai's Department of Economic Development and Sharjah Municipality. International organisations that are also engaged in the anti-piracy drive in the UAE are the Motion Pictures Association (MPA) the Business Software Alliance (BSA) and the International Federation of the Phonographic Industry (IFPI).

In July 1999 thousands of pirated audio and videocassettes, compact discs and computer playstation tapes confiscated in a series of government raids were destroyed and some shops selling the goods were shut down. The raids on video and CD shops in Dubai and the Northern Emirates were carried out by the Ministry of Information and Culture, Dubai Police Economic Crime Section and the Business Software Alliance.

In August, a trader who had been convicted of selling pirated videocasettes had his sentence increased from the original Dh 5,000 fine to three months' imprisonment following an appeal brought by the Motion Picture Association Middle East.

Reduction in piracy levels

In the last few years the UAE has achieved tremendous results in fighting piracy at the local and federal levels. As a result the UAE continues to have the lowest piracy level in the Middle East according to statistics released by the Business Software Alliance (BSA). Of the US $190 million revenue estimated to have been lost by the IT industry on account of illegal copying of software in the Middle East, the UAE's contribution was a mere US $3.6 million. On a global scale, the estimated loss of revenue in the UAE is not even 1 per cent of losses perceived to be suffered by IT companies due to software piracy in countries such as the UK, Canada, Germany and France.

E-COMMERCE

In order to keep abreast of commercial trends worldwide, the UAE intends to set up an Internet-based central financial forwarding and clearance facility known as the Payment Gateway Server (PGS). Several top companies are working with government departments to establish the facility which is expected to be the first of its kind in the AGCC area. PGS, a major step in the introduction of e-commerce, is the equivalent of central clearing and forwarding of financial transactions carried out on the Internet. The server, which will permit secure electronic transactions, is an intermediary between Web-based merchants, financial institutions and consumers.

FINANCIAL SERVICES

Developments in the financial services sector are designed to foster a properly regulated business environment in which economic development, especially diversification, can continue unabated.

STOCK MARKETS

Efforts to establish an official stock exchange to regulate the informal market gathered momentum as the draft federal stock exchange law was approved by the federal Cabinet at the end of June 1999. The UAE has been working on setting up a formal bourse for some years. The draft law envisages the establishment of a Securities and Commodities Commission to be based in Abu Dhabi which will have the authority to license trading floors. The exchange is expected to have electronic trading based on two trading floors in Abu Dhabi and Dubai.

Stock market volatility

The UAE informal stock market witnessed a 26.74 per cent surge in market capitalisation in 1998, suggesting that investors had fared reasonably well despite the mid-year volatility and the prolonged downturn in the fourth quarter. Market capitalisation on 1 January 1999 was Dh 116.42 billion, as compared with Dh 91.86 billion on 1 January 1998. It had, however, reached a peak of Dh 182 billion at the end of August 1998, at which point a correction occurred, sparking off the subsequent slide. In 1997 investors had witnessed a return of over 30 per cent, while 1996 had seen a 5 per cent dividend yield and a 20 per cent surge in market capitalisation.

By late May 1999, the UNB Market Index had fallen to 111.4 points, 14.5 per cent lower than it was at the beginning of 1999, despite the fact that corporate results for 1998 were generally good. Market capitalisation stood at Dh 105.44 billion. However, stock values began to recover towards the end of the summer and in the first week of September as many as 28 of the 43 stocks monitored recorded a rise. The UNB Market Index had also risen to 114.09 points, reflecting the improved market sentiment.

Stock brokerage

There was a significant increase in the number of applicants seeking licences to operate brokerage houses following the approval of the stock exchange law by the Cabinet. More

than 34 applications were forwarded to the office concerned within a day of Cabinet approval for the local stock exchange. The Central Bank issued around 20 new brokerage licences at the beginning of 1999, which increased the total number of brokerages to 57. The requirements stipulated by the Central Bank for granting brokerage licences are stringent and it is up to the Central Bank to decide whether the market can accommodate more brokers or not.

It was announced in July 1999 that the UAE Securities and Commodities Commission (SCC) is likely to authorise some UAE banks to undertake trading in stocks. Many of these banks already have operational stock-trading departments. Investors in emirates other than Abu Dhabi and Dubai, which will have trading floors, could conduct deals through banks nominated by the SCC.

Saadiyat financial centre

The official UAE stock exchange had yet to be formally established at the time of writing this review (October 1999), but the Saadiyat International Stock Exchange (SISE), a completely separate bourse, was due to open in Abu Dhabi towards the end of 1999, initially functioning from a temporary location.

SISE is expected to become a fully electronic, order-driven market with 'straight-through processing' capabilities should market participants require. SISE will be fully supervised by a regulatory commission.

In July 1999 the Saadiyat Free Zone Authority (SFZA) signed a 50-year renewable concession agreement with Emirates Global Capital Corporation (EGCC) to develop the US $3.3 billion offshore financial market centre, including SISE, Saadiyat Futures and Options Exchange, Saadiyat Commodities Exchange and Saadiyat Clearing House (for more information see section on Business Environment).

The new commodities trading hub, the first in the region, is expected to net annual revenues totalling Dh 1.46 billion (US $398 million) by the year 2005 from commodities trading alone.

Feasibility studies predict that the Saadiyat market, which will serve a consumer market of about 1.5 billion people in the Middle East, Central Asia and East and North Africa, could emerge as the world's fifth largest capital market after those of New York, London, Tokyo and Singapore. The Saadiyat market will open on Saturdays and Sundays and will also cover the time zone gap of about three to five hours between markets in London, Singapore and Hong Kong, thus offering 24-hour global trading.

The issue date has not been set as yet for the IPO which will be open to both UAE national and foreign investors. The Japanese bank Nomura was appointed to manage the international listing while the First Gulf Bank (FGB) and the National Bank of Abu Dhabi (NBAD) are jointly handling the local issue. The Abu Dhabi Government will be one of the major shareholders and it has already committed US $400 million to the capital raising programme.

With projected indirect revenues of US $170 billion over 25 years, the project is expected to play an important role in the UAE's strategy for economic diversification.

BANKS AND INSURANCE

The UAE's banking and monetary system has made significant progress in recent years due to the Central Bank's increasingly strict control of financial institutions. In particular, 1998 was a year of impressive growth in the banking sector, attributable to some extent to adherence to the guidelines laid down by the Central Bank. In the last ten years, the Central Bank has played an important role in supervising the banking industry and has contributed in a measurable way to improving the quality of services and performance of a number of banks.

The number of locally incorporated banks increased to 20 in 1998 from 19 the previous year following the licensing of the Abu Dhabi Islamic Bank. Bank branches and cash offices rose from 262 (223 branches and 39 cash offices) in 1997 to 284 (243 branches and 41 cash offices) in 1998. In 1998 there were 27 foreign banks in the UAE, the same as the previous year, with branches and cash offices of these banks also remaining unchanged at 110 (109 branches and one cash office). Banca Commerciale Italiana continued to be the only restricted-licence bank and the number of investment banks was unchanged at two.

The number of foreign bank representative offices in the UAE has risen steadily over the last couple of years, a trend ascribed to the flotation of a number of new companies and to the UAE's membership of the WTO. The Central Bank issued eight licences for new representative offices in 1998, bringing the total of licensed representative offices of foreign banks and other financial institutions to 38, compared with 30 in 1997. The new representative offices licensed in 1998 were Bank Gesellschaft Berlin AG, Qatar Islamic Bank, MID-MED Bank Plc, Abbey National Plc, Unit Trust of India, Prudential Bache International Ltd, Natexis Banque-BFCE and Union Bancaire Privee (CBI-TDB).

New administrative and accounting systems

National banks are now required to adopt a new administrative structure which stipulates specific functions for top executives and in which top-level appointments will be subject to Central Bank approval.

All banks and financial and investment companies in the UAE have also been directed by the UAE Central Bank to prepare their financial results in accordance with the International Accounting Standards (IAS) with effect from 1 January 1999. Considered to be a major initiative with far-reaching implications for the financial markets in the country, this move will bring about a quantum leap in the area of public disclosures by banks and financial and investment companies.

IAS implementation in the banking sector is believed to be essential to ensure fiscal transparency and consistency and to enhance the sector's potential for integration with global financial institutions. The Central Bank will also implement IAS by the end of 1999.

Bank regulations for Saadiyat Free Zone

New regulations governing banks and financial institutions in the Saadiyat Free Zone have been adopted by Saadiyat Free Trade Zone Authority. Although functioning as offshore

units, all banks will require a licence to operate in the free zone. The general regulations and requirements for financial institutions reflect standards operating in international markets such as North America and Europe, while the code of conduct sets out the general controls which the Authority requires participants in its market to adopt in the course of their transactions.

Banks and insurance companies may be incorporated in the free zone as private or public limited companies. The minimum paid-up capital for a bank or insurance business starting operations in the zone is fixed at Dh 100 million and minimum capital for an insurance broker is Dh 1 million.

Financial and commodities brokers may be incorporated as private or public limited companies with a minimum paid-up capital of Dh 50 million. The regulations stipulate that banks or insurance companies incorporated outside the Saadiyat Free Zone may set up branches in the free zone, but must have the consent of the home regulator to do so. The authority must satisfy itself on the nature and scope of supervision, including capital, other financial resources and liquidity requirements conducted by the home regulator. The minimum capital for a branch is also Dh 100 million.

Exemptions from corporate taxation and bank reserve requirements and the absence of restrictive legislation as regards staffing and deposit-taking, as well as the ability to set its own price for the major currencies, stocks and commodity groups, will ensure that Saadiyat emerges as a major international banking centre.

Abu Dhabi Islamic Bank

The Abu Dhabi Islamic Bank (ADIB), the world's biggest Islamic banking institution, was officially opened in the capital by Sheikh Abdulla bin Zayed Al Nahyan, Minister for Information and Culture, in April 1999. The bank is fully committed to becoming a major contributor to the social and economic development of the UAE. A team of profes-sional, experienced bankers with a thorough knowledge and understanding of Islamic banking will manage the bank in accordance with international banking standards. In contributing to the local economy through Islamic financing, the bank provides opportu-nities for both commercial investment and service projects, thereby improving the returns on investment for its customers.

The ADIB with a paid up capital of Dh 1 billion was founded as a joint stock company under an Emiri decree issued by Sheikh Khalifa bin Zayed Al Nahyan, Crown Prince of Abu Dhabi and Deputy Supreme Commander of the UAE Armed Forces. Fifty-five per cent of its capital has been raised through public issues of shares with a par value of Dh 10, and the remainder is distributed between the Abu Dhabi Government (10 per cent) founders' subscriptions of Dh 390 million and the Private Department of President His Highness Sheikh Zayed bin Sultan Al Nahyan which has invested Dh 50 million. The bank, which opened its doors to the public on 11 November 1998 at premises on Najda Street, provides a range of retail and corporate banking services and carries out its business activities in strict conformity with the principles of sharia.

Money Supply & Domestic Liquidity   Bn. AED's

120
100
80
60
40
20
0

1975   1980   1985

- Currency with the public
- Money Supply
- Private Domestic Liquidity
- Overall Liquidity

Loans, Advances & Overdrafts to Residents by Sectors

Sector		%
Commercial & Industrial	☐	62%
Others	■	24%
Government	▨	12%
Financial Institutions	☐	2%

Emiratisation

The UAE Central Bank and the Human Resources Development (HRD) Committee for Banks will assist in implementing Cabinet Decree No.10/1998 which requires banks to increase national employment by 4 per cent annually. Implementation of the decree is of major importance since the sector is strategic to the national economy.

The annual increment of 4 per cent was arrived at after due consultations with all the banks, which felt they could comfortably accommodate this level every year.

In fact, the number of UAE citizens working in banks jumped from 1,068 in 1995 – when the HRD Banking Committee started operating – to 1,650 by the end of 1998. The number of nationals employed by UAE banks rose from 736 to 1,187, and those in foreign banks operating in the UAE from 328 to 463. While the UAE banking sector has an average 12 per cent national staff component the figure varies markedly between individual commercial banks. Nine banks have more than 15 per cent, 17 have a 10–15 per cent component, eight have a 5–10 per cent component, and around 15 banks have a national staff strength of less than 5 per cent. The committee sought explanations from the bottom-placed 15 banks for their below-par performance.

Banks have welcomed the Cabinet resolution and have made serious efforts to attract national employees. The Central Bank, which is empowered to penalise banks failing to meet the target, will address the committee every six months to brief it on progress in implementing the decree.

As the emiratisation process gains momentum there is a move to widen the scope of the HRD Banking Committee from the present twin-pronged focus on banks and educational institutes.

OIL AND GAS

Oil and gas production has been the mainstay of the economy in the UAE and will remain a major revenue earner long into the future, due to the vast hydrocarbon reserves at the country's disposal. Proven recoverable oil reserves are currently put at 98.2 billion barrels or 9.5 per cent of the global crude oil proven reserves. As for natural gas, the proven recoverable reserves are estimated currently at 5.8 billion cubic metres or 4 per cent of the world total. This means that the UAE possesses the third largest natural gas reserves in the region and the fourth largest in the world. At the current rate of utilisation, and excluding any new discoveries, these reserves will last for over 150 years.

The UAE's oil production is limited by quotas agreed within the framework of OPEC to 2 million barrels per day (mbd). Production capacity, however, will rise to around 3 mbd in the year 2000. There are plans to boost that level to 3.6 mbd in the year 2005 and 4 mbd in the year 2010.

Gas production is being expanded to meet a forecast doubling of demand to 3.7 billion cubic feet per day (bn cfd) by the year 2000. Domestic demand is expected to increase from 813 million cubic feet per day (mn cfd) in 1996 to 1.137 bn cfd by the year 2000, while gas used for reinjection is projected to double to 1.8 bn cfd.

The value of oil exports dropped from Dh 49.1 billion in 1997 to Dh 35.7 billion in 1998 (-27.3 per cent) due to the deterioration in oil prices which fell by 34 per cent during 1998 compared with 1997 levels, to reach US $12.4 a barrel. The value of liquefied gas exports also dropped from Dh 8.5 billion in 1997 to Dh 6.5 billion in 1998, due to the fall in its prices which are closely linked with oil prices and owing to the fact that the value of gas exports in 1997 included a one-time payment of Dh 1.5 billion made to ADGAS by its main importer Tokyo Electricity Power Company.

The UAE exports 62 per cent of its crude oil to Japan making it the UAE's largest customer. Gas exports are almost entirely to Japan, the world's largest buyer of liquefied gas, with the UAE supplying almost one-eighth of Japan's entire requirements.

INTERNATIONAL MARKETS

The UAE plays a vital role in achieving stability in international oil markets through its positive and balanced attitude within OPEC. The UAE participated in two production cuts in 1998 and also played an important role in the agreement adopted by OPEC member

states in March 1999 to reduce production by 1.7 mbd. The UAE agreed to reduce its production by 157,000 bd to a low of 2 mbd.

By early September 1999 international benchmark Brent crude oil was trading at a new high of US $21.03 per barrel. Oil prices were expected to continue rising in the fourth quarter of 1999 when winter weather in the western hemisphere is expected to increase demand. The UAE welcomed a proposal to hold an OPEC summit meeting in Venezuela in late 1999 or the year 2000 in order to reinforce rationalisation of the world supply of oil.

ABU DHABI

Abu Dhabi is by far the biggest oil producer in the UAE, controlling more than 85 per cent of the UAE's total oil output capacity and over 90 per cent of its crude reserves. Principal offshore oil fields are Umm Shaif, Lower Zakum, Upper Zakum, Al Bunduq and Abu al-Bukhoosh. The main onshore fields are Asab, Bab, Bu Hasa, Sahil and Shah. Almost 92 per cent of the country's gas reserves are also located in Abu Dhabi and the Khuff reservoir beneath the oil fields of Umm Shaif and Abu al-Bukhoosh ranks among the largest single gas reservoirs in the world.

Abu Dhabi National Oil Company

Oil companies from Japan, France, Britain and other countries own up to 40 per cent of the energy sector in Abu Dhabi, the only Gulf oil producer to have retained foreign partners on a production-sharing basis. More than half of Abu Dhabi's oil production is generated by the Abu Dhabi Company for Onshore Operations (ADCO), one of the 10 largest oil companies worldwide and the largest crude oil producer in the southern Arabian Gulf. The second main producer is Abu Dhabi Marine Operating Company (ADMA-OPCO). The output of oil and gas from ADMA-OPCO fields is transported to its centre of operations on Das Island for processing, storage and export. Both ADCO and ADMA-OPCO are part of the Abu Dhabi National Oil Company (ADNOC) group of companies.

ADNOC, established in 1971, is a fully owned government company controlled and supervised by the Supreme Petroleum Council (SPC), which is responsible for formulating Abu Dhabi petroleum policy and overseeing the emirate's oil and gas operations and related industry.

ADNOC group of companies

In addition to its own concession areas and operations ADNOC has major shareholdings in 15 ventures forming the ADNOC group. These include the three main oil and gas operating companies (ADCO, ADMA-OPCO and ZADCO), five support companies providing services to the oil and gas industry, two natural gas processing companies (GASCO, ADGAS), two maritime transport companies for crude oil, refined products and LNG (ADNATCO, NGSCO), a refined product distribution company (ADNOC-FOD) and two chemical and petrochemical companies (FERTIL, BOROUGE). ADNOC also owns and operates two refineries at Umm al-Nar and Ruwais, the gas treatment plants at Habshan, gas pipeline distribution network and the chlorine industries at Umm al-Nar.

ADNOC restructuring

ADNOC announced a major management restructuring plan in November 1998 shifting the firm's refinery and gas operations to two new wholly-owned subsidiaries and bringing the number of subsidiaries up to 17. The two new ADNOC companies, Abu Dhabi Oil Refining Company (TAKREER) and the Abu Dhabi Gas Company (ATHEER), were formally established on 19 June 1999.

Along with the creation of refinery and gas subsidiaries the company has set up five business line directorates (BLDs) to carry out upstream and downstream activities. Another three directorates will provide support services for various operations. The new management structure also creates an executive committee, chaired by a chief executive officer, to oversee the company's businesses.

DOLPHIN PROJECT

The Dolphin project was launched in March 1999 following an announcement by the UAE and Qatar of plans for a joint venture aimed at transporting gas from Qatar's huge reserves to industrial consumers in the UAE, Oman and other countries. Dolphin, which is being developed under the auspices of the UAE Offset Group (UOG), is intended to provide a framework to stimulate investment in a variety of related industries throughout the value-added gas chain. (For more information see section on Business Environment). Economic forecasters predict that the UAE's demand for gas will double over the next decade.

Memorandums signed with Oman and Pakistan

In June 1999 Oman signed a Memorandum of Understanding with the UOG that would enable it to receive gas at an estimated 300–600 mn cfd through the Dolphin project. Muscat's involvement in Dolphin, which will be of great assistance in meeting anticipated demand for energy in the sultanate well into the next century, will include the construction of pipelines in Oman. Another memorandum was signed between UOG and Pakistan to supply much-needed natural gas to Pakistan. The memorandum provides for the offsets group to submit a firm proposal to supply between 1 and 1.5 bn cfd to Pakistan as part of a broader programme of substantial investment in Pakistan's energy sector.

Dubai joins Dolphin

The Dubai Government also joined the multi-billion dollar Dolphin initiative with the signing of a memorandum with the UOG whereby the Dubai Supply Authority (DSA) agreed to purchase its requirements for Qatari gas from Dolphin. Under the terms of the agreement, Dubai plans to purchase gas in the amount of 200–700 mn cfd. The Dubai Government and the UOG also agreed to cooperate in identifying and maximising opportunities for investment arising out of the supply of gas. The Dolphin gas will bridge the gap between energy supply and demand which will develop over the next five years as Dubai's economy expands.

UAE Crude Oil Production & Exports   **Thousand bls/Day**

Legend: ■ Production ■ Exports

Source: *Development Indicators in the UAE 1999*, Crown Prince Court – Research and Studies Dept., Abu Dhabi.

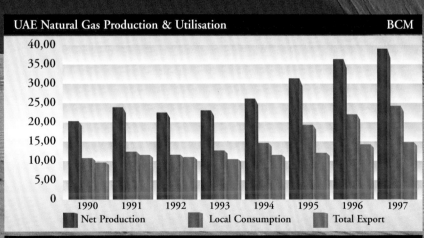

UAE Natural Gas Production & Utilisation   **BCM**

Legend: ■ Net Production ■ Local Consumption ■ Total Export

Source: *Development Indicators in the UAE 1999*, Crown Prince Court – Research and Studies Dept., Abu Dhabi.

DUBAI

Dubai's oil reserves have reduced over the past decade and are now expected to be exhausted within 20 years. The main fields are offshore: Fateh, Southwest Fateh and two smaller fields, Falah and Rashid. The only onshore deposit is the Margham field. Dubai Petroleum Company (DPC) is the main operator. Dubai has a 2 per cent share of the UAE's gas reserves. Dubai's Margham gas/condensate field can deliver up to 140 mn cfd for domestic use and offshore fields can provide another 100 mn cfd. Sharjah also supplies Dubai with 430 mn cfd through a pipeline installed in 1992. The state-owned Dubai Natural Gas Company (DUGAS) is responsible for processing natural gas produced in Dubai's offshore oil fields as well as the gas piped from Sharjah.

SHARJAH

Sharjah owns 5 per cent of the UAE's gas reserves, mostly non-associated gas which is being utilised domestically. The emirate's most important gas deposits are at the offshore Mubarak field and the onshore Saja'a, Moveyeid and Kahaif fields. Gas reserves are estimated at 10,000 billion cubic metres and around 800 mn cfd of gas are produced. Sharjah's offshore Mubarak field, operated by the local Crescent Petroleum Company, produces around 30,000 bd of condensate. In July 1999 Crescent Petroleum began drilling Sharjah-2 some 30 kilometres offshore of Sharjah where gas has already been discovered. The site is located 800 metres from the Sharjah-1 well. Any gas finds are expected to contain valuable liquid condensates.

Crescent operates the concession area along with London-based Atlantis. Crescent–Atlantis also announced in July that they were about to begin major seismic work in the gas-proven areas of Sharjah's interior desert and this would be followed by drilling.

The onshore Sajaa and Moveyeid fields, operated by BP–AMOCO, produce 35,000 bd of condensate in addition to natural gas.

Sharjah Natural Gas project

The Sharjah Liquefied Gas Company (SHALCO) was formed to increase exports of liquefied natural gas (LNG). The first phase of a Dh 300 million project to supply natural gas to residences, commercial and industrial premises in Sharjah was officially inaugurated in March 1999. Natural gas was supplied to buildings in Abu Shaghara in Sharjah marking the beginning of Phase I which is due for completion in May 2000. A 172-kilometre network of pipes, three pumping stations and the internal connections for a total of 25,000 domestic, commercial and industrial consumers will be completed in the first phase. Phase II is due to supply the remainder of the city of Sharjah.

RAS AL-KHAIMAH

Ras al-Khaimah's reserves are estimated at 400 million barrels of oil and condensate and 1,200 bn cfd of natural gas. In September 1997, Ras al-Khaimah awarded Norway's Atlantis Technology Services and Petroleum Geo Services a permit to explore the offshore Baih field. The Ras al-Khaimah Oil and Gas Company, set up in 1996, has exclusive hydrocarbon rights to the rest of the emirate.

REFINERIES

In the UAE there are six refineries operational at present and the existing refining capacity in the region is estimated to be around 800,000 tonnes.

Development of downstream industries such as refineries and petrochemical plants is a central part of UAE efforts to move away from crude oil exports. Major plans are under way to construct new refineries and increase the capacity of existing ones in order to attain production of 180,000 bd by the year 2000.

Abu Dhabi is presently in the middle of a five-year (1997–2002) development project aimed at boosting refining capacity. ADNOC's US $600 million Ruwais refinery upgrading project is just one of the many downstream projects that are included in the programme. Others include a 35,000 bd refinery plant in Fujairah and the Dh 600 million Sharjah refinery at Hamriyyah Free Zone, which commenced operations in mid-1999.

EPPCO

The Emirates Petroleum Products Company (EPPCO) condensate and light crude refinery in Jebel Ali was commissioned in May 1999. Up to 50 per cent of the refinery's output – comprising naphtha, marine diesel oil, diesel, kerosene, jet fuel and LPG – will be exported. The plant will have a capacity of 60,000 bd, with naphtha comprising more than half. LPG will be supplied to Emirates Gas, a wholly-owned subsidiary of Emirates National Oil Company (ENOC), which holds a majority stake in EPPCO. Caltex of the US holds the remainder.

PETROCHEMICALS

As part of an ambitious plan to expand its energy sector the UAE is planning to make a major investment in petrochemicals in the next few years. The Abu Dhabi Government plans to establish four petrochemical plants with a total investment of Dh 10.6 billion: the Dh 3.67 billion Borouge joint venture, the Dh 1.83 billion Ruwais EDC plant, the Dh 1.46 billion Ruwais fertiliser project and a Dh 3.67 aromatics venture.

Polyethylene plants

Work on the Borouge gas-based downstream complex is on schedule to start production late in the year 2001. The project is a joint venture between ADNOC (holding 60 per cent of shares, and Borealis (holding 40 per cent) is located at Ruwais. It envisages a petrochemical complex with two major segments – an ethylene cracker plant with a designed capacity of 600,000 tonnes per year and two of the world's most sophisticated polyethelene units, each with an output of 225,000 tonnes per year of low density polyethylene. The ethylene cracker will have an annual capacity of 600,000 tonnes of which 450,000 tonnes will go as feedstock to the proposed polyethylene plants and 150,000 tonnes will be allocated to the planned ethylene dichloride (EDC) plant wholly owned by ADNOC, which will also be sited at Ruwais. The complex will be close to both the ADNOC refinery and the Abu Dhabi Gas Industries Ltd (GASCO) facility which will supply the ethylene cracker with ethane.

Borouge was established in 1997 to construct, own, operate and maintain the ethylene and polyethylene plants. The company awarded a contract in January 1999 to a two-member team comprising Germany's Linde and Eastern Bechtel Company of the US to build the ethylene cracker plant. The Dh 1.47 billion (US $400 million) contract to build the polyethylene plants was awarded to Italy's Tecnimont SpA in June 1999.

When completed, Ruwais will be one of the largest polyethylene production facilities in the Middle East and the first significant downstream petrochemical investment in the UAE.

A sales and marketing company Borouge Pte Ltd, 50 per cent of which is owned by Borealis, has been set up in Singapore and pre-marketing has begun in the Middle East, East Asia, China and the Asia-Pacific.

Formaldehyde manufacturing

Emirati Investor Company is establishing a petrochemical plant to manufacture formaldehyde and formaldehyde derivatives such as UFC85, resins, glues and urea formaldehyde, the first plant of its kind in the UAE. Construction will begin in 1999 and the plant is expected to go on stream in the year 2001. The production capacity for formaldehyde is 42,000 tonnes per year, urea formaldehyde 57,000 tonnes per year and UFC85 26,000 tonnes per annum. These products, which are presently imported, are mainly used in making fertilisers, chipboard and formica board. The products will be marketed locally and exported to neighbouring AGCC markets such as Oman and Qatar. Emirati Investor Company was founded by 11 prominent UAE nationals three years ago and is a wholly owned national company.

MANUFACTURING INDUSTRIES

The discovery of oil ushered the UAE into the industrial age. This process of industrial-isation gathered momentum following the formation of the Federation. During the last two decades, with the Government's increasing emphasis on diversification and basic components such as capital and energy readily available, the manufacturing sector has made significant progress in the UAE.

Free zones have played an instrumental role in attracting manufacturing industries (see section on Business Environment) and today, hundreds of factories covering a wide range of manufacturing are distributed throughout the country. Cement, building materials, aluminium, chemical fertilisers and foodstuffs industries top the list, followed by garments, furniture, paper and carton, plastics, fibre glass and processed metals.

SECTORAL DISTRIBUTION

In 1999 1,695 factories employing more than 145,000 people and with investments estimated at more than Dh 14 billion were operating in the UAE.

Sharjah has the largest number of firms followed by Dubai, Abu Dhabi and Ras al-Khaimah. Nearly 140 units were established in 1998 – roughly the pace at which new manufacturing units were formed in 1997 – and employment saw a 20 per cent increase. The strongest growth was in chemicals (see section on Oil and Gas). The chemicals and non-metallic industries had the greatest number of establishments and employed the most people. Food and beverages — in the consumer goods sector – were most successful at substituting imports. Industry in the Northern Emirates focused on small factories especially textiles, most of them in Ajman.

CEMENT INDUSTRY

Dating back to the mid-1970s, the cement industry is one of the oldest manufacturing industries in the UAE. The first factory, Al Ittihad Cement Company of Ras al-Khaimah, started commercial production in 1975. This was followed by the construction of several other factories in Al Ain, Sharjah, Dubai, Fujairah, Ajman and Umm al-Qaiwain.

The total number of cement factories throughout the country had reached nine by the end of 1998. Eight of these produce Portland cement, and one factory in Ras al-Khaimah manufactures white cement. The total capacity of the eight Portland cement factories is

estimated at 9 million tonnes. These factories employ 2,999 workers, representing a total investment of approximately Dh 1.8 billion. Ras al-Khaimah Company for White Cement and Construction Materials is expanding its production capacity to 450,000 tonnes per year.

New cement factories

Test production at a new Dh 550 million cement plant in Ras al-Khaimah commenced in mid-August 1999. The plant, the fourth in Ras al-Khaimah, is owned by Ras al-Khaimah Cement Company. It will have a production capacity of 1 million tonnes per year of Portland cement.

A Dh 80 million cement plant in Dubai's Jebel Ali industrial area was fully operational by mid-September 1999. Plans are under way to raise production capacity immediately from the initial 250,000 tonnes per annum to 400,000 tonnes. Falcon Cement is the first purpose-built ground, granulated blast furnace slag processing plant in the Middle East.

CHEMICAL FERTILISERS INDUSTRY

Chemical fertiliser production began in the UAE with the establishment by the Abu Dhabi National Oil Company (ADNOC) of Ruwais Fertiliser Industries (FERTIL) which has a capacity of 1,050 metric tonnes of ammonia and 1,500 metric tonnes of urea per day. The complex, situated in the industrial zone at Ruwais in western Abu Dhabi, also comprises an integrated production unit, storage, packing and cargo units.

Abu Dhabi Fertiliser Industries' Dh 5 million chemical fertiliser plant was set up as a joint venture in June 1998 between the UAE-based International Technical Trading Company (ITTC, with a 64 per cent stake) and SQM of Chile (36 per cent). Annual production is 40,000 tonnes of fertiliser, mainly water soluble and granular compound products. The company, which has an annual capacity of 200,000 tonnes, also produces liquid and suspension fertilisers. Other fertiliser manufacturing projects are located in Jebel Ali Free Zone.

PHARMACEUTICAL INDUSTRY

The UAE-based pharmaceutical industry is emerging as a major force in the local, Gulf and the Arab markets. Despite intense international competition many local companies are successfully marketing their products even in the highly competitive European arena. Local pharma companies such as the Ras al-Khaimah-based Gulf Pharmaceutical Company (Julphar) and the Jebel Ali-based Gulf Inject Company are at the forefront of the industry.

Julphar

With a capital of Dh 165 million and 855 workers, Gulf Pharmaceutical Company (Julphar), which has a production capacity of 1 billion units annually, manufactures 275 varieties of medicine, only 7 per cent of which are consumed locally. The rest is exported to 30 countries.

The company's new factory, Julphar 2, which produces antibiotics, was opened in March 1999. Julphar, founded in 1985, now has five factories, three of which are in Ras al-Khaimah, one in Ecuador and one in Germany.

Gulf Inject

Specialising in the production of intravenous solutions, Gulf Inject has become a major regional player in this segment of the Middle East's pharmaceuticals industry. With a capital base of Dh 55.05 million (US $15 million), Gulf Inject was set up by a group of local and Gulf businessmen. High quality production standards are helping the company to market its products effectively in international markets. In the past three years it has produced and exported over 10 million bottles of solution to around 26 Arab, African, Asian, CIS and East European countries.

Following a growing demand from the international market the company has raised its output in recent years. In the first six months of 1999, the company produced over 6.3 million bottles of intravenous (IV) fluids. Current international orders are in excess of 25 million bottles. Since demand is far in excess of the company's production capacity, it has entered into a production contract with other Gulf-based intravenous fluid manufacturers to fill the supply gap.

DUBAI ALUMINIUM COMPANY

Dubai Aluminium Company (DUBAL) was established in 1975 with a capacity of 135,000 tonnes of aluminium per year. The company has since expanded its capacity to reach 380,000 tonnes of aluminium annually. Total investment has reached Dh 3.114 billion. The factory employs a workforce of 2110 and depends on imported alumina as raw material.

DUBAL sold 402,000 tonnes of aluminium worth Dh 2.46 billion (US $670 million) during 1998. This sales figure was achieved in the face of difficult circumstances, with a marked 20 per cent downturn of prices at the London Metals Exchange exacerbated by shrinking markets due to the economic turmoil in the Far East. Asia's share of 1998 sales declined from 80 per cent to 50 per cent. Exports destined for Asia were diverted to Europe where sales rose from 20,000 to 80,000 tonnes despite the 6 per cent EU tax on primary aluminium imports

In 1999 the company is planning to sell 430,000 tonnes and expects to see a slow return to the old levels of sales in Asia. Exports to Europe in 1999 are expected to reach 100,000 tonnes compared with 83,000 tonnes in 1998 and to rise to approximately 150,000 tonnes once a new phase of expansion is completed. DUBAL was awarded an ISO 14001 environmental certificate on 10 May 1999.

Condor

The first reduction cell of DUBAL's Condor expansion programme, comprising approximately 25 per cent of the project, was energised in May 1999 ahead of schedule. By the year 2000, when Condor is completed, DUBAL will be one of the biggest stand-alone smelting complexes outside the former USSR with a hot metal capacity of around 530,000 tonnes.

The Condor project has involved expenditure of Dh 1.1 billion with local industries and suppliers. The number of nationals in senior positions also increased in 1998 and citizens of the UAE now occupy 45 per cent of senior management posts.

AL AIN VEGETABLE PACKING FACTORY

Al Ain vegetable packing factory, owned by the Department of Agriculture and Animal Resources in Abu Dhabi's Eastern Region, started operation in 1987 with the aim of establishing a solid food industry using local raw materials in the form of a portion of the huge agricultural surplus in the area. The factory comprises lines for pickled vegetables with an annual capacity of 3,000 tonnes and frozen vegetables with a capacity of 500 tonnes and tomato paste producing 60,000 tonnes. Investment in this project has reached Dh 54 million and the workforce numbers approximately 180.

HOUSEHOLD GLASS EQUIPMENT INDUSTRY

This new industry commenced in 1995 with the establishment in Jebel Ali Zone of Al Tajer Glass Factory, which is entirely financed by local investors, followed by two other factories in Dubai and Ras al-Khaimah. The Jebel Ali glass factory in the Jebel Ali Free Zone, a Gulf joint venture and one of the biggest projects, started production in 1997. Al Manal glass factory in Ras al-Khaimah commenced production in 1999 as a joint venture with 96 per cent of the capital being supplied by local investors. The capacity of the three factories is estimated at 900 million units, with investment of Dh 370 million and employing 425 workers.

DUBAI CABLE COMPANY

Dubai Cable Company's (DUCAB) Dh 77 million expansion programme was completed in mid-1999. DUCAB has installed the most up-to-date computer-controlled extrusion line in the world in order to manufacture high-voltage cables. This will allow them to move into the range of higher voltage cables to support and supply the utilities sector not only in the UAE but throughout the AGCC. DUCAB has also increased capacity for its low-voltage cables of up to 3.3kV and medium-voltage cables of up to 33kV. The new facility will increase DUCAB's production capacity by 130 per cent from 20,000 tonnes.

Established in 1979, DUCAB is a joint venture between the Dubai and Abu Dhabi Governments (35 per cent each), and the UK-based BICC (30 per cent).

ABU DHABI FLOUR AND FODDER MILL

Production capacity is 400 tonnes of flour per day. Animal and poultry fodder production reached 20 tonnes per hour, while silo storage capacity is 60,000 tonnes of grain.

Expansion during 1999 included a new mill with a capacity of 400 tonnes per day and construction of additional silos with a capacity of 90,000 tonnes, together with installation of new equipment for discharging grain at a capacity of 800 tonnes per hour. Studies are also under way to raise capacity of the fodder mill to meet increasing demand.

REINFORCED STEEL FACTORY

Work has begun on the construction of a reinforced steel factory with a capacity of 500,000 tonnes of 10–32 mm diameter steel per annum at Mussafah Industrial Area. The factory is currently dependent on importing and processing of raw material. Expansion plans include the construction of a 205,000 tonnes per year smelter, a 351 megawatt power station and a desalination plant with a capacity of 2,000 cubic metres of fresh water per day. Gas will be supplied to the project through a newly constructed pipeline.

FIREFIGHTING EQUIPMENT

In April 1999 the UAE Offsets Group announced the formation of UTS-Burnstop LLC, a new venture between the local group United Technical Services (51 per cent), Burnstop Ltd from Finland (40 per cent) and Dassault Investments, a sister company of Dassault Aviation (9 per cent). The new company will be capitalised at Dh 5 million. UTS-Burnstop LLC, which will manufacture firefighting and prevention equipment will have its offices in Abu Dhabi and its manufacturing facility in Mussafah Industrial Zone.

This venture will release the UAE fire-related industries from their current dependence on imported alternatives, as the establishment of the manufacturing facilities will be the first of its kind within the UAE. The unit will also export to the Middle East, Europe and Asia.

COOLING PLANT

A Dh 45 million cooling plant room installed by National Central Cooling Company (TABREED) commenced operations in May 1999 at Zayed Military City in Sweihan. The energy efficient system comprises gas-driven chillers producing 3,000 tonnes of chilled water which is supplied to a number of buildings within a radius of 1.5 kilometres.

Tabreed, another offset project, is also examining several similar projects in Sharjah, Al Ain and Ras al-Khaimah and is working on two major projects in Dubai. Working on an economy-of-scale basis, Tabreed plans to build cooling systems with a capacity between 75,000 and 100,000 tonnes.

MAGNESIUM ALLOY PLANT

Construction of a Dh 734 million magnesium alloy plant is planned for Sharjah's Hamriyyah Free Zone. The magnesium smelter project is being promoted by the Sahari Group of Abu Dhabi and Normans of Albania, both of which hold a 50 per cent stake in the project. The plant will have an initial capacity to produce 20,000 tonnes per year of magnesium products, to be increased to 60,000 tonnes upon completion. The market demand for magnesium is estimated to be increasing at a rate of 15 per cent a year. Raw material (magnesium) will come from mines in Albania which are estimated to have reserves of over 400 million tonnes. Magnesium products made at the Sharjah plant will be sold to buyers in Japan, the US and Europe.

EDIBLE OIL PLANT

Dubai Investments PJSC announced a US $50 million edible oil project in the Jebel Ali Free Trade Zone in partnership with the Swiss-based CAM Group. The seed-crushing plant for the production of edible oil and meals is the largest facility of its kind in the Middle East and is expected to go on stream at the end of the year 2000. Edible Oil (Dubai) LLC–Dubai Investments holds a 70 per cent equity stake with the remaining

30 per cent being held by the CAM Group, a world leader in the supply of agro-industrial processing lines. The crushing plant will have an initial capacity of 300,000 tonnes which could be expanded to 450,000 tonnes.

With this new project, the total investment in some 19 projects initiated by Dubai Investment Company., which was established in 1996, has exceeded Dh 6 billion. Other projects at the planning stage include a Dh 370 million unit for manufacturing of aluminium sheets and a Dh 100 million unit for the manufacture of wood panels. The company will also take over four operating projects in the UAE.

FRUCTOSE SYRUP

A Jebel Ali-based company has introduced new technology to produce fructose syrup – a key sweetening ingredient for food and beverage manufacturing industries – from dates. Concept Food Industries (CFI) FZE claims that it is the first company in the world to use this technology which also delivers a high protein animal feed as a by-product. The production of sweetener at Concept's facility in Jebel Ali Free Zone is expected to reduce reliance on imports and the product is also being marketed in the Middle East and worldwide. The facility has the capacity to extract high fructose syrup from dates at the rate of 35,000 tonnes a year. The new facility is expected to boost government-sponsored efforts to improve palm date cultivation within the UAE.

STEEL WIRE AND ROD PLANT

The Abu Dhabi-based private company Abu Dhabi National Industrial Projects (ADNIP) is setting up a Dh 170 million plant to manufacture steel wire and rod with German collaboration. The project will be implemented in two phases. In the first phase 80,000 tonnes of steel wire, rod and reinforced mesh will be produced. These products will be used by 12 other industries to be set up in due course.

ADNIP, established in 1997, has several other projects under construction including a medical equipment project, a carpet factory and a tissue paper plant in Dubai.

PAPER MILL

The paper mill owned by ADNIP which will be located in Dubai Investment's Industrial Park, is expected to become operational in September 2000. It will have a capacity of 22,000 tonnes per year of fine paper rolls of all specifications and weights. The advanced technology to be used in this plant is being introduced in the AGCC for the first time.

TRADE

Preliminary data analysed by the Central Bank indicate a decrease, for the second consecutive year, in the trade balance surplus, which reached Dh 11.6 billion in 1998, as compared with Dh 27.2 billion in 1997 (-57.5 per cent). The contraction was mainly attributed to a decline in the value of oil exports (-27.3 per cent) and liquefied gas exports (-23.5 per cent). Despite the increase in values of commodity exports and re-exports by 3.8 per cent and 2.4 per cent respectively in 1998, compared with 1997 levels the total value of exports (oil, gas and other) and re-exports dropped from Dh 124.9 billion in 1997 to Dh 111. 5 billion in 1998 (-10.7 per cent). Interestingly, the value of exports from the Free Zones maintained its upward trend to reach Dh 16.5 billion in 1998, an increase of 12.9 per cent over 1997 levels, while the value of commodity exports dropped by 5.6 per cent as a result of the drop in the value of petroleum product exports whose prices are closely linked with oil prices.

The value of imports, however, registered a new record level of Dh 99.9 billion in 1998, compared with Dh 97.7 billion in 1997. This was mainly attributable to population increase, higher demand for imports to meet re-export requirements and a higher level of individual expenditure partly due to the increased commercial activity associated with the shopping festivals held throughout the year. The increase in value of imports also involved an increase in volume resulting from appreciation of the US dollar and hence the UAE dirham against most major currencies and also against the currencies of the UAE's trade partners in Asia. Low commodity prices caused by fierce competition among Asian countries eager to maintain external markets also had an upward effect on volume.

Data on imports classified by major groups of commodities show that in 1998 consumer goods had a 52.1 per cent share of the market, capital goods 35.6 per cent and intermediate goods 12.3 per cent, these percentages being identical to the 1997 figures.

With regarded to geographical distribution based on import value, European countries had a 35 per cent share of the market, up from 33.8 per cent in 1997. Within this group the UK's share remained the highest, although it fell from 8.6 per cent to 7.5 per cent. Asian countries increased their overall market share by half a percentage point to 45 per cent, however, the US's share decreased from 13 per cent in 1997 to a low of 11.2 per cent in 1998.

RE-EXPORTS

A report by Emirates Industrial Bank (EIB) issued in May 1999 ranks the UAE as the third most important re-export centre in the world (after Hong Kong and Singapore respectively). Re-export trade forms a substantial one-third of the entire trading sector in the UAE. In Dubai, where a large part of the re-export trade is concentrated, it forms an even greater proportion of that emirate's total income.

The re-export strength of the UAE lies in bulk purchases, low taxes, good infrastructure and an historical concentration of traders. Reduced delivery lead times are also a major reason for the success of the trade. Although Iran (machinery, textiles, vehicles) and India (silver, silver jewellery) feature prominently as destination countries there is a fairly even spread of re-exports across at least 35 countries.

After expanding very rapidly in the mid-1990s, there has been a slowdown in the growth of re-export trade in recent years, due in part to an economic decline in key destination countries. Overall re-exports in the 1990s have grown at a much faster rate than imports. Currently more than 25 per cent of imports are for re-export, compared with less than 17 per cent as recently as 1994.

NORTHERN EMIRATES

The Northern Emirates' contribution to the UAE's total non-oil foreign trade has increased by over 59 per cent in the four years from 1993 to 1997. Statistics released by Dubai Chamber of Commerce and Industry indicated that the combined foreign non-oil trade of four emirates (Sharjah, Ras al-Khaimah, Fujairah and Umm al-Qaiwain) was Dh 9.29 billion in 1993, rising to Dh 14.79 billion at the end of 1997. During the corresponding period the UAE's total foreign non-oil trade was Dh 94.21 billion in 1993, rising to Dh 118 billion four years later.

Of the four emirates the highest cumulative growth was achieved by Fujairah (219.2 per cent), where trade was Dh 968 million in 1993, rising to Dh 3.09 billion in 1997. This was primarily due to increased industrial activity. Fujairah is one of the world's largest bunkering ports and being on the Arabian Sea, it is emerging as a popular port for ships plying between Europe and East Asia. During the same period Ras al-Khaimah showed a growth of 86.3 per cent from Dh 1.4 billion to Dh 2.6 billion, Sharjah 38.2 per cent (Dh 6.8 billion to Dh 9.06 billion) and Umm al-Qaiwain 34.2 per cent (Dh 35 million to Dh 47 million).

DUBAI

Major categories of imports into Dubai in 1998 were machinery, audio equipment, TVs and videos (Dh 3.8 billion); textiles and textile articles (Dh 2.8 billion); vehicles, aircraft, vessels, etc. (Dh 1.6 billion); and, base metals and articles of base metal (Dh 1.32 billion). The major categories of exports were base metals and articles of base metal (Dh 573.3 million) and textile and textile articles (Dh 233.8 million). As far re-exports were concerned, the major items were textile and textile articles (Dh 875.2 million), machinery, audio equipment, TVs, etc. (Dh 792.4 million); and vegetable products (Dh 355.42

Trade Balance 1975-1997   Bn. Dh.

- Total Exports
- Total Imports
- Trade Balance

Source: *Development Indicators in the UAE 1999*, Crown Prince Court – Research and Studies Dept., Abu Dhabi.

million). Of Dubai's direct trade (non-oil) by regions, the highest exports were to east and southeast Asia, followed by western Europe and south and west Asia. For imports, east and southeast Asia led the segment, followed by western Europe.

GOLD TRADE

In 1998 Dubai's gold imports plunged 45.6 per cent to 359.8 tonnes from a record 660 tonnes in 1997. The first five months of 1999 (219.8 tonnes) showed a further decline on the 1997 figures (261.7 tonnes), although July and August figures are much more promising.

According to Dubai Department of Ports and Customs (DP&C), several factors contributed to the slump in gold bullion imports. These include the drop in value of the Indian rupee against the dollar affecting the Indian demand for gold bullion re-exported from Dubai. India has been the top market for Dubai's gold for decades. Another factor behind the decline in imports from Dubai is the Indian Government's new policy allowing local banks to directly import gold bullion from European countries such as Switzerland (the main exporter) the UK and South Africa, South Korea and Russia.

Although bullion trade was poor, demand for gold jewellery was stimulated by the Dubai City of Gold promotion during the Shopping Festival and other promotional activities such as the World's Longest Gold Chain. The Gold Festival held during the Abu Dhabi Festival of Sales in combination with bargain priced gold, also contributed to higher consumer purchases.

CUSTOMS

UAE Customs Council

Agreement has been reached between Abu Dhabi, Dubai and Sharjah customs departments for a series of joint measures to be undertaken as part of the process of streamlining customs procedures. Although each emirate operates customs procedures independently, they meet and discuss federal and AGCC issues under the auspices of the UAE Customs Council.

Abu Dhabi Customs

Abu Dhabi Customs Department plays a vital role in the national economy by providing rapid procedures to expedite trade movement. In the past few years a comprehensive development plan has been implemented which seeks to modernise all the department's custom posts. The department has been provided with advanced computer systems to further facilitate customs procedures. It has also installed a shared database for taxed or exempted commodities which can be accessed by the customs departments of other emirates.

New advanced equipment has also been introduced at the Ghuwaifat border crossing point. The equipment, the first of its kind in the Middle East, helps to accelerate custom procedures by allowing inspection of trucks and containers without having to unload them.

In addition, the Customs Department is implementing a number of programmes to improve work practices. Nationals are offered training course opportunities at home and abroad as a positive step towards implementation of GATT.

Statistics issued by the department reflect the progress made in Abu Dhabi's trade. Total import volumes of non-oil products reached 1,656,338 tons in the first five months of 1999, compared with 1,405,046 tons during the same period last year, an increase of 17.8 per cent. Total imports in the first five months of 1999 were valued at Dh 9.1 billion compared with Dh 7 billion during the same period last year, an increase of 30 per cent.

AGCC customs unification

Until 1994, the customs tariff was fixed at 1 per cent, with basic products, food items and building materials being exempted from custom duties. At present a tariff of 4 per cent applies to basic goods, with 6 per cent being levied on other goods. However, discussions have been under way for some time on the standardisation of customs tariffs for all AGCC states. This would involve an increase in customs duties to 6 per cent on basic goods and 9 per cent on other goods. Negotiations are also taking place on whether to add spare parts and automobiles to the 'others' category.

The UAE is reluctant to increase customs duties because of the potential impact on business and has proposed a more detailed study on the issue with the assistance of the World Bank and Maxwell Stamp, a UK consultancy. The deadline for agreement on the new tariffs is December 1999.

Dubai Customs

Dubai Customs has contracted with the US-based Cisco Systems to market the trademark-registered Mirsal throughout the Middle East and with the potential to target other international markets. Mirsal, a tailor-made system developed after a thorough study of customs clearance systems, links customs online with cargo and clearing agents for speedy, secured and efficient movement of shipments among the system members in the cargo community.

AGRICULTURE AND FISHING

I always had faith in God, a desire to change things and a determination to meet challenges. We became dutiful towards the country and people and with the help of God we managed to change the desert into green gardens and provide the people with a comfortable life.

Sheikh Zayed

GREENING THE DESERT

The UAE has made major strides in developing its agricultural sector and, due to the determination of Sheikh Zayed, the desert has undergone a remarkable transformation. Concerned authorities like Abu Dhabi Municipality and Town Planning Department and Sheikh Zayed's Private Department have played significant roles in spreading afforestation and establishing farms to increase agricultural production, thereby meeting local market requirements as well as providing surplus production for export abroad.

Under instructions from Sheikh Zayed, Abu Dhabi Municipality has been extremely busy beautifying the emirate's cities. The municipality has also planted extensive green belts in order to protect these cities from the devastating effects of sandstorms. Examination of the vast areas which the municipality has cultivated under beautification projects, totalling 92,500 hectares in 1998, proves that the difficulties posed by the country's harsh climate have been successfully overcome by the municipality's use of advanced technology.

To date a total of 39 public parks, occupying an area of 3.7 million square metres, have been established in the emirate. Some of these leisure and entertainment parks are reserved especially for women and children, such as Al Khalidiya Park, Al Mushrif Park and the Women's Beach, all in Abu Dhabi city. The municipality has also planted approximately 2,450 hectares of greenery and flowers on the verges of internal roads and highways. Other projects include Baynunah Forest, which covers an area of 20,000 hectares. In Abu Dhabi, the municipality has also planted 2,500 hectares with palm trees, as at Ras al-Akhdar and Al Ghaf Park.

Special nurseries set up by the municipality produce a total of 1.5 million tree saplings, 20 million flowers and 30,000 plants each year, supplying the raw material for the beautification process.

Agricultural production	1986	1997
Agricultural produce (tonnes)	332,292	10,335,544
Fruit growing area (donums)	25,087	25,503
No. of date palm trees (millions)	4.6	35
Date production (tonnes)	59,718	388,190
No. of greenhouses		7,358
Livestock	822,343	1,722,918
Fresh milk production (tonnes)	41,434	46,000
White meat production (tonnes)	1,348	28,017
Egg production (millions)	160	256.3

Private agricultural production	1997
Vegetables (tonnes)	2,004
Animal fodder (tonnes)	5,500
Private dairy farms	22
Milk production (tonnes)	46,000
Private poultry farms	31
Egg production (millions)	256

Source: Ministry of Agriculture and Fisheries 1998

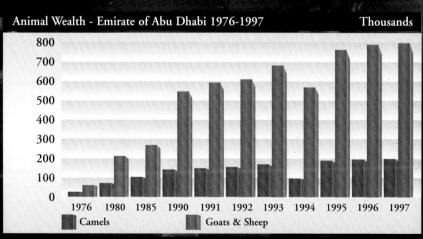

Source: *Development Indicators in the UAE 1999*, Crown Prince Court – Research and Studies Dept., Abu Dhabi.

Distribution of farms

In accordance with Abu Dhabi's long-term urban development plan, scheduled for implementation by the year 2010, the Ruler's Representative in the Western Region and Chairman of the Abu Dhabi Municipality and Town Planning Department, Sheikh Mohammed bin Butti Al Hamed, has instructed that farms in Liwa, Ghiyathi and Bida Zayed be established for distribution to UAE nationals. Around 3,000 farms are also being created around Al Ajban where Abu Dhabi Municipality has levelled a 30-kilometre desert area to transform it into cultivable land. These farms will also be distributed to nationals. With the completion of the project, productive farms in Abu Dhabi and adjoining areas should increase to around 15,000. Meanwhile over the past six years the number of farms has grown 12-fold from approximately 1,000 to more than 12,000. The total number of farms distributed among nationals so far totals 12,021 covering an area of 27,704 hectares. The municipality also provides farmers with financial assistance to purchase equipment, fertiliser and seeds.

As a result of the programme the country's once small-scale traditional farming has been complemented by investment that has seen more than 100,000 hectares of land being brought under the plough.

DATE PALM CULTIVATION

	1986	1997
No. of date palm trees (million)	4.6	35 million
Date production (tonnes)	59,718	388,190 tonnes

As the above figures indicate, Sheikh Zayed's initiatives in date palm cultivation have led to a qualitative and quantitative breakthrough, the production of rapidly growing trees and the introduction of effective control to combat palm diseases. The UAE has become a world leader in the production of palm tissues having established a tissue culture laboratory at the Emirates University for this purpose. The Ministry of Agriculture and Fisheries plans to develop all aspects of palm cultivation and to improve productivity through the creation of experimental farms, provision of guidance services and equipment, generation of high quality varieties, studies of palm populations and establishment of date processing plants.

Offset tissue culture laboratory

One new project which will assist in achieving the Ministry's goal is the Dh 5.75 million bio-technology joint venture, Al Wathba Marionnet LLC, which has been set up by France's Giat Industries as part of its military offset obligations. The project, the first of its kind in the UAE, will cultivate date palm seedlings using advanced tissue culture techniques. The cloning of date palms began in January 1999 in the Al Ain laboratory and the process is expected to take about three years before the high-yield trees bear quality dates. The new company, which will produce an initial 200,000 date palms annually 50 per cent of which will be exported, will assist in providing the UAE and the Arab world with disease-free, well rooted plants of selected varieties.

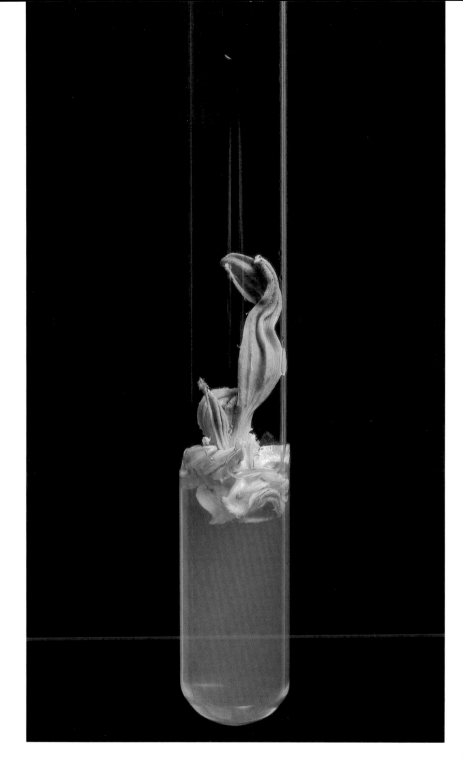

CHELSEA FLOWER SHOW

Sheikh Zayed's entry in the Royal Horticultural Society's Chelsea Flower Show held in London from 25 to 28 May, has won a gold medal for the second consecutive year. The 1999 show, one of the world's top horticultural events, was inaugurated by Queen Elizabeth who toured the displays, stopping off to inspect Sheikh Zayed's entry. This year's garden, which was inspired by an eighteenth-century poem, featured 12 large date palms specially flown to London from the UAE. At the head of a rectangular reflective pool stood a piece of perfect white Carrera marble supporting a tablet of black granite, inlaid with an intricate design in 22-carat gold leaf. Hand-wired arbours placed between the palms and bedecked with black and gold cushions provided tranquil areas for peaceful meditation. The garden was designed to promote the importance of horticulture as a means of breaking down barriers between cultures. Sheikh Zayed is an Honorary Fellow of the Royal Horticultural Society.

HORTICULTURE EXPORTS

The UAE's entry in the Chelsea Flower Show highlights the increasing importance of horticulture as a UAE export. The National Horticulture Management Company, which was set up in 1997 to provide marketing and technical assistance to farm owners, has started marketing flowers produced by Franserre UAE under the brand name Shams. The company targets the local market and exports mainly to the Middle East, Europe and Asia. Last year Shams exported 70,000 flowers a month to Riyadh and Beirut. Franserre UAE, another military offset project, was set up by Dassault Investments, Thomson Compensation International and Al Hamed Enterprises. In the first phase of the Dh 50 million project, high-tech greenhouses were established on 50,000 square metres of land near Sweihan in Abu Dhabi. Production is controlled by a centrally computerised system which regulates temperature, humidity, water for irrigation and the distribution of fertiliser.

The project is part of the UAE's strategy to create a high, value-added agricultural sector which maximises profits while reducing water consumption, subsidisation and the foreign work force.

NEW IRRIGATION TECHNIQUES

Major developments in the agricultural sector outlined above have placed huge demands on scarce water supplies, 70 per cent of which are consumed by agriculture. The need for a cost-effective source of water is therefore high. This has resulted in the implementation of a series of projects aimed at cutting expenditure on irrigation, the first of which was carried out in the 1980s when city planners decided to recycle waste water. The Mafraq sewage treatment plant which was commissioned in 1982 has an output of 18.5 million gallons of water per day. Abu Dhabi Municipality, however requires 29 million gallons of water to maintain its 45 public parks and gardens as well as its many roadside and pavement plantings.

The latest in a series of experimental water projects is under way at the Rahba farming belt in Abu Dhabi. The main objective of the experiment is to vapourise saline underground water from deep wells by using solar energy. The saline water is stored in pools 2 metres deep covered by plastic. Water with a salinity of up to 40,000 ppm is desalinated by evaporation and subsequently collected through condensation. The experiment, which will be completed in two years, is being carried out by Abu Dhabi Municipality in cooperation with the Japanese Government.

Two-thirds of the country's agricultural area is presently irrigated by modern methods. While the water-conserving drip method is most extensively used, other methods include bubbler, sprinkler and flood irrigation. Areas being irrigated by sprinklers are being supplied with desalinated water to safeguard the public from possible pathogens which may be present in the recycled waste water. The proposed new system should help ease pressure on old water treatment plants and ensure that the pathogens problem is solved.

GROUNDWATER PROJECT

The first phase of a large-scale groundwater project has been completed in the Al Khazna–Remah area between Al Ain and Abu Dhabi. The indications are that the 51 wells can produce up to 50 million gallons per day suitable for irrigation. The second phase of the project, which includes supplying farmers in the region with 50 million gallons per day free of charge to assist them in expanding cultivated areas, is under way. Plans are also in place to prospect for water in other areas.

Many companies had previously prospected for underground water in the region and and had met with very little success. Sheikh Zayed insisted, however, that the exploration continue.

DAMS

Dams in the UAE	
No. of dams	40
Total capacity	100 million cubic metres

A number of ways of conserving precious water supplies are under discussion at federal and local level and these include building more dams in valleys to trap rainwater. Construction of the Dh 30 million Wadi al-Basirah dam between Dibba and Masafi in the Hajar mountains was finished in July 1999. The dam, which took 22 months to build, is 855 metres long and 10.7 metres in height and has a capacity of 1.7 million cubic metres of water. Three main barriers, retaining 100,000 cubic metres of water each were built around the reservoir. Wadi al-Basirah and other dams will help to resupply underground water reserves on both sides of the Hajar Mountains. The dam will also help reduce water salinity and protect farm produce from being destroyed during heavy rains in winter.

FISHING

1997	
No. fishing boats	6,341
Total fish catch (tonnes)	114,358
Total value	Dh 617 million
Per capita consumption	33 kilos

YEAR	1993	1994	1995	1996	1997
Total fish catch (tonnes)	99,600	108,600	108,600	107,000	114,358
No. of fishing boats	4,303	4,303	4,464	6,341	

YEAR	1986	1997
No. of fishermen	10,600	17,286

Source: Ministry of Agriculture and Fisheries

In view of its lengthy coastline it is not surprising that the UAE has a successful indigenous fishing industry. In fact, it ranks fourth in the Arab world and second among AGCC states in the volume of its annual catch. Around 20 fishing ports and 25 repair workshops have been established along the coastline to provide facilities for fishermen.

New investment in the fishing industry (as opposed to fish farming) is largely confined to the field of refrigeration. Somewhere between 10 to 15 medium-sized establishments are currently engaged in refrigeration and packaging part of the local catch.

With the fish catch rising, but the average catch per boat declining, the Ministry of Agriculture and Fisheries is keen to protect the fishing industry and has therefore placed legal restraints on fishing to conserve fish stocks. Fish must not be caught during the spawning season and undersized fish must be returned to the sea. The ministry plans to publish a spawning timetable for each commercial fish species to encourage fishermen to suspend fishing at those times. Limits will also be set on boat registration. The fishing of shrimp in UAE waters has been banned since 1980 because of the impact of trawlers on spawning grounds. A ban ordered by HH Sheikh Hamad bin Mohammed Al Sharqi, Supreme Council Member and Ruler of Fujairah, on the use of the hayali fishing method has also been effective in preserving fishery resources. Before the ban fishermen caught quantities of both large and small fish using a 1,500-metre net. The preponderance of small fish in the catch affected the reproduction and size of the fish population. Having sold the big fish, the fishermen would dry the small ones and sell them for food or as fertiliser for palm trees.

ARTIFICIAL REEFS

Some areas in the UAE have also undertaken proactive projects to help increase stocks. For instance, Dibba Al Fujairah Municipality plans to place 300 new cone-like cement 'caves' as artificial habitats at three marine reefs about 800 metres offshore of Dibba. Each metre long 'cave' has a 58-centimetre opening to allow small fish to enter and live within

the protection of the 'cave', with eight small holes punched in the cave to facilitate water exchange. The total weight of each artificial habitat is 1.5 tonnes. These 300 new 'caves' are additional to the 270 installed by Dibba Al Fujairah Municipality in 1995 and 1998 at the same sites in Dibba, Al Aqqah and Al Faqit, near Dhadna. The building and placing of the artificial reefs, which it is hoped will help to promote tourism, is being carried out under the supervision of Fujairah and Dibba Al Fujairah municipalities and the Dubai International Marine Club.

FISH FARMING

Warm seawater that allows a year-round growing cycle, easy access to the coast and low labour and energy costs give the UAE, especially the Northern Emirates, a major advantage in aquaculture over other parts of the world. With regional and international fisheries shrinking, high-tech fish farming methods are used to enhance the UAE's traditional role as a seafood producer.

A Dh 300 million public joint stock company, International Fish Farming Company (Asmak) was incorporated in May 1999, following an initial public offering in January 1999. The lead founders of the aquaculture venture are the UAE Offsets Group, Oasis National Food Company, a subsidiary of the Abu Dhabi Investment Company, Union Cold Stores, Dassault Investissements, Athens-based Nireus Chios Aquaculture SA, Baldwin International Ltd and Gulf Investment Corporation.

Asmak plans to build two hatcheries – one in Abu Dhabi and one in the Northern Emirates. The hatchery in the capital will produce 12.5 million fin-fish hatchlings annually. The second facility will have a production capacity of 25 million fin-fish hatchlings and 360 million post-larval shrimp. Asmak also plans to build and operate three grow-out cage fish farms, two in the UAE and one in Oman, with an annual capacity of 2,000 tonnes of high-value fin fish. The company also proposes to build shrimp ponds in the Northern Emirates. Processing will take place at the company's Dubai plant. Targeted annual production will be 5,750 tonnes of full-grown marine fin-fish and 2,500 tonnes of full-grown shrimp.

In July Asmak signed a 10-year management service agreement with Nireus Chios Aquaculture, one of its shareholders.

Earlier in 1999 Dassault Investissements, Nireus Chios Aquaculture SA along with Oasis National Food Company and Union Cold Stores, set up another military offset project, Ocean Fish Processing LLC, with an initial investment of US $1.5 million.

Ras al-Khaimah

In July 1999 Asmak signed a fish-farming agreement with Ras al-Khaimah under which Asmak will be allocated an area of 450 hectares 8 kilometres offshore from the Al Mataf district for cage-farming. The site will be serviced from a 2,000 square metres onshore facility. Commencing in the year 2000, the project will produce 3,000 tonnes of sea bream and other marine fish estimated to be worth Dh 50 million at harvest. Production will be primarily for export to Europe and Japan.

TOURISM

Due to its location the UAE has been able to act as a connecting link between Europe and the Indian subcontinent, the Far East and Africa since time immemorial. It is still playing the role of intermediary between these vastly different cultures, the only difference being that air travel has significantly increased the number of visitors who come to the UAE. Traditional Arab hospitality and a delightful winter climate complemented by a highly sophisticated infrastructure and crime-free environment, have also contributed in recent years to creating an ideal atmosphere for the development of tourism.

The UAE is also endowed with an extensive coastline, sandy beaches and varied landscape, where a wide variety of activities can be indulged, ranging from powerboat races to sand-skiing. Manicured golf courses provide ready enjoyment and for the less active shopping opportunities abound. In addition, the country's deep-rooted cultural heritage, accessible in the many cultural centres and at traditional sports such as falconry, camel- racing and horse-racing, has been a powerful attraction for tourists. The UAE has also become a much sought after venue for conferences, regional and international exhibitions and major sports events such as the Dubai World Cup, the Dubai Desert Classic Golf Tournament, and polo and cricket competitions.

FEDERAL COORDINATION

Tourism organisations in the individual emirates actively market their own special attractions, frequently attending international holiday fairs as well as encouraging travel agents and tour operators to visit the UAE to experience the rich seam of Arabian life for themselves.

Minister of Information and Culture Sheikh Abdullah bin Zayed Al Nahyan announced at the ATM 99 (Arabian Travel Market) that the Ministry is studying a plan to set up a federal body to coordinate the promotional activities carried out by tourism authorities in individual emirates in order to integrate tourism promotion in the UAE as a whole. Sheikh Abdullah called on local authorities to concentrate on developing elite tourism and to focus on the country's heritage and culture. He noted that the selection of the UAE as one of the nine prominent destinations in the Middle East at the 1999 ITB Berlin travel and tourism show was an acknowledgement that the country's tourism infrastructure and facilities were rated among the best in the world. Sheikh Abdullah

infrastructure and facilities were rated among the best in the world. Sheikh Abdullah stressed the importance of promoting inter-Arab tourism and also mooted the idea of Arab countries coming together to form a pan-Arab tourism body in the Middle East.

ABU DHABI

Abu Dhabi emirate was little known as a tourist destination until the discovery of oil financed its major development programme. A thoroughly modern infrastructure of air and sea ports, highways, telecommunications systems, five-star hotels, restaurants and entertainment complexes has turned the emirate into an active tourist centre. Dubbed the Garden City of the Gulf, Abu Dhabi now offers visitors a variety of options ranging from green parks, clean beaches, a range of marine and other sports, exotic adventures in the desert, or the pleasure of shopping in its diverse shopping centres and malls. Tourists can also pay a visit to the oasis city of Al Ain and enjoy a sightseeing tour to archaeological and leisure sites such as Al Hili Fun City, Ain Al Faydha Resort, Al Jahili Fort or the National Museum. In 1997 some 937,717 visitors from neighbouring countries spent a memorable time in Abu Dhabi city.

Abu Dhabi National Hotels Company

Established in 1978 the Abu Dhabi National Hotels Company (ADNHC), plays an important role in the promotion of tourism in Abu Dhabi emirate. The total assets of the company were Dh 1.175 billion for the year ending 1998. ADNHC owns six hotels in the emirate and manages seven other hotels and a number of tourism outlets such as the Abu Dhabi Icerink, as well as several rest houses. It also supervises the duty-free complexes at Abu Dhabi and Al Ain international airports and is involved in the development of several new facilities.

The company operates divisions for hotel management, catering and contract services, purchasing and tourism services and provides transport services through Al Ghazal, a wholly-owned subsidiary.

New tourism projects

The development of tourist-related projects in Abu Dhabi continues to gather speed, with a major new hotel and leisure complex being built on reclaimed land on the Breakwater, just off the Corniche. Led by the Abu Dhabi Marine International Sports Club, the complex will also include shopping facilities, and is designed to provide a focal point for tourist activities in the capital.

Work is also nearing completion on the international class Umm al-Nar golf club, close to the island, which is designed to attract visitors as well as local residents.

GLOBAL TRAVEL AWARDS

Worldwide acknowledgement of the great strides made in the tourism industry in the UAE was underlined when the UAE was awarded several international travel industry awards in March 1999, the most significant of which was the world's safest holiday

country. The UAE was also voted the best overall destination and best shopping venue, as well as runner-up in the dining out category, scoring just one point less than Italy. Emirates airline was voted the best international airline. The Travel Oscar awards were organised by Germany's travel magazine GLOBO which surveyed 13,000 readers. The UAE had also received the safest destination award for 1996.

DUBAI

Independent studies show that the tourism industry has accounted for a steadily increasing percentage of Dubai's GDP, with some estimates putting it as high as 20 per cent. In fact tourism is expected to overtake oil exports as an important source of revenue in the near future. Dubai's 255 hotels have a total of 17,253 rooms and occupancy in 1998 averaged 49.3 per cent.

Since January 1997 when the Department of Tourism and Commerce Marketing (DTCM) took over from the Tourism and Trade Promotion Council, there has been renewed focus on worldwide promotion of Dubai as an ideal tourist destination and a thriving commercial centre. This has involved setting up the DTCM representative offices in many countries across the globe as well as participation in numerous international tourism fairs. In addition, the DTCM has launched very successful advertising campaigns worldwide.

The DTCM also organises tourism-related exhibitions in Dubai. Early in 1999 it hosted the Arabian Marine Tourism Conference, the first of its kind to be held in the region. In May more than 500 exhibitors from 40 countries participated in the Arab Travel Market 99, which was also held under the auspices of the DTCM.

Not surprisingly, since the number of tourists is expected to reach three million by the end of the year 2000, Dubai has a number of major tourism-related projects coming on-stream.

Al Maha

The endangered Arabian oryx is one of the showpieces of what is billed as the first ecotourism project in the UAE. The oryx also lends its Arabic name 'Al Maha' to the new resort, a luxury desert hideout and nature reserve. Al Maha resort, which opened its doors to its first guests in March 1999, is also home to other wildlife, such as gazelles, Arabian foxes and small cats, which have been reintroduced to the region, along with indigenous grasses and other flora. The resort, wholly-owned by Emirates Airline, lies 45 minutes by four-wheel drive car from Dubai airport. Covering about 25 square kilometres, it is surrounded by an electrified perimeter fence to keep the more exotic wildlife in and the camels which roam freely in the Arabian desert out. The resort consists of a main reception area and 30 suites which can house a total of 66 guests. Tented roofs and predominant use of 'arish or palm fronds for fencing and ceilings are intended to evoke traditional bedouin camps, although the living conditions are rather more luxurious than those to which the original desert nomads would have been accustomed.

The Emirates Group is planning two more five-star properties in the UAE. One of the luxury properties will be a 200-room hotel in the Emirate of Fujairah (see below) while the other will be located in Hatta.

Arabian Tower

Another major tourism project recently completed is the soaring 52-storey Arabian Tower, with its huge atriums, colossal supporting cross braces and acres of double glazing and aluminium cladding rising 321 metres from a concrete base on the seabed off Jumeirah beach. The impressive dhow sail-shaped building, the world's tallest hotel, contains 202 luxurious two-storey suites and a restaurant with spectacular views of Dubai. The hotel is part of a complex which includes the award-winning 26-storey Jumeirah Beach Hotel, the 40,000 square metre Wild Wadi Park (see below), conference facilities, a marina, sports centre, beach restaurant, tennis courts and a variety of swimming pools.

Royal Mirage Hotel

The Royal Mirage, an opulent 250-room beach resort, opened in mid-1999. Located on Jumeirah beach, the resort has been designed to reflect the splendour of a rediscovered Arabian fortress. With a majestic 70-foot gilded dome, the hotel promises to link Arabia's enticing culture with the demands of twenty-first-century leisure. Focus is on the most highly prized virtues of the Arab world, hospitality and courtesy. The hotel has 64,000 square metres of manicured desert landscape and 800 metres of private beach with a dedicated water sports and recreational facility, including sailing, kayaks, windsurfing, pedalos, water-skiing, snorkelling and water polo.

Wild Wadi Park

In addition to developing luxury hotels and restaurants, the UAE has focused on providing superlative entertainment and leisure facilities. Wild Wadi Water Park, which claims to be the world's leading water adventure theme park, is one of the most recent projects in this field. Located adjacent to the Jumeirah Beach Hotel, the water park draws on the rich heritage of Arabian myth and legend for its design and resident cast of characters. Situated on 5 hectares of land, the park is built to resemble a typical wadi with water rides extending for a hair-raising 1.7 kilometres. Lush green vegetation amidst the ruins of a long-lost civilisation add a touch of scenic beauty.

FUJAIRAH TOURISM BUREAU

Fujairah Tourism Bureau was established in 1996 to market the emirate's considerable tourist attractions, which include such diverse activities as watching bloodless bull-wrestling, visiting mangrove forests and bird-breeding sites, or navigating the steep mountain roads and narrow gorges of the Musandam peninsula.

The area between Al Faqit and Al Aqqah, just south of Dibba, is already a popular destination for holidaymakers, thanks to its long, sandy beaches and many snorkelling and scuba-diving sites.

Fujairah Tourism Bureau recently signed a contract with the Belgian Three Corners Emirates Company to build a 150-room resort in Al Faqit. The Dh 34 million Fujairah Resort will be constructed on 35,000 square metres. In addition, Emirates plans to build a five-star, 200-room hotel in Al Aqqah which will be operated by Meridien Hotels. Several other projects are also set to commence in the near future: a spa in Ain Al Ghammour, two diving centres in Dibba Al Faqit and a large marina and golf course in Al Aqqah near the Sandy Beach Motel.

AJMAN RESORT

Other emirates are also developing their tourist facilities. For example, the Ajman Kempinski Hotel and Resort, a new 200-room 5-Star beachfront property, opened in October 1998. With extensive leisure facilities, including deep sea fishing and wreck diving from the hotel's own boats, water-skiing, parasailing, windsurfing, bowling, tennis, fitness centre and spa, the Ajman Kempinski also offers a range of business and conference facilities.

YOUTH HOSTELS

Tourism in the UAE is not entirely about luxury for there are youth hostels in Dubai, Sharjah, Ras al-Khaimah and Fujairah and several new hostels are planned for the year 2000. An agreement between Dubai's travel and tour operator, DNATA, and the Youth Hostels Association (YHA), concluded in May 1999, making it the first UAE travel agency to sell international membership in YHA.

URBAN DEVELOPMENT

Infrastructural development in the UAE at federal and local level has been phenomenal in view of the relatively brief period since the country's establishment. Modern cities have risen like phoenixes from the barren desert, connected by a vast network of first-class roads and linked to the outside world by modern airports and ports. Houses, schools, hospitals, shopping centres, telecommunications, electricity and water, luxury hotels and recreational facilities have all been provided for the people in a remarkably short space of time. As the country enters the third millennium a process of consolidation is taking place, with the private sector taking more of an active role in infrastructural development.

MINISTRY OF PUBLIC WORKS AND HOUSING

The Ministry of Public Works and Housing, which has been actively developing infrastructure in the UAE, is overseeing numerous projects throughout the country, including construction and maintenance of 13 mosques in Fujairah, 16 mosques in Sharjah, Umm al-Qaiwain Hospital, Fujairah Hospital, Saif bin Ghubash Hospital in Ras al-Khaimah, the Ministry of Finance and Industry premises at Al Khubeira Palace in Abu Dhabi, the Abu Dhabi Radio and TV building, the Health Care Centre in Umm al-Qaiwain and three health care centres in Dubai. Twenty-seven schools, three kindergartens and two mosques in Ajman are also being refurbished, in addition to four mosques in Ras al-Khaimah, two mosques in Umm al-Qaiwain, as well as annual maintenance works on buildings in all areas. Fifty-six projects are at the planning stage and 80 others under review.

ABU DHABI PUBLIC WORKS DEPARTMENT

A number of major infrastructural projects executed by Abu Dhabi's Public Works Department have contributed enormously to the development of the UAE. These include the modern road network which links many parts of the country, bridges, housing, schools, institutes, mosques, hospitals, clinics, sports clubs, government departments, hotels and recreation facilities. All have been aimed at ensuring the comfort and welfare of the people. More building and services projects are planned in all parts of the country as part of the Department's efforts to implement an ambitious development programme.

To date, the Department has embarked on projects totalling Dh 11,477 million, of which Dh 5,157 million has been spent on roads and bridges, Dh 1,150 million on seaports and excavation projects, Dh 5,100 million on government buildings and Dh 70 million on airport development.

Projects totalling Dh 2,790 million were completed by the Department in 1998: Dh 4 million was spent on extending and renovating the VIP lounge at Abu Dhabi International Airport. Dh 96 million was spent on seaports, excavation works and land cultivation projects, which include extension work on jetties at Al Jarf and Ras Sadr ports. The Department also spent Dh 1,165 million on government buildings, including the construction of Abu Dhabi Women's College, part of the Higher Colleges of Technology (HCT), as well as a number of schools and low-cost houses, villas for police officers, a new block for the Ministry of Health's Preventive Medicine Department, a public hospital in Medinat Zayed and the Al Mushrif premises of the UAE Women's Federation.

The Department is currently undertaking a number of projects costing approximately Dh 8,687 million in various parts of Abu Dhabi emirate: Dh 3,636 million has been allocated for the construction of roads and bridges, Dh 66 million for airports, Dh 1,054 million for seaports, excavation works and land cultivation and Dh 3,937 million for government building projects.

ABU DHABI MUNICIPALITY

Abu Dhabi Municipality and Town Planning Department has prepared the comprehensive development plan for Abu Dhabi emirate to be implemented by the year 2010, including a number of projects to be carried out in cooperation with the United Nations Development Programme (UNDP). The plan, many aspects of which are starting to take shape, is designed to reduce pressure on the capital by developing and populating outlying areas.

In recent years significant improvements have been made to the road network in and around Abu Dhabi to improve traffic flow. In particular major work on the Eastern Ring Road has now reached its final phase. Other major transportation projects completed in 1999 include the Dh 112 million new Al Maqta bridge, linking the island of Abu Dhabi to the mainland, at the end of July 1999 and completion of the beautification and expansion of Abu Dhabi Corniche at a cost of Dh 200 million. The municipality is also spending Dh 148 million on 27 other projects. These include construction of a branch of the Abu Dhabi Women's Association in Al Wathba and a large fruit, vegetable and fish market in Medinat Zayed.

With regard to public health and environmental protection, the municipality implemented 14 projects at a total cost of Dh 938 million in 1998, while another 21 projects costing Dh 581 million are under construction.

As part of its beautification drive the municipality has demolished old areas and buildings in the city, having given adequate compensation to the owners. Around 1,350 houses are currently under construction in Al Rabha, Al Shahama, Al Samha, Al Wathba, Al Sila, Medinat Zayed and Liwa, and are scheduled to be distributed to citizens upon their completion. In the past the municipality has created 39 parks and built approximately 150 fountains in various parts of the emirate. A major focus of the municipality is the creation of a green

belt around the city and the planting of roadside verges and parks with trees and flowers. Major afforestation and farming projects in the desert are also undertaken by the municipality. (For more information see section on Agriculture and Fishing).

As far as public transport is concerned, approximately 250 modern buses equipped with air conditioning have been placed at the service of 1.2 million commuters. To cater for the growing need for car parking facilities in the capital, the municipality is investing more than Dh 300 million in building four new underground car parks, taking the number of new car parks that the capital will have in the coming years to eight.

The municipality's revenue from rents on industrial land, fees at abattoirs and entry fees at public gardens amounted to Dh 38.56 million in 1998.

INFRASTRUCTURE AT AL AIN

Al Ain is undergoing a major development of its infrastructure, including a Dh 220 million airport expansion project; the construction of a major hospital costing Dh 900 million, housing, tree planting and small farm projects. A luxury hotel is under construction and a second complex is planned. Other projects include a championship golf course, museum (Dh 200 million), souq (Dh 70 million), an upgrade of the zoo (Dh 58.72 million for the first phase), veterinary hospital, redevelopment of the town centre and leisure and recreation facilities. The private sector is also being invited to build and operate shopping malls.

HOUSING

The provision of adequate housing for nationals with the aim of enhancing social stability has been a focus of government policy since the establishment of the federation. The number of low-cost houses distributed to nationals in Abu Dhabi has climbed steadily throughout the 1990s. In 1991 some 18,652 homes were distributed; by 1997, the latest year for which statistics are available, the number had risen to 21,344.

The Zayed Housing Programme, which has been allocated an annual budget of Dh 640 million, also aims to assist UAE nationals in acquiring suitable housing. The most significant part of Federal Decree No. 10 of 1999, which was issued by Sheikh Zayed, established a corporate body of ten members to be appointed by the Cabinet to oversee the provision of housing under the Zayed Housing Programme. The programme will allocate housing to nationals whose average monthly income is less than Dh 10,000. It will also give UAE nationals easy-term loans, not exceeding Dh 500,000, and payable within a period of 25 years.

In June 1999 the federal Cabinet approved a memorandum from the Minister of Planning and the chairman of the Permanent Projects Committee for financing a Dh 22.9 million project for 50 housing units in Sharjah.

KHALIFA COMMITTEE

A Dh 6 billion construction plan for 438 commercial buildings in Abu Dhabi is also under way. The Department of Social Services and Commercial Buildings, otherwise known as the Khalifa Committee, is implementing the plan and has indicated that an additional

632 multi-million dirham projects are in the pipeline. Since the Committee's inception, it has completed more than 6,000 projects throughout the capital at an estimated cost of Dh 26 billion. These include about 74,000 housing units. In 1998 the Department constructed 219 commercial buildings. The houses built by the Department are given to nationals through an easy-loan scheme. The loans division of the Department has also advanced billions of dirhams to nationals to build houses as well as commercial buildings since 1990.

One hundred and nine commercial buildings, comprising 3,176 residential units, were built during the first half of 1999 at a cost of Dh 983 million. Of these 65 buildings are in Abu Dhabi, 34 in Musaffah, eight in Al Ain and two in Bani Yas. Another project, comprising 46 commercial buildings, has been completed in Medinat Zayed at an estimated cost of Dh 53 million.

The Department is working on 20 other major projects in various parts of Abu Dhabi. Work on 938 smaller projects is also in progress throughout the emirate – 548 in areas adjoining the capital, 25 in Al Ain, 273 in Mussafah, two in Al Shahama, five in Bani Yas, 46 in Medinat Zayed, 15 in Sila, 11 in Abu Rahma and 14 in Dalma. As a result of this activity rents have fallen significantly in the large number of high-rise buildings which have been built in Abu Dhabi.

DUBAI MUNICIPALITY

Dubai Municipality has been instrumental in the transformation of Dubai emirate into a modern, efficient commercial and tourist centre. In view of the expected increase in Dubai's population by the year 2011 to more than double the present number and the consequent increase in the number of vehicles, Dubai Municipality has prepared a comprehensive transportation master plan for traffic flow in the emirate, commencing in 1991, with the medium-term phase of the plan culminating in the year 2001 and the long-term plan in the year 2011. Key aspects of the plan are construction of new roads between Dubai and Sharjah, construction of a ring-road around Dubai, replanning of traffic circulation, especially the flow of traffic crossing the Creek and construction of parking lots.

Phase 1 of the the Dubai bypass road linking Sharjah with the Dubai-Abu Dhabi highway was completed in 1999. The two-lane expressway, which is planned as a direct link between Sharjah, the Northern Emirates and Abu Dhabi, will allow Abu Dhabi-bound traffic to avoid entering the traffic-clogged urban limits of Dubai.

A new three-level interchange is also under construction opposite the Dubai Cargo Village. The new interchange, which is scheduled for completion by August 2000, is part of the Dh 140 million restructuring of the approach roads to the airport.

Dubai Municipality's Horticulture and Public Parks Department is responsible for the development and maintenance of all of Dubai's numerous public parks and public recreational facilities, roadside planting and afforestation and date palm projects. It operates its own extensive nursery to provide a ready supply of the colourful plants which grace Dubai's roadsides and parks.

AIRPORTS AND SEAPORTS

Considering the important role that airports and ports play in economic progress it is no wonder that the UAE has developed a highly sophisticated air and sea network, with six major international airports and 15 modern, well-equipped seaports connecting the country to global markets.

ABU DHABI

Abu Dhabi Civil Aviation Department was established 30 years ago, with the aim of promoting air transport in the emirate. The Department's open skies policy is designed to assist the emirate to take a strong competitive position in the field of civil aviation at both a regional and international level.

Abu Dhabi's strategic location has also played a major role in helping it to become one of the most important traffic centres in the region and a vital crossroads between Europe and Asia. In addition to Abu Dhabi International Airport (ADIA), another international airport was opened in 1994 in Al Ain city to meet the increasing needs of the region and enhance economic and tourist development projects.

New city terminal

A new city terminal for air passengers was opened in Abu Dhabi in 1999, the first ever in the UAE and Gulf region. The terminal, which is provided with first-class facilities and services including duty-free shopping, is intended to facilitate checking-in procedures. Passengers can check in at the city terminal up to eight hours prior to departure and report at the international airport approximately 35 minutes before departure. Passengers travelling with the local carrier Gulf Air may check in 24 hours before their flight leaves.

Abu Dhabi Airport

Studies indicate that the number of passengers using ADIA will exceed 7 million by the end of the second decade of the twenty-first century. Between 50 to 60 airlines are expected to use the airport, connecting it with approximately 70 other international airports. These projections have prompted the Civil Aviation Department to embark on a Dh 2.5 billion (US $660 million) expansion and refurbishment masterplan, comprising short-and long-term strategies designed to put the airport at the forefront of aviation in the new millennium.

Developments during the current phase (1998 to 2002) include the construction of a new 100-metre diameter satellite building with 11 aircraft parking bays. The satellite, which will be connected to the main building by a high-tech shuttle service, will have the best duty-free shopping complex in the region and sophisticated, modern passenger facilities, encompassing business and first-class lounges, cinemas and restaurants. With the construction of the new satellite building, Abu Dhabi International Airport will be able to handle approximately 2,000 passengers per hour. Another 4,000-metre long, 60-metre wide runway, equipped with state-of-the-art safety devices is scheduled for completion by the end of the year 2000. Other secondary runways are also planned, as well as 18 well-equipped aircraft hangars, 11 of which will serve larger aircraft such as Boeing B 747-400s, Boeing 767s and airbus A 320s. There are also seven hangars for Boeing 747-400 and Boeing 767 aircraft. In the meantime upgrading of the present aircraft safety system is ongoing.

A new 200-room hotel for transit passengers is also scheduled for completion in the year 2000. It will be built overlooking the car parking areas and will be surrounded by extensive gardens, a swimming pool, a health club and a floodlit golf course which will be open on a 24-hour basis.

Abu Dhabi Duty Free

Abu Dhabi Duty Free (ADDF) won 'the best travel retailer in the Middle East' award for the second consecutive year. ADDF has maintained its growth rate with an 11 per cent increase in revenues for the first quarter of 1999 over the corresponding period of the previous year. In 1998 ADDF had a sales turnover of Dh 296 million, up 12 per cent over 1997 and it expects another increase of 10–15 per cent in 1999.

The new airport satellite will provide an extra 4,000 square metres of retail space, thus dedicating a total of 7,200 square metres for duty-free shopping. The new extension will host 50 branded and 20 speciality boutiques. To date the brand name boutiques and shops introduced by ADDF have been a great success.

Al Ain Airport

Al Ain Airport has two runways, each 4,000 metres long and 45 metres wide, five parking areas for Boeing 747 aircraft and another two for cargo planes. The airport is equipped with excellent facilities and services including duty-free shopping. A Dh 220 million (US $60 million) expansion plan is under way, including extension of the terminal building, cargo, catering and duty-free areas.

DUBAI

Dubai's Department of Civil Aviation is expecting around 12 million passengers to travel through Dubai International Airport in the year 2000, 19.3 million in the year 2005 and 31.4 million in the year 2010. A futuristic concourse presently under construction is due to open early in the year 2000 to cater for the increased passenger numbers. Access to the airport has been radically improved and the airport parking area has undergone major restructuring, with space for 1,000 cars and a link to the main terminal by two air-conditioned bridges.

SHARJAH

Sharjah International Airport was awarded the title of 'Global Air Cargo Airport 1999' by the UK's Institute of Transport Management. The award was made in recognition of the airport's 'outstanding standard' in respect of air cargo facilities. This is the first ever international award of its kind to be presented to an international airport for its cargo operations. The award, which followed a thorough investigation by the Institute's research team and intense global competition, is a vindication of the airport's efforts to improve its cargo facilities.

Sharjah Airport handled a mere 30,000 tonnes of cargo in 1990, rising to an astonishing 430,000 tonnes in 1998. Figures for 1999 are set to break the 500,000 tonnes mark. Overall the UAE's air freight and air express market is growing at a rate of 15–20 per cent each year.

AVIATION

In line with developments in air passenger and freight traffic, the UAE has nurtured a thriving aviation industry in the past few years.

Gulf Air's worldwide line maintenance operations have been transferred to Abu Dhabi's Gulf Aircraft Maintenance Company (GAMCO), 60 per cent of which is owned by the Abu Dhabi Government and 40 per cent by Gulf Air. The US $450 million five-year contract is expected to result in considerable cost savings for Gulf Air. GAMCO's joint venture in Bahrain, GAMCO Bahrain, in which GAMCO holds a 51 per cent stake and Bahrain Airport Services the remainder, will become operational by the end of the year 2000. A Dh 295 million (US $80 million) four-bay maintenance facility will be operational by the year 2001. GAMCO is also planning a joint venture with Oman Air Services in Muscat, maintaining Oman's A310s as well as its turboprop aircraft.

In May 1999 GAMCO signed a technical support contract with FR Aviation Ltd to provide UK station support for Royal Air Force L1011 aircraft. The contract is for working party and casualty support in the UK for the RAF aircraft and the work will be completed at FR Aviation's facility at Bournemouth International Airport where FR Aviation's hangars are located. GAMCO is contracted to support the RAF's nine TriStars, covering scheduled and unscheduled aircraft maintenance for five years.

GAMCO is in talks with Boeing to handle its aircraft maintenance in the Gulf region. Successful conclusion of these negotiations will make GAMCO Boeing's regional centre for aircraft maintenance. Initially GAMCO will act as support agents for Boeing's business jets. The company is also negotiating with original equipment manufacturers on a number of projects, all of which will bring technology and expertise to the UAE.

Air Safety Award

The London-based Guild of Air Pilots and Air Navigators has bestowed the honorary position of Liveryman on Sheikh Hamdan bin Mubarak Al Nahyan, Chairman of the Abu Dhabi Civil Aviation Department. Sheikh Hamdan was decorated with the official apparel of Liveryman of the Guild at a ceremony in London in June 1999. The Guild

recognised the dedication and success of Sheikh Hamdan in promoting aircraft safety at
an international level, not only in his role as Chairman of the Civil Aviation Department
and Abu Dhabi Aviation, but also as Chairman of GAMCO. There are only eight honorary
liverymen worldwide.

Emirates Group

The Emirates Group announced a net profit of Dh 429 million for 1998, achieving a
growth rate of 15.6 per cent over the previous year. Total group revenue jumped 8.8 per
cent to Dh 4,827 million by the end of March 1999. Profits by the airline increased 19.3
per cent to Dh 313 million. Emirates airline contributed Dh 4,443 million to the group
revenue with DNATA's contribution being Dh 564 million, achieving increases of 8.7
and 10.8 per cent respectively.

The Emirates network has expanded to 47 destinations with the addition of three north
Pakistan cities. Having surpassed its previous record of 4 million passengers, Emirates is
expected to continue its profitable track record during 1999–2000. The airline has forecast
that it will carry 11 million passengers in 1999.

Emirates' fleet expansion and renewal programme has increased its passenger-carrying
capacity. The carrier operates nine Boeing 777-200s and has confirmed leases for three
Boeing 777-300s. There are also 18 A330-200s on firm order, three of which have been
delivered, as well as new orders for long-range A340-500s.

Middle East Person of the Year Award

The Chairman of Emirates and President of Dubai Civil Aviation Department, Sheikh
Ahmed bin Saeed Al Maktoum, was named 1999's Middle East Person of the Year in the
airline category by the US *Travel Agent* magazine. Nominees for this distinction are selected
from a variety of categories including airlines, hotels, cruises, destinations, retail agents
and tour operators. Since 1990 the award has gone to leading figures in the travel industry.

Training

The Emirates Group plans to strengthen its emiratisation programme by spending Dh
37 million (US $10 million) to train 200 UAE nationals annually for jobs with the airline,
commencing in 1999. Twenty-six per cent of the group's senior positions, from Grade
8 to management level, are occupied by nationals. However, the group's total staff strength
of 12,000 includes only 450 nationals.

Airline of the Year

The global Airline of the Year 1999 title was presented to Emirates at the prestigious *Official
Airline Guide* (OAG) – formerly the *Executive Travel* – awards. This is the third time and
the second consecutive year that Emirates has won this title – first in 1994, then 1998
and 1999. Emirates was also named Best Middle Eastern and Indian Subcontinent Airline.
The airline has won this award consistently since 1988. The OAG awards were based on
nominations by over 19,000 frequent flyers worldwide who subscribe to OAG Worldwide's

print and electronic travel information services. Emirates was also named Best Airline to the Middle East at the Travel Weekly Globe Awards 1999, as voted by readers of *Travel Weekly*, one of the UK's premier travel trade publications. Emirates has won this title every year since 1994. The airline was named Best Business Airline Middle East at the Business Travel World Awards 1999. The award is based on votes by readers of the monthly magazine for business travel professionals. Emirates has won nearly 170 awards in its 13-year history.

PORTS
Abu Dhabi

The Abu Dhabi Seaports Authority supervises the operation of Mina Zayed, Abu Dhabi's main gateway to the outside world and one of the most important seaports in the UAE, in addition to a number of small branch seaports such as the dhow harbour, Mussafah port, Umm al-Nar port and Ras Sadr port.

Mina Zayed, established in 1968 and officially inaugurated in 1972, is located in the northeast section of Abu Dhabi city. Covering an area of 510 hectares it comprises 21 berths with depths ranging from 6 to 15 metres and a total length of 4,375 metres. These berths enable Mina Zayed to receive huge transocean commercial vessels and it is also well equipped for vessels of more than 60,000 tonnes load.

Since 1991 efforts have been successful in persuading more than 50 major shipping lines to use Mina Zayed regularly. Now more than 2,000 freight ships berth there each year and more than 4 million tonnes of cargo is handled annually.

Mina Zayed provides its customers with one of the best equipped stevedoring services in the region providing efficient loading and unloading operations at cost-effective prices.

In light of the increasing importance of containers as a safe and economic means of freight a sophisticated and well-equipped container terminal was established in 1982. Covering an area of 41 hectares, the terminal has a storage capacity of 15,000 TEUs at any given time. Four deep water berths are provided with a total length of 931 metres and 15 metres depth. The berths are equipped with five 40-tonne cranes.

Mina Zayed's throughput in 1998 increased 34 per cent in container volume and 25 per cent in general cargo over 1997. The port's capacity to hold chilled, cool and frozen products was significantly increased when a 15,000 tonne cold store became operational in 1999.

The Seaports Authority has adopted a comprehensive plan for the development of Mina Zayed and other affiliate ports over a 20-year-period from 1993 to 2013 at a total cost of Dh 2.8 billion (US $765 million). This is divided into two stages: the short-term development plan begun in 1993 and continuing to the year 2000 and the long-term plan from 2000 to 2013. Some of the major projects under the 10-year development plan are reconstruction of berths, dredging, construction of new buildings and workshops and cold storage.

Located close to Mina Zayed the dhow harbour has been developed as a free port for dhows which promote business between Abu Dhabi, the Gulf states, East Africa, the Middle East and the subcontinent. The facilities at the free port include 34 berths with

2,000 metres of quayside for offshore supply boats and barges. Meanwhile, Mussafah port is scheduled to be in operation by the end of 1999 easing the growing pressure on Port Zayed. The port development plan includes a new channel and berths for Mussafah.

Sharjah's ports

In 1998 Sharjah Ports Authority's twin container terminals at Mina Khalid and Khor Fakkan recorded a 5.58 per cent rise in throughput to 863,527 TEU. The jump in traffic was achieved against the backdrop of the economic downturn felt in many parts of the globe. Container throughput through Mina Khalid rose to 80,176 TEU from 64,564 TEU the previous year, a record 24.18 per cent growth. Traffic through Khor Fakkan on the UAE's east coast rose 4.33 per cent to 750,817 TEU, the performance being attributed to the quality of services. Statistics show sustained growth in overall throughput, rising 26.68 per cent from 500,700 TEU in 1994 to 634,284 TEU in 1995, to 708,462 TEU in 1996, up 11.69 per cent, and 815,381 TEU in 1997, up 15.09 per cent.

The newly-commissioned 350-metre long deepwater berth at Khor Fakkan will increase the port's annual throughput capacity to more than 1.5 million TEU, confirming the Khor Fakkan Container Terminal (KCT) as one of the leading container transhipment facilities in the region. Part of a multi-million dollar rolling improvement programme, the berth extension brings KCT's total quay length to 1,060 metres and adds a further 100,000 square metres of paved stacking area.

During the berth construction a comprehensive dredging programme was completed, and the depth alongside berths, the enlarged turning circle and port approaches, are all now 15 metres at MLW, enabling the world's largest container ships to access the port with ease. Progressively, over the past few years, new container handling equipment has been introduced to maximise handling efficiency. The port now has eight Post Panamax and Super Post Panamax ship-to-shore gantry cranes, the two recent and largest of which can handle vessels stowed 18 containers across. KCT has four rail-mounted yard gantries and six state-of-the-art rubber tyred gantries (RTGs) and is taking delivery of four more RTGs from Liebherr.

Dubai Ports Authority

Dubai Ports Authority, which operates Port Rashid and Jebel Ali port, the biggest man-made port in the world, won two top awards for the Middle East region as the Best Seaport and the Best Container Terminal Operator at the Thirteenth Asian Freight Industry Awards for 1999. DPA facilities have a total of 102 deepwater berths, 23 container gantry cranes and four Super Post Panamax cranes, covering 10 container terminal berths. More than 100 shipping lines are served by DPA.

In 1998 DPA reported an increase of 8 per cent in handling container cargo reaching a record of 2.8 million TEU, while a total of 11,316 vessels called at DPA's twin terminals, including 4,898 container vessels, 6 per cent more than the previous year. The total tonnage handled in 1998 rose to 36,424,403 tonnes.

Dubai Ports Authority has predicted that its annual cargo volume will not be affected in 1999 despite a reduction of 250,000 containers each year due to a decision by Maersk and Sealand to shift some of their operations to a neighbouring port in Oman.

Other emirates

Fujairah's port is strategically located just outside the Straits of Hormuz and expansion of its bunkering facilities will make it one of the world's top three bunkering ports, after Rotterdam and Singapore. The port's business is supplemented by the adjacent free zone and the nearby international airport.

The success achieved by the free zone in Umm al-Qaiwain has also encouraged the emirate's government to increase the port's area, along with that of the zone, to more than 215,000 square metres. Port facilities have also been radically improved in Ajman to support the free zone.

Located in the Straits of Hormuz, Ras al-Khaimah's Mina Saqr has always enjoyed high levels of transhipment trade. It has improved its container facilities and is poised for growth.

SHIPBUILDING

Abu Dhabi Shipbuilding Company

ADSB is a joint venture set up in 1995 between the Abu Dhabi Government and Newport News Shipbuilding of the US. Abu Dhabi holds 20 per cent equity, Newport News Shipbuilding 40 per cent and the remaining 40 per cent is held by UAE nationals. ADSB announced profits of Dh 13.3 million on revenues of Dh 87 million for financial year 1998, a rise of 19 per cent in profits and 16 per cent in revenues.

In 1997 ADSB, created under the UAE's offset programme, completed the mid-life refits of the first two UAE navy 45-metre fast patrol boats under a six-ship contract. Two ships were delivered in 1999 and the remaining two will be completed during the year 2000. ADSB also completed the construction of five firefighting tugboats – three for the UAE coastguard and two for the navy.

ADSB signed a contract with the UAE Government to develop and install a new computerised logistics software system for the navy for use in fleet maintenance, purchasing and inventory control.

Once ADSB's new multi-million shipyard facility in Musaffah becomes fully operational in the year 2001, the workforce will be doubled and ship-lifting capacity will increase from the current 500 tonnes to over 2,000 tonnes. This will allow the shipyard to build and repair vessels between 85 and 100 metres in length. New production and outfitting workshops will manufacture and overhaul components required to build and repair military and commercial vessels. A new quay will be built for new ship outfitting and commissioning and additional pier space and three large ship repair dry berths will also be added.

Adyard Abu Dhabi

Adyard Abu Dhabi LLC, a subsidiary of the Oman-based Topaz Energy and Marine SAOG (Team), was granted two major contracts for the refurbishment of drilling rigs. The

contracts were awarded by ENSCO, a leading drilling contractor. The rigs, ENSCO 96 and 97, were towed to Adyard's jetty at the Mussafah waterfront. Adyard is also under contract to construct two vessels at Mussafah. These include a service barge, an addition to Team's fleet. It is also engaged in a range of fabrication and repair projects to support customers in the marine and energy service sectors. Adyard is pre-qualified as a supplier to the major UAE and other Gulf oil and gas industry operators.

Rig construction

A multi-million dollar project to build the first self-propelled, self-elevating utility support jack-up rig was completed at Maritime Industrial Services' quayside facility in Sharjah in 1999. The project, which involved the conversion of a conventional ship into a jack-up, is believed to be the first of its kind in the region. The rig, whose four legs each measures 240 feet, has been designed to operate in over 150-foot depths.

Gulf Craft

In a major expansion programme, Ajman-based shipbuilder Gulf Craft has budgeted Dh 25 million as initial investment to set up a second boat-building facility in the UAE. Further investments could eventually total another Dh 15 million which would make it the largest such unit of its kind in Asia. Capital requirements for the expansion are to be met by a mix of equity and financing from local financial institutions. The new facility will have a capacity to build 50 yachts annually while the existing production units at Ajman will be confined to smaller vessels. Gulf Craft had sales of Dh 35 million in 1998, producing 220 units, mostly leisure boats. Exports constituted 70 per cent. The company claims 60–70 per cent share of the UAE boat market and between 50–60 per cent in the wider Gulf.

ELECTRICITY AND WATER

The services offered by the federal Ministry of Electricity and Water have grown very substantially over the years and now match those offered in developed countries. Electricity has reached every dwelling in the UAE. However, demand has also spiralled in the intervening years, so much so that maximum demand in Abu Dhabi emirate was 2,686 MW in 1998.

Water supplies have also been under pressure to meet the needs of 75,000 consumers. Current consumption levels stand at approximately 250–300 million imperial gallons per day (migd), with Dubai accounting for up to 107 migd during peak periods and up to 100 migd in winter.

An independent federal authority is being established under the chairmanship of the Minister of Electricity and Water to manage the electricity and water sector as well as supervise projects and planning in the future. A draft federal law to this effect was approved by the federal Cabinet in June 1999. The authority is due to be in operation by the end of 1999.

NEW INTERNAL GRID

In order to cope with the demands of more than 124,000 energy consumers the Ministry is linking all its generating plants in a single grid. The first and second phases of the grid linked areas of the east coast, Fujairah, Qidfa, Khor Fakkan and Dibba, and the west coast, Ajman, Umm al-Qaiwain and Ras al-Khaimah, to the Central Zone.

The Ministry has also signed a Dh 75 million contract for the third phase of the project which covers the linking of Dhaid power generation station in the Central Zone with the main station in Fujairah in the Eastern Zone.

The new grid will facilitate the distribution of power to the stations according to the needs of each area, at the same time meeting the growing demand of electricity in the Northern Emirates. On completion of the grid the UAE will be linked to the AGCC grid throughout the Arabian peninsula.

In addition the Ministry finalised a Dh 220 million contract on 6 August 1999 for the installation of 200 megawatt gas turbines in Qidfa in Fujairah and Nakheel in Ras al-Khaimah, all of which will increase output to the Northern Emirates, stabilising power supply and meeting the increasing demand for power in the area. The final phase of the project is scheduled to be completed by the end of the year 2000.

PRIVATISATION IN ABU DHABI

At present desalination plants in Abu Dhabi emirate are currently operating near their design capacities of 218 migd and the capital's power requirements are expected to reach 4,500 MW by the year 2010. To meet current needs and plan for the future Abu Dhabi Government has embarked on a comprehensive programme to privatise its water and electricity sector which is expected to be completed within the next 10 years.

The ambitious privatisation plan is well under way with the formation of 11 companies under the Abu Dhabi Water and Electricity Authority (ADWEA), thereby bringing to an end the old Water and Electricity Department (WED). The 11 companies will operate on a commercial basis, each with its own budget and objectives, under the leadership of Sheikh Dhiyab bin Zayed Al Nahyan, ADWEA chairman. The Government will retain control of the 11 companies for some time, but the plan is to ultimately permit foreign investors to buy stakes in the generating and distributing companies.

Four of the 11 companies will be involved in power generation: the Al Mirfa Power Company, Umm al-Nar Power Company, Bainounah Power Company and Al Taweelah Power Company. The two new distribution companies are the Abu Dhabi Distribution Company and Al Ain Distribution Company. Other new firms are the Abu Dhabi Company for Servicing Remote Areas, Abu Dhabi Transmission and Despatch Company (Transco), Abu Dhabi Water and Electricity Corporation, Al Wathba Central Services and Emirates CMS Power Company. Transco will be responsible for scheduling and despatching, maintaining the integrity of the transmission networks (water and electricity) and administering the settlement system. All the companies will be subsidiaries of ADWEA and will be supervised by the Regulation and Supervision Bureau for Water and Electricity which will grant or withdraw licences for operating companies, establish quality standards and develop the tariff structure. The immediate aim is to trim the 14,000 staff in the Water and Electricity Department and develop new revenue sources through investment in infrastructure. Long-term objectives are to promote the efficient use of resources, to send cost reflective price signals to consumers and provide clear incentives for producers to manage costs.

Privatisation of electricity projects will eliminate government subsidies: currently electricity consumption is heavily subsidised by up to 75 per cent of the cost for nationals and up to 50 per cent for non-nationals and business. Privatisation will also reduce public expenditure on the provision, maintenance and expansion of power projects, which will free financial resources for other development expenditure.

Taweelah A2

Financial closure of the Dh 2.75 billion (US $750 million) contract for the Taweelah A2 project, the first independent water and power project in either the UAE or the Gulf, took place at the end of April 1999. Taweelah A2, located northeast of Abu Dhabi city, will have 710 MW of power capacity and 50 migd water capacity.

Based on limited resource financing, the US-based CMS Energy Corp has a 40 per cent stake in Taweelah A2 with ADWEA represented by Emirates Power Company, holding a 60 per cent stake. The latter has signed an agreement with Abu Dhabi Water and

Power Generation & Water Production Abu Dhabi Emirate 1969-1998

Year	Employees Nos.	Max. Demand MW	Derated MW	Power Generation kWh	Water Prod. MG
up to 1969	37		25		
1970	61		76		
1971	103		76		
1972	121		91		
1973	174		91		1,536.32
1974	231	121.9	158	490,715,000	1,908.62
1975	346	164.3	206	690,187,000	2,058.14
1976	547	227.3	292	916,951,000	2,647.82
1977	677	304.2	446	1,341,535,000	3,887.14
1978	868	397.6	631	1,669,926,000	5,294.13
1979	1030	514.0	779	2,170,062,160	7,701.63
1980	1300	656.8	1000	2,818,666,550	10,965.16
1981	1443	748.3	1092	3,394,513,700	13,098.36
1982	1578	852.8	1086	3,891,979,865	14,962.42
1983	1690	966.8	1213	4,336,555,035	15,511.34
1984	1798	973.3	1196	4,727,561,875	16,836.65
1985	1805	1062	1443	5,123.859,635	17,905.82
1986	1833	1163	1603	5,624,846,145	20,379.66
1987	1828	1213	1607	6,095.822,581	23,449.28
1988	1883	1301	1750	6,627,781,664	26,902.14
1989	2098	1411	1988	7,004,133,282	28,589.38
1990	2185	1524	1988	7,839,246,741	33,156.98
1991	2201	1616	1973	7,937,365,512	33,583.34
1992	2169	1641	1973	8,308,392,664	34,600.00
1993	2169	1766	2115	9,102,151,203	36,240.55
1994	1804	1900	2317	9,901,151,203	38,852.39
1995	1863	2008	2561	10,444,872,255	42,918.53
1996	1837	2207	3009	11,842,024,758	49.449.67
1997	1865	2420	3112	12,755,449,534	56,321.81
1998	1639	2686	3097	14,993,251,010	63,085.97

Electricity Company to purchase electricity and water for 20 years. Contracts for the engineering works, provision of material and construction were awarded to Siemens of Germany and Hanjung of South Korea. Work at the Taweelah site started in January 1999 and the first gas turbine is expected to become operational by May 2000, with full commercial operation scheduled for August 2001.

DUBAI

Peak loads in 1998 were 1,989MW of electricity and 107 migd, while in 1997 this figure was only 96 migd. The total quantity of water pumped into the networks in 1998 was 37,728 mig against 33,335 mig in 1997. The annual growth in demand for power and water in Dubai is estimated at 10 per cent respectively. Although in 1998 growth in demand was 14 per cent and in the first quarter of 1999 it was 12 per cent, these are considered to be exceptional cases.

The Dubai Government spent Dh 2.6 billion during 1997–1999 on energy projects and expects to invest Dh 2.61 billion in the near future to increase local power generation and desalination capacity, as well as development of transmission and distribution networks.

Jebel Ali

In the context of this overall strategy, Dubai's Electricity and Water Authority (DEWA) signed a Dh 526 million contract for the construction and commissioning of three desalination plants with a total capacity of 27.5 migd. The first unit ,which has a capacity to produce 7.5 migd of desalinated water, will be installed at Jebel Ali Power and Desalination Station (G Station) and will be commissioned before summer 2000, and the other two, each with a capacity to produce 10 migd of desalinated water, will be installed at the New (K Station) at Jebel Ali. One will be commissioned before the end of the year 2000, and the other unit will be commissioned at the beginning of January 2001. DEWA's total production capacity of desalinated water will increase to approximately 143 migd on completion of this project.

The electrical generation plant at K Station, Jebel Ali aims to produce 500 MW of electricity, of which 400MW will be by means of gas turbines and waste heat recovery boilers. The latter will be used in operating the back pressure steam turbines that produce 100MW.

DEWA also signed a Dh 930 million contract with South Korea's Hyundai Engineering and Construction Company in August 1999 for the installation of a 360 MW re-engineering power project and a desalination plant at Jebel Ali (Station 'D' Phase 11). After completion of the project, the total output of 'D' Station Phase II will be 585 MW, compared with the existing output of 225 MW. It will be commissioned in stages between the years 2001 and 2002, taking DEWA's total power generation capacity to 3,260 MW, including the Satwa power station ('C' station).

Natural gas from Sharjah is used as feedstock for Dewa's D, E, G and H power and desalination plants. The gas is supplied by BP-Amoco. The giant Al Aweer gas turbine energy plant, built at a cost of Dh 1.082 billion, was commissioned in March 1999.

DEWA announced in July 1999 that its Power Stations and Planning and Projects Department (Generation) has been awarded the ISO 9002 quality certification for the fifth consecutive year through adhering to the comprehensive quality systems required by the certificate. The Power Stations Department also earned the ISO 14001 in 1998 for environment management.

SHARJAH

Sharjah Electricity and Water Authority (SEWA) has secured finance for the purchase of two gas turbines for the second phase of the Wasit power station. The turbines, with a combined output of 200 MW, are being supplied by the French company Alsthom.

RENEWABLE ENERGY IN FUJAIRAH

Fujairah has embarked on a Dh 42 million programme to harness renewable energy resources. In 1998 six meteorological stations were set up across Fujairah to measure wind speed and solar radiation. The emirate aims to harness these resources to generate electricity for lighting remote villages and pumping water for drinking and irrigation. Subsequent stages in the programme will involve the use of solar energy for industrial purposes and photovoltaics and air turbines to pump water for irrigation and desalination processes.

TELECOMMUNICATIONS

The UAE is entering the twenty-first century with a sophisticated telecommunications sector which provides its citizens with a highly efficient and cost-effective communications network. Emirates Telecommunications Corporation (ETISALAT), one of the largest and most successful companies in the Middle East, controls the telecommunications business in the UAE. Although ETISALAT recorded a a net profit of Dh 2.012 billion for 1998 and revenues surged by 23 per cent to Dh 5.07 billion surpassing its performance in 1997 by Dh 157 million, the company faced many challenges in 1998. Not least of these were the crises in East Asia and Russia, coupled with the steep fall in oil prices, all of which had a negative impact on business and trade, regionally and globally.

Nevertheless, developments in Africa and Asia were of considerable interest to ETISALAT and decisions were made not only to invest but also to actively participate in telecommunications projects in Zanzibar and Sudan as well as in projects closer to home.

ETISALAT holds slightly over 34 per cent of its associate UAE-based Thuraya Satellite Telecommunications Company and has continued to expand its position in global markets through acquisition of a further 3.1 per cent stake in ICO Global Communications Holdings Ltd as well as 1 per cent in Qatar Telecom (Q-Tel).

INTERNET

ETISALAT has provided Internet services to the UAE since August 1995. The country now has one of the highest rates of Internet usage in the Middle East.

At the end of March 1999 ETISALAT launched its value-added Internet roaming service which allows Internet dial-up customers to travel anywhere in the world and access their home Internet Service Provider (ISP), read and retrieve e-mail messages and browse the World Wide Web, all at the cost of a local call. This was made possible through the Global Roaming Internet Centre (GRIC), a worldwide alliance of ISPs of which Emirates Internet is a member.

Price reductions

As part of its programme to encourage Internet usage, in July 1999 ETISALAT announced a major shake-up in its Internet service charges with immediate effect. The new revised flat-rate represented a 50 per cent reduction in the previous rate. Major reductions on the Internet for businesses and educational institutions also took immediate effect: these included reductions of 50 per cent for government schools and about 30 per cent for business, private schools and academic institutions.

Free Internet training

Free Internet training for UAE nationals was offered by ETISALAT in Abu Dhabi and Dubai. Conducted by specialised instructors from the ETISALAT training centre, the two-hour sessions included a theoretical and hands-on workshop aimed at addressing various applications of the service and its benefits. The seminars and workshops attracted nationals from the diplomatic, government, commercial, academic and tourism sectors.

E-commerce

ETISALAT launched its e-commerce services in October 1999 through its new business unit Comtrust. The e-commerce facility, which is being set up with a phase one investment of Dh 30 million, will serve the entire region and is due for completion in the fourth quarter of 1999. As the first in the region to offer a complete, secure e-commerce platform, Comtrust will offer online payment solutions. A host of new telecommunication services and bill payments will be available to customers through its Web Shop, an integral part of this new venture.

HIGH-CAPACITY NETWORK

In June 1999 Fore Systems, a leading global supplier of networking solutions, was awarded the contract to supply the new high-capacity equipment for the Etisalat Asynchronous Transfer Mode (ATM) network including LAN and WAN. This scalable network equipment will enable ETISALAT to deliver high-speed network connectivity to all its branches in the UAE.

TELEPHONE CARDS

ETISALAT has completed the first phase of a state-of-the-art manufacturing facility for Smart and SIM cards.The first phase of the project caters for in-house requirements for GSM SIM cards and as a pilot unit for payphone Smart card requirements. The second phase will provide for the wide scale manufacture of these cards with an initial annual production target of 65 million cards.

MOBILE PHONE SERVICES

By November 1998 the UAE had more than 450,000 subscribers connected to the mobile network nationwide with penetration levels reaching 17 per cent. Future expansion plans aim to double this penetration figure through increasing network capacity to one million subscribers by the year 2000. This will be achieved by continued review of prices and enhancement of the GSM service in accordance with the most up-to-date developments in the field.

In order to achieve these objectives ETISALAT has signed a Dh 240 million contract with Ericsson for a microcell expansion of the GSM system. The project will enlarge the network around Dubai and Al Ain as well as extending the existing GSM microcell network. In April 1999 ETISALAT awarded a Dh 100 million contract to Motorola's Network Solutions Sector (NSS) for the expansion of the GSM900 MHz network in Sharjah and the Northern Emirates.

Roaming deal with ICO

Satellite communications firm ICO Global Communications signed a roaming agreement with ETISALAT in July 1999. ICO and ETISALAT have agreed to implement bilateral roaming, allowing ETISALAT's cellular customers to use the ICO global satellite system and customers of ICO to use ETISALAT's cellular network. Similar deals have already been signed with Saudi Telecommunications Company, Bahrain Telecommunications Company (BATELCO) and Kuwait's Mobile Telecommunications Company. ETISALAT has invested US $140 million in ICO and will develop and operate one of 12 satellite access nodes and distribute ICO's products and services. ICO expects to begin commercial operations of its mobile satellite services in the third quarter of the year 2000. One of the 12 satellite access nodes being set up worldwide is in the UAE. The main difference between the ICO and the UAE's Thuraya satellite project, in which ETISALAT is also a shareholder, is that the former is international while the latter is regional.

THURAYA SATELLITE SYSTEM

Thuraya is the region's largest satellite telecommunication project. The mobile satellite communications network system will cater to 1.8 million users in 49 countries in the Middle East, north Africa, eastern Europe, central Asia and the subcontinent. The first Thuraya satellite is scheduled to be launched in May 2000 and will begin commercial operations in September. Thuraya services will be offered via handheld, vehicular and fixed terminals. Thuraya's flexible dual-mode (GSM and satellite) handsets will provide advanced voice, data, fax, messaging and location determination services. The system will further enhance telecommunications services for millions of people in the areas covered by its satellites.

In July 1999 Thuraya Satellite Telecommunications Company signed a Dh 2. 2 billion (US $600 million) financing package with a consortium of local and international banks to fund the system. The complex financial structure is a combination of conventional and Islamic financing which will be used on top of the company's equity of Dh 1.835 billion (US $500 million) to complete the capital requirements of the project outlay of Dh 4 billion (US $1.1 billion).

In September 1998 ETISALAT became the first service provider for Thuraya's regional services. ETISALAT will provide Thuraya's mobile satellite services in the UAE with rights to distribute and market user terminals, SIM cards, pricing, billing and other customer care aspects. Countries which have signed service provider agreements include Iran and Libya, following the suspension of UN sanctions. All AGCC countries are also partners in Thuraya.

CHANNEL TV

From the end of 1999 thematic channels catering to the diverse demographic groups in the UAE will be available on ETISALAT's cable television network in addition to the 100-odd channels beamed directly into subscriber homes through hybrid fibre coaxial technology. These 'exclusive' channels will be created by ETISALAT for specific audiences with a focus on events with local relevance.

The 100-odd channels are being selected by ETISALAT TV from among thousands on offer. The channels will be in 10 different languages, including Arabic, English and Asian languages. Subscribers will be given options of choosing bouquets of 40 or more channels. The basic difference between ETISALAT's cable channels and the existing satellite channels is that ETISALAT will offer distortion-free reception and clear sound without the need for satellite dishes.

The network will eventually cover the whole of the UAE and in its initial phase will be able to provide services to 20,000 residential units in Abu Dhabi and Dubai.

FIBRE OPTIC CABLE

ETISALAT's submarine cable unit is a separate company called Emirates Telecommunications and Marine Services FZE (E-Marine). The wholly-owned subsidiary was set up in the Jebel Ali Free Zone in Dubai and is the only company in the region to have two strategically located, fully functional cableships, the *C.S. Etisalat* and *C.S. Umm Al Anber*. ETISALAT and Marine Services FZE (E-Marine) recently announced completion of the installation of the FLAG (Fibre Optic Link Around the Globe) extension to Jeddah and Aqaba. FLAG is the world's longest operating submarine cable system, linking Europe, Asia and the Far East. ETISALAT's submarine cable unit has been providing services not only to domestic submarine cables but also other submarine cables in the region which link the UAE to India, Iran, Pakistan and all the AGCC countries.

SOLAR ENERGY PAY PHONES

ETISALAT has installed a number of solar energy payphones in rural areas of Ras al-Khaimah. The move was necessary to resolve communication problems in those areas especially along the major roads which needed such facilities for emergency cases.

EMIRATISATION IN THE TELECOMMUNICATIONS SECTOR

A major objective of ETISALAT's emiratisation drive is to ensure that by the end of the year 2000, 46 per cent of its employees will be UAE nationals. ETISALAT, with a Dh 40 million annual training budget, has begun several specialised training programmes to encourage nationals to enter its workforce. In 1998 ETISALAT recruited 770 nationals, both male and female. This was the highest number recruited in any single year, earning the company the 'Employer of the Year Award for 1999'. ETISALAT employs a workforce of 8,000, 28 per cent of which are nationals. Eighty-eight per cent of its senior staff are nationals.

EMPLOYMENT AND SOCIAL SECURITY

In tandem with rapid economic development, the UAE's workforce has grown from 288,414 in 1975 to 1,378,390 in 1998. The nature of work is also changing: in 1975 the largest sector was construction, which accounted for 26 per cent of the workforce, followed by the wholesale, retail, restaurant and hotel sector, which made up 18 per cent. By the end of 1998 the wholesale, retail restaurant and hotel sector constituted 22 per cent of the work force, pushing construction into second place with 14 per cent. Forty-one per cent of the workforce is based in Abu Dhabi, followed by Dubai with 30 per cent; 15 per cent work in Sharjah, 6 per cent in Ras al-Khaimah, 4 per cent in Ajman, 3 per cent in Fujairah and just 1 per cent in Umm al-Qaiwain.

A major change since the early 1970s has been the huge increase in the numbers of educated nationals who are entering the workforce every year: by the year 2000 an estimated 200,000 high school students will graduate in the UAE with a further 46,000 graduating in higher education. The challenge is to develop a dynamic labour policy to absorb this large outflow of national graduates and to tap both human and natural resources for the welfare of the country. A key element of this policy is a renewed focus on educational curricula and training so that graduates are equipped with the specialities and skills required in the job market. Emiratisation of the workforce, a process which has already commenced in the public sector, is also a high priority on the national agenda.

EMIRATISATION

The process of emiratisation has been pursued aggressively by the Ministry of Labour and Social Affairs over the last two years with some success, as we have seen, in sectors such as telecommunications and banking. In April 1999 an agreement giving priority to graduates of the Higher Colleges of Technology (HCT) in recruitment for jobs in both the public and private sectors was signed between HCT and the Ministry of Labour and Social Affairs. However, the Ministry is in favour of simultaneous development of the economy and human resources and is reluctant to alienate the private sector by forcing a quota for employment of nationals.

Nearly 1,000 nationals seeking work registered with the ministry in 1998, of which approximately 80 per cent were women. The difficult task ahead is to assist jobseekers in finding suitable employment. In the past national graduates have shown a reluctance

Labour Force by Economic Sectors*	1996**	1997**	1998**
Agriculture, Live Stock and Fishing	95,476	99,498	101,800
Mining and Quarrying			
A. Crude Oil	19,566	20,544	21,900
B. Others	3,353	3,558	3,700
Manufacturing Industries	161,065	169,730	173,800
Electricity, Gas and Water	21,855	23,044	23,935
Construction	242,180	250,600	255,800
Wholesale/Retail Trade and Repairing Services	212,670	227,759	234,700
Restaurants and Hotels	47,170	49,857	52,850
Transportation, Storage and Communication	94,906	95,795	98,710
Financial Institutions and Insurance	19,093	19,476	20,866
Real Estate and Business Services	32,475	33,285	35,440
Social and Personal Services	58,383	60,850	63,450
Producers of Government Services	140,465	144,017	153,659
Domestic Services	125,093	131,490	137,880
Total	**1,273,750**	**1,329,503**	**1,378,490**

Source: Ministry of Planning. * Preliminary Data. ** Figures do not include employees in the armed forces and visitors to the country.

Workers by Economic Sectors 1975

Agriculture & Fishing	8%
Mining and Quarrying	1%
Manufacturing	6%
Electricity & Water	2%
Construction	26%
Wholesale/Retail & Catering	18%
Transport, Storage & Comm.	11%
Finance, Insur. & Real Est.	2%
Other Services	8%
Government Services	15%
Domestic Services	3%

Workers by Economic Sectors 1997

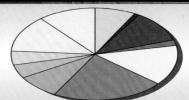

Agriculture & Fishing	8%
Mining and Quarrying	1%
Manufacturing	11%
Electricity & Water	2%
Construction	14%
Wholesale/Retail & Catering	22%
Transport, Storage & Comm.	8.5%
Finance, Insur. & Real Est.	4.5%
Other Services	5%
Government Services	13%
Domestic Services	11%

Source: *Development Indicators in the UAE 1999*, Crown Prince Court – Research and Studies Dept., Abu Dhabi.

to enter private sector employment. This was borne out by a recent study entitled 'Attitudes to the Private Sector' which showed that 96.5 per cent of students at Abu Dhabi Women's Higher College of Technology wanted to work after graduation, of which 62 per cent favoured the oil sector, a further 48 per cent said they would like to work in the government sector and only a meagre 11.5 per cent opted for the private sector. Most students cited high salaries, greater benefits, job security and shorter working hours as their reasons for preferring the state and semi-state sectors.

PANDE

The Government has sought to tackle the employment issue by setting up the Public Authority for National Development and Employment (PANDE), an autonomous body under the supervision of the Minister of Labour and Social Affairs. Established in mid-1999, the authority is responsible for matching the real needs of employers to the qualifications of UAE nationals seeking employment. The Labour Market Information System (LMIS), also under development, will advise nationals on emerging job opportunities and trends in the employment market. The service will be free of charge. LMIS will collect information about the UAE's labour market, track changes and carry out planning and research.

Job website

The Ministry of Labour and Social Affairs is also launching a new website, comprising a data bank on job vacancies in the country's private and public establishments and on available job seekers. The site will provide potential job applicants with a chance to file their application forms and CVs directly with the website. Alternatively, private companies or government establishments looking for employees in specific specialisations will be able to access the data bank. The ministry will not be actively seeking jobs for the unemployed registered in its system.

However, job seekers will also be able to access the Ministry's site looking for job vacancies advertised on the site by companies registered with the Ministry. The service for both job seekers and companies is free of charge. Although the Ministry will not be directly involved in the recruitment process it plans to allocate a computer at its premises to enable job seekers to visit its site and submit their applications. In addition to the recruitment service, the site will also provide information on UAE Labour Law. Queries on labour related issues can also be submitted.

Reorganisation of the workforce

Another significant difference between the 1970s and the 1990s is that today there is a surplus of unskilled manpower in the UAE. The Ministry of Labour and Social Affairs has started a major reorganisation of the labour market in order to discourage a further influx of foreign unskilled manpower and to try to absorb the present surplus of manual workers. New guidelines have been issued to all visa committees for processing applications to import foreign manpower. In 1996 the Government granted an amnesty to all those foreigners who were staying illegally. They were given a chance either to obtain new employment under a sponsor or leave the country without facing a fine or punishment. As a result 150,000 expatriate workers found new jobs and sponsors, and 170,000 left with the help of their embassies. Despite all these efforts there are still violations of the labour law, a situation which the Ministry is addressing, for example with the introduction of new high-tech labour cards. These cards will help the Ministry update its files and obtain an accurate picture of the labour market.

PENSIONS AND SOCIAL SECURITY

From September 1999 UAE nationals working for private companies are entitled to the same social security and pension benefits as UAE nationals working for the Government. Through the provision of benefits in the private sector, the Government hopes to attract more nationals to non-government jobs, thereby speeding up emiratisation of the workforce.

Under the new national pension and social security scheme, which took effect in the public sector in May 1999, nationals who have contributed to the scheme will be eligible for retirement benefits, disability benefits and compensation on death. Current end-of-service entitlements for government employees have been transferred to the new programme.

The General Authority for Pensions and Social Security (GAPSS), an independent entity which invests employer and employee contributions to fund the social security programme, was set up to operate the scheme. The Government allocated the required capital of Dh 500 million in the 1998 budget for the establishment of the authority, which commenced functioning as an investment body from 15 December 1998.

Detailed information on the scheme is available on the following web site: <www.uae.gov.ae/gpssa/index.htm>

SOCIAL WELFARE

Recognising that even in a prosperous country such as the UAE there will always be vulnerable members of society who need assistance, the Government has instituted a comprehensive social welfare system operated by the Ministry of Labour and Social Affairs. The Ministry also makes specific allocations to the country's women's organisations to ensure that all those in need, particularly women in rural areas, have access both to an economic safety net and to assistance in adapting to a fast-changing world.

Social welfare assistance is extended in accordance with the Social Security Law which came into effect in 1977. According to official statistics the Ministry of Labour and Social Affairs spent Dh 5,860 million on social welfare from 1986 to 1997. The total cost in 1997 was Dh 660 million. Of the families receiving social assistance, 25 per cent were in Abu Dhabi, 23 per cent in Dubai, 21 per cent in Sharjah, 7 per cent in Fujairah, 5 per cent in Ajman and 3 per cent in Umm al-Qaiwain. Among those who benefited from the assistance the elderly were the largest group representing 43 per cent of the total. They were followed by widows, divorcees, the deserted, the unmarried, expatriate wives, orphans, families of prisoners and married students. Today almost 40,000 nationals benefit from social security and nearly 9,000 receive pensions totalling Dh 720 million annually.

In July 1999 the Federal National Council approved new legislation regulating social security benefits. Under the new law people entitled to monthly social benefits include national widows and divorced women, the disabled and handicapped, the elderly, orphans, single daughters, married students, relatives of a jailed dependent, estranged wives and insolvents. Under the law all widowed and divorced national women who were married to foreigners are also eligible for social security benefits. The Social Security Committee may also consider an application from a national woman whose foreign husband is unable to earn a living for reasons beyond his control or if his income is less than that needed to run the home (Dh 5,000).

EDUCATION AND YOUTH

State-funded educational opportunities in the UAE have blossomed since the establishment of the Federation when only a tiny minority of the population had access to formal education. A comprehensive free education system is now available to all students, male and female. At the start of the 1999/2000 academic year, 336,135 students enrolled in over 640 government schools throughout the country. Substantial progress has also taken place in the private sector which accounts for nearly 40 per cent of the student population at kindergarten, primary and secondary level.

In addition the UAE's youth have ready access to higher education, both federally-funded and at the many internationally accredited private institutions that are being established throughout the UAE. Generous grants are also available for those wishing to study abroad.

EDUCATIONAL STRATEGY

Although the UAE has achieved much in the field of education there is a real awareness that constant updating of policy and continual investment in infrastructure is required to ensure that graduates are properly equipped to enter the workforce and assist in the country's development. To this end, the Ministry of Education has released a draft policy document outlining a strategy for educational development in the UAE up to the year 2020 based on several five-year plans. The strategy aims to introduce the latest information technology at all levels including a computer for every 10 students at kindergarten, every five students at primary school, every two students at preparatory school, and a computer for every student at secondary school.

The primary focus of attention will be on the needs of students, especially through the promotion of self-learning and continuous education programmes. There will also be training programmes for teachers since surveys have shown that although the majority of students can use computers and the Internet, their teachers were less familiar with this technology.

Cooperation between the public and private sectors at this stage in the country's progress is considered to be essential and so the draft policy document features the establishment of a council for educational development, comprising senior education-alists, government officials and businessmen to assist in raising finance for infrastructure and information technology projects. It also envisages the setting up of a special fund comprising governmental and private bodies.

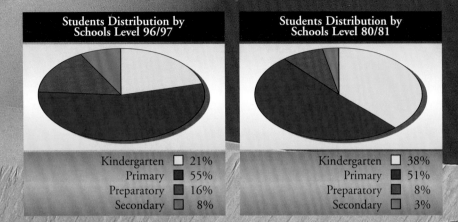

Students Distribution by Schools Level 96/97

Kindergarten	☐	21%
Primary	■	55%
Preparatory	■	16%
Secondary	☐	8%

Students Distribution by Schools Level 80/81

Kindergarten	☐	38%
Primary	■	51%
Preparatory	■	8%
Secondary	☐	3%

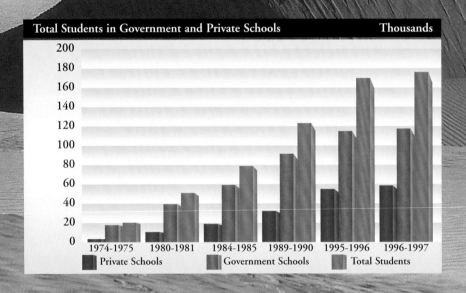

Total Students in Government and Private Schools — Thousands

Private Schools — Government Schools — Total Students

Source: *Development Indicators in the UAE 1999*, Crown Prince Court – Research and Studies Dept., Abu Dhabi.

Graduates of Higher Colleges of Technology by Sex and Year

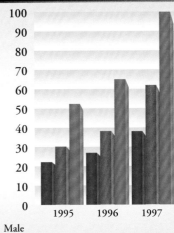

■ Male
■ Female
■ Total

University Students by Faculty 96/97

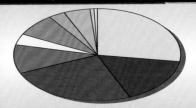

Humanities & Social Science	☐	28%
Science	■	16%
Education	■	25%
Economics & Admin. Sc.	☐	10%
Law & Sharia	☐	4%
Engineering	☐	8%
Agricultural Science	☐	3%
Medicine & Health Science	☐	5%
Graduate Studies	☐	1%
	☐	0.1%

Source: *Development Indicators in the UAE 1999*, Crown Prince Court – Research and Studies Dept., Abu Dhabi.

The emiratisation of teaching staff is scheduled to reach 90 per cent by the year 2020, a necessary development if the UAE's Islamic traditions and principles are to be safeguarded.

SECONDARY SCHOOL CERTIFICATE

Women in the UAE have enthusiastically embraced the educational opportunities provided by them in recent years. (For more information see the section on Women.) This was evident yet again in the General Secondary School Certificate results in 1999 where female students outshone their male counterparts for the third consecutive year. The results showed a good overall performance by girls in both the science and literature subject groups. Fifteen girls were in the top 10 places in the literature group, while 16 girls and 10 boys shared the top 10 positions in the science group. The pass percentage of government schools was 96.2 per cent in science and 82.6 per cent in literature while private schools' pass percentage was 84 per cent in science and 77.9 per cent in literature.

HIGHER EDUCATION

More than 80 per cent of national students who graduated from secondary school in 1999 took up a place in higher education in September 1999. According to the National Admissions and Placement Office (NAPO), 90 per cent of female students and 73 per cent of their male counterparts commenced courses at the federally funded Higher Colleges of Technology (HCT), established in 1987, Zayed University for women, established in 1998, and UAE University at Al Ain, established in 1977.

A total of 16,000 students, including 4,000 new recruits, commenced the new academic year 1999/2000 at Al Ain University, whilst 1,692 students enrolled at Zayed University, where the entire educational process is computer-based, 742 at the Abu Dhabi campus and 950 at the Dubai campus. In 1999, 4,944 students were granted admission to the 11 constituent colleges of the HCT network, compared with 4,154 at the beginning of the 1998–1999 academic year. Of these admissions, 1,675 were male and 3,229 were female, the latter figure being nearly double that for 1998.

Higher Colleges of Technology

The courses provided by the HCT are designed to prepare nationals for professional and technological careers in both government and private sectors. Since their foundation, the colleges have grown dramatically, with staff and students increasing by about 30 per cent each year. At present over 10,000 students are taking advantage of the educational opportunities offered by HCTs in Abu Dhabi, Dubai, Sharjah, Al Ain and Ras al-Khaimah. HCT courses are grouped under four main programme headings: engineering, technology, health science, communication technology and business.

During the period under review, Sheikh Zayed issued Federal Law No. 17 of 1998 dealing with the re-organisation of the HCTs. The law stated that these institutions should henceforth be administered under an independent central body which will have its headquarters in Abu Dhabi but with branches in other towns.

HCT in Fujairah

The HCT opened a new campus for women in Fujairah in September 1999. Fujairah Women's College will be followed by a new men's college. Initially some 350 students joined programmes leading to certificates, diplomas and Bachelor of Arts degrees. Later new programmes will be created according to the needs of the region, such as business, information technology, health science, education and engineering. The Fujairah Women's College is the HCT's eleventh campus.

'Intelligent Building' at CERT

At the end of April 1999, Sheikh Nahyan bin Mubarak Al Nahyan, Minister of Higher Education and Scientific Research, inaugurated the technologically sophisticated 'Intelligent Building' at the Centre of Excellence for Applied Research and Training (CERT) the training arm of the HCT. This is CERT's first joint venture in the region as part of its policy to form a series of strategic alliances with a variety of multi-national partners.

The Electronic Learning Resource Centre at the new building, equipped with the fastest computers available in the country and the latest plasma flat screens, illustrates CERT's Distance Education connectivity to higher education opportunities all over the world in a real-time video or Intranet format.

CERT has been extremely successful in reaching into the community through its programmes to develop a national workforce with information technology skills. It also seeks to enhance the productivity of companies through applied and sponsored research, information and technology transfer.

The HCT, for its part, intends to develop and maintain strong working relationships with all relevant institutions in the country in addition to creating a bridge between local institutions and international corporations as sources of necessary expertise.

CERT cooperative training programmes

The UAE armed forces, CERT and Thomson-CSF signed a memorandum of understanding in March to set up a training institute in Abu Dhabi, commencing in September 1999. The CERT-Thomson Institute (CTI) will develop training programmes in advanced technologies and management methods. The institute will be open to other AGCC countries. Under the plan, 300 students will be trained from the armed forces and the civilian sector in the first year.

Harvard University, which opened its Harvard Institute at CERT early in 1999, held a series of training courses for leading educationalists in the AGCC states as a means of developing educational services.

New regulations

Following a comprehensive study of higher education in the emirates, a new law to regulate private and government colleges and universities was proposed. The law will deal with a number of issues including licensing of colleges and universities as well as

their organisation and supervision. Greater emphasis is to be placed on scientific research as a means of supporting economic development. Agriculture and construction are two key areas where focused research is likely to be highly productive.

LITERACY

The UAE's illiteracy rate has dropped dramatically in the 20 years from 1975 to 1995. In 1975 the illiteracy rate among males was 45.8 per cent and among females 69.1 per cent. By 1995 it was down to 12.1 per cent among females and 18.4 per cent among males. The UAE's illiteracy rate of 16.3 per cent in 1995 is low compared to that of other countries in the Arab world.

The declining illiteracy rate has been largely due to the widespread availability of literacy classes at adult education centres spread throughout the state. The 54 centres and 4,912 students of 1972 rose to 98 centres and 11,017 students in 1975. By 1997 there were 139 centres and 18,163 students. Improvements in literacy are continuing and the UAE has pledged to stamp out illiteracy by the dawn of the third millennium.

SPECIAL NEEDS

Centres for people with disabilities supervised by the Ministry of Labour and Social Affairs cater for those with hearing, mental and physical disabilities, as well as the visually impaired. The Ministry is improving its facilities while at the same time emphasising the role of the family in caring for members with disabilities. The percentage of people with disabilities in the UAE is similar to the worldwide average, i.e. 8–10 per cent of the population.

A number of major new developments are under way in this field including a large centre in Abu Dhabi with 70 classrooms and 20 training workshop, due to open in the year 2001 and the Al Thikka Club which was officially opened in Sharjah in July 1999.

Arabic sign language

A 10-day workshop organised by the Arab League's Social Development Department to assist in creating a unified Arabic sign language ended with 400 standardised signs being agreed upon by 70 specialists from 13 Arab countries. One of the workshop's recommendations was that equipment should be made available to enable every person with acute hearing loss to learn sign language. It also suggested that people be trained as specialist instructors and every effort be made to enable those with hearing impairments to merge into mainstream society.

YOUTH MOVEMENT

In addition to providing wide-ranging formal educational opportunities the UAE Government has expended a good deal of effort in promoting youth and sports activities through national social, scientific, art and cultural clubs. Special attention has been paid to developing youth voluntary work. Scout and Girl Guide societies have been established throughout the country and a special camp, the Zayed Scout Camp, has been constructed near Abu Dhabi. The Girl Guide Society organises cultural, religious, social, scientific and educational programmes for its members and participates in regional and international meetings, conferences and camps. In recent years scientific clubs with an emphasis on the environment have spread throughout the UAE and scientific exhibitions are organised on a regular basis.

Youth hostels were established in Dubai, Sharjah, Ras al-Khaimah and Fujairah to serve as suitable venues for youth activities. The hostels are also used as training camps for local teams as well as providing accommodation for youth delegations on exchange visits. Youth groups are also encouraged to participate in activities abroad.

Several specially equipped and supervised youth centres have also been set up in Abu Dhabi, Dubai, Sharjah, Ras al-Khaimah and Fujairah. Over the years the numbers visiting these centres has risen from 7,000 in 1985 to 82,000 at the end of 1998.

HEALTH SERVICES

Since its inception the UAE has seen remarkable progress in health care. Over the past 28 years government health strategies have paid special attention to the welfare of UAE citizens who are considered to be the country's major resource and the prime target of all national development. To this end comprehensive health programmes have been adopted to meet the needs of UAE society, compatible with global objectives of achieving health for all. Currently the UAE has a comprehensive, government-funded health service and a developing private health sector. This progress is clearly reflected in the positive changes in health statistics which indicate that the UAE has taken its place among the developed nations of the world.

In fact the latest United Nations Human Development Report released in July 1999 ranked the UAE forty-third out of 174 industrial and developing countries, up five places from the previous year. The UAE is also listed as the fourth most developed Arab state. The Human Development Index (HDI), on which the report is based, measures overall achievements in a country in three basic areas of human development: life expectancy, education and general standard of living.

Preventive medicine campaigns, which have been launched to combat and control more than 36 infectious diseases in the UAE, have had a major impact on life expectancy and constitute a key element of health care strategy.

PREVENTIVE MEDICINE

Nine preventive medicine centres have been established throughout the country in a major move to widen immunisation, health scanning, public awareness, research and educational programmes. As a result of these measures, as well as broader access to general health services and sanitation the infant mortality rate has dropped to less than 9 per 1,000 in 1998 and under fives mortality to about 2.23 per 100,000. The UAE now ranks second among developing countries which have achieved the fastest progress in reducing mortality among children below five years of age. The mortality rate among mothers has also declined dramatically to 1 per 100,000 newborn babies. In 1998 figures showed the decline of tetanus to almost 1 per 1,000 infants while the incidence of diptheria was actually nil. Among the most important preventive medicine strategies are those briefly described below.

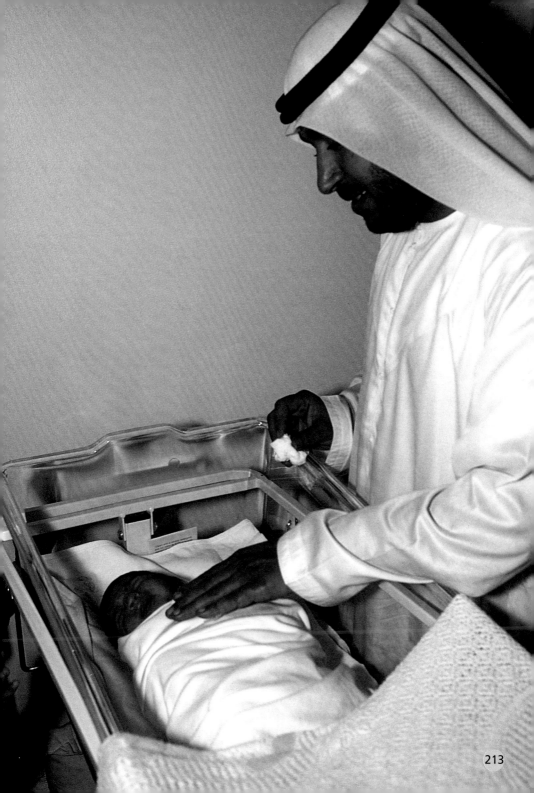

Fighting epidemic diseases

This programme is aimed at protecting the country from introduced epidemic diseases, such as pulmonary tuberculosis, AIDS, salmonella, intestinal worms, hepatitis (B) and leprosy. Expatriates are not issued with residence visas unless given a clean bill of health by the relevant medical authorities.

Fighting AIDs

A special preventive programme to combat AIDs has been adopted since September 1984. AIDs tests are carried out in 16 laboratories throughout the country with about 5 million tests being conducted between 1985 and early 1999. The programme has been very successful in preventing the spread of AIDS.

Fighting malaria

A central administrative unit set up in Sharjah in 1972 to combat malaria has succeeded in reducing the disease spread rate to less than 1 per cent of the registered cases up to early 1999. More than 58,000 people were tested during 1998, of which 2,700 were carriers. As in the previous years, 99 per cent of positive cases came from abroad.

Expanded immunisation programme

Established in 1981 the programme to eradicate childhood communicable diseases, targeting children under five, started with immunisation against tuberculosis, measles, diphtheria, polio, whooping cough and tetanus. In 1986 measles, mumps and rubella vaccines were added to the list, followed by hepatitis B in 1991, and haemophilis influenza B (HIB) in March 1999.

As a result of the programme, cases of measles dropped to less than 20 per 1,000 in 1998. A massive vaccination programme, targeting the over-sixes, is under way with the objective of making the UAE measles-free by the year 2002.

Three other vaccines have also been added to the immunisation programme, namely vaccines against meningitis, cholera and yellow fever, the latter for those leaving the country on holidays or business.

Polio eradication programme

The Ministry of Health has completed four anti-polio vaccination programmes, covering 250,000 patients annually and using about 1 million vaccines. The strategy has been a total success and the country has not had a reported case of polio since early 1993. The immunisation programme against polio covered all children and students from the age of 9 months to 18 years (i.e. 750,000 from October 1998 to April 1999).

Maternity and child care

Nine specialised centres, 95 clinics, four specialised maternity hospitals and 14 general hospitals provide medical services to women and children throughout the country and more than 97 per cent of births now take place in hospitals. This has helped greatly in reducing newborn mortality rates to 1 per 100,000 births, an achievement matching that of developed countries. Ninety-five per cent of pregnancies are checked regularly at the maternity, child care and medical centres. Post-natal services include checking infant growth, immunisation, fighting hereditary diseases, early detection of cancer and encouraging breast feeding.

School health

The UAE is a regional pioneer with regard to school health. The school health services commenced in 1971 with only four physicians, two dentists and 30 nurses providing medical services to about 40,139 students in 129 schools. In 1986 the number of physicians rose to 83 with 14 dentists and 319 nurses. In 1996, with the expansion in school health services, the number rose to 87 physicians, 22 dentists and 365 nurses providing services to 295,000 students. There are also plans to extend school services to private schools, which accommodate 195,000 students in 388 schools. During the academic year 1997–98 the number of students visiting school health clinics reached 250,000.

Health education

The Ministry of Health has paid special attention to health education as an effective tool to alter those forms of behaviour that might have a negative impact on the safety and health of individuals and society at large. To this end, it has established a central health education department with branches in all medical zones.

Within the framework of the Ministry's training programme, eight graduate citizens were sent abroad for post graduate studies in health education. This was complemented by the organisation of 15 general training courses and 10 specialised courses attended by more than 750 trainees. More than 600 students participated in health education training courses during the summer vacation.

No-smoking programme

One of the prominent programmes in the field of health awareness is the no-smoking campaign which includes the issuing of legislation to regulate the tobacco trade. A special committee was formed for this purpose and it has already prepared an anti-smoking draft law which will be submitted to the competent authorities for approval.

A key element of the campaign is the establishment of Quit Smoking units at the departments of preventive medicine in each of the nine medical districts throughout the country. The aim is to reduce the prevalence of smoking and associated illness and death and to encourage people to adopt a healthier lifestyle as well as to support smoke-free policies. Initially, a Quit Smoking unit was established in October 1998 in the Abu Dhabi Preventive Health Department providing assistance to 100 people monthly. Sharjah's anti-smoking clinic was scheduled to commence operations in September 1999.

The units, which will be provided with all necessary personnel, equipment and auxiliary materials, will target all smokers in the community who are willing to quit smoking. There will be a particular emphasis on the prevention of smoking in adolescents. Strategies for the units will include clinical smoking cessation techniques which will be used through group counselling sessions, as well as nicotine replacement therapy.

The UAE actively participated in the Gulf No Tobacco Week in October 1998 as agreed by the Gulf Anti-Smoking Committee. The Ministry of Health has also launched a nationwide study of smoking habits and attitudes in the country in cooperation with the Ministry of Planning which will cover 1,500 UAE national households. Research is under way on whether to include lessons on the dangers of smoking in the school curriculum, and to ban smoking in public places.

As a further disincentive, the UAE raised import taxes on cigarettes to 70 per cent, with plans to further increase it over the next few years, as part of the GCC health plan to curb the smoking habit in the region.

Health conferences

The Health Education Department has organised several conferences, seminars and training courses on cancer, nutrition and chronic diseases, among other topics.

The first Gulf conference on health and awareness held in Abu Dhabi in 1997, was attended by a number of distinguished experts from the Gulf countries and abroad. Its recommendations have helped significantly in the development of health awareness in the Gulf region.

INFRASTRUCTURE

Health care infrastructure has kept pace with other health care developments over the past 28 years to ensure that adequate services are provided in the Emirates. For example, the number of government hospitals has risen to 30, with 4,681 beds, compared with only seven hospitals and 700 beds in 1971. The number of physicians has also risen to 1,535, and nursing staff to 4,664. These hospitals are furnished with the latest medical equipment.

Specialised treatment centres, such as open heart surgery and transplant units, have also mushroomed throughout the country: the total number of operations in the various specialisations rose to 66,000 in 1998. Al Mafraq Hospital open heart unit performed some 298 open heart operations in 1998, 106 of which were performed on children. In addition there are now 67 dialysis machines distributed in six centres nationwide, used by 272 patients.

Diagnostic services have also improved and the Ministry of Health has provided its laboratories with sophisticated equipment to keep abreast of the latest developments in conducting a wide range of tests. It also introduced international standards in the fields of virology and blood transfusions in 1997–98, in cooperation with Germany and also in the field of bio-chemistry, in cooperation with Saudi Arabia.

In 1964 there was only one X-ray machine in Abu Dhabi emirate, operated by a team of six specialists and technicians. By 1981 a radiography department was established at the Ministry's premises and all hospitals had made remarkable progress in radio-diagnostic services. In 1978 the first CT SCAN machine was installed at Al Jazeirah Hospital in Abu Dhabi and by 1998 radio-diagnostic services covered all medical zones.

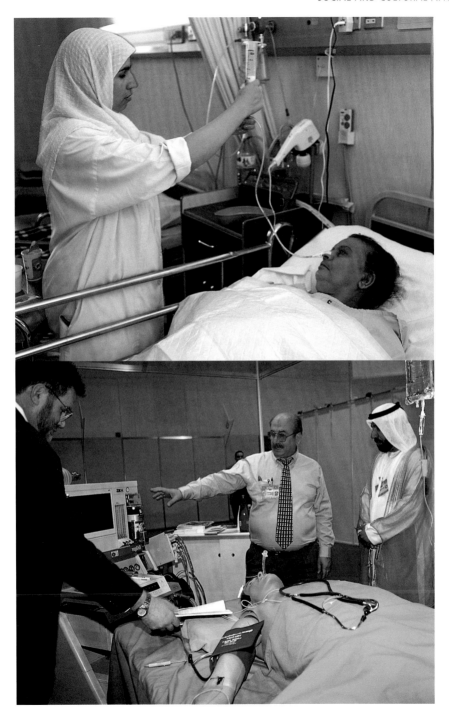

Other specialised services operating across the country include specialised laboratories, such as the in-vitro fertilization laboratory in Tawam hospital in Al Ain: some 82 in-vitro deliveries have been successfully conducted in this department. Al Tawam is also the site of a major oncology treatment centre which cooperates with other AGCC states. So far the centre has received about 380 cases from outside the state for treatment at the centre.

The Zayed complex for herbal research and alternative medicine has also been established in the Mafraq area. It utilises advanced technology to conduct research into herbal medicine with the purpose of establishing an advanced pharmaceutical industry, wholly dependent on natural remedies.

New hospitals

Developments in infrastructure are ongoing. The construction of 17 public hospitals including extensions to existing hospitals will add 1,800 beds in various medical disciplines, nearly doubling the bed capacity of public hospitals in the UAE over the next 10 years. Landmark projects already completed include Sheikh Khalifa bin Zayed Hospital for surgery and emergency cases in Abu Dhabi, a general hospital at Medinat Zayed in the Western Region, and the Sheikh Khalifa bin Zayed Hospital in Ajman. All have been provided with the latest in medical equipment.

Primary health care centres

An increased emphasis on the provision of primary health care throughout the country has seen the number of primary health care centres rise from 12 in 1971 to 98 by early 1999. In addition, as many as 10 new primary health care centres are scheduled to open in the Northern Emirates in 1999.

Telemedicine

The UAE has always been eager to adopt the latest in medical technology and so a wide-ranging telemedicine service has opened at Al Mafraq Hospital to improve patient care and reduce the cost of foreign travel for patients. The system links Al Mafraq Hospital to the Mayo Clinic in Minnesota and enables the exchange of digitised data and high-resolution, diagnostic video images. Al Mafraq Hospital is also purchasing an electronic medical records system which will make it possible to establish physician-to-physician contact via the telemedicine link.

The telemedicine system will enable physicians at Al Mafraq Hospital to consult 1,600 physicians and scientists at the Mayo Clinic and its associates in Minnesota, Arizona and Florida. Consultations will initially focus on cardiovascular diseases, but the scope will quickly be broadened to cover neurosurgery, orthopaedics, dermatology, oncology and other disciplines. The Mayo Clinic will also establish similar links with Al Jazeirah Hospital in Abu Dhabi and Tawam Hospital in Al Ain. The Ministry for Health also plans similar links at other hospitals including Al Qasimi Hospital in Sharjah, Al Baraha Hospital in Dubai and Al Ain Hospital.

INFORMATION TECHNOLOGY

Fully aware that information technology can be of major assistance in improving efficiency, the Ministry of Health is engaged in a project to develop a central database at its premises in Abu Dhabi linking all hospitals, health centres and medical zones in the country. In 1999 Dh 120 million was spent on the project. The Ministry has also implemented a Dh 70 million plan for modernising its computer network and a Dh 4 million project to replace medical equipment incompatible with the year 2000. It has also modernised medical registration services, particularly in Al Ain hospitals, laboratory testing and administrative services at a cost of Dh 40 million. The Ministry also prepared a database on psychiatric services in all medical zones in preparation for developing these services.

PHARMACEUTICAL SERVICES

Progress in other areas of health care is also reflected in the pharmaceutical services. In 1998 more than 5.2 million medicines were prescribed by 154 government pharmacies, employing 742 pharmacists and assistants compared with only nine pharmacists in 1973. The total number of pharmacies and stores administered by the Ministry of Health reached 683 in 1998, employing 1,294 pharmacists and assistants.

TRAINING

Developments in healthcare infrastructure necessitated the recruitment and training of healthcare professionals. As a result the total number of nursing staff increased from 1,900 in 1978 to 5,854 by the end of 1998, about 3 per cent of whom are UAE nationals. In line with the Ministry of Health's efforts to improve nursing services a central department was established in 1992 to deal with nursing affairs. The number of nursing schools has risen to five in the past few years and a special strategy has been formulated to upgrade standards and improve services during the period 1994–2004.

The first class of national medical students has recently graduated from the Faculty of Medicine and Health Sciences at UAE University and several public hospitals have obtained academic recognition from internationally-recognised scientific establishments such as the British Royal College of Internal Medicine and the Royal College of Surgeons in Glasgow.

PRIVATISATION OF HEALTH CARE

At present the UAE Government finances 81 per cent of the cost of health care. The federal Government and Abu Dhabi emirate have taken steps to begin the privatisation of healthcare and several initiatives are taking place as a joint effort between the Ministry of Health and the UAE Offsets Group (UOG).

As a first step, the offsets group is launching the Emirates Health Care Company to provide healthcare management, healthcare investments and healthcare consultancy services. Several other projects are planned including a day surgery centre, sports rehabilitation facility and a diabetes and heart surgery centre. The healthcare division has launched one project, Associates for Advanced Care (AAC), which recruits healthcare workers. On a wider national scale the subject of adequate healthcare insurance coverage will be addressed.

AWARDS

One of the most prominent aspects of cooperation between the UAE and the World Health Organisation (WHO) is the UAE Health Award, created through the initiative of Sheikh Zayed. This award is presented annually at the World Health Assembly to international scientists and experts in recognition of their contribution in different fields of medicine.

On the occasion of the fiftieth anniversary of the WHO, Sheikh Zayed was awarded a gold medal and certificate of appreciation, received on his behalf by the UAE's Permanent Representative to the UN, during the fiftieth session of the WHO Assembly in May 1998.

WOMEN

Women in the UAE have had the complete support and commitment of Sheikh Zayed and the UAE Government in their quest to play a full role in the development of the country. The belief that women are entitled to take their place in society is grounded in the UAE Constitution which states that the principles of social justice should apply to all. Under the Constitution women enjoy the same legal status, claim to titles, access to education and the right to practise professions as men. The guarantees enshrined in the Constitution have been incorporated into implementing legislation.

However, a legislative framework by itself, although valuable, would not have been sufficient to achieve emancipation. The President's wife Sheikha Fatima bint Mubarak, therefore, has worked tirelessly since the establishment of the Federation to implement Sheikh Zayed's vision of a modern society based on Arab and Islamic traditions, recognising that it was only by organising women that real progress could be made.

UAE WOMEN'S FEDERATION

Sheikha Fatima founded the first women's society in the country in 1972, the Abu Dhabi Women's Society. The success of the Abu Dhabi association led to the creation of the Dubai Women's Development Society, the Sharjah Women's Development Society, the Umm al-Mou'meneen Women's Development Society in Ajman, the Umm al-Qaiwain Development Society and the Ras al-Khaimah Women's Development Society. These societies were subsequently linked together under the UAE Women's Federation which was established on 28 August 1975, again headed by Sheikha Fatima. To date, the Federation has played a highly significant role in assisting the women of the UAE to realise their full potential.

The UAE Women's Federation is an autonomous body with its own budget. It has a number of committees to run its activities, such as religious affairs, mother and child care, social affairs, cultural affairs, sports, heritage and the arts.

Depending on the geographical size of the emirate, the individual societies may have more than one branch and there are now a total of 31 branches of the six societies, many operating in remote areas of the country. Activities undertaken by the individual branches include, illiteracy eradication, nursery classes, housekeeping, dressmaking and handicraft classes, art classes, child care advice, health education, vocational training projects, job placement programmes, religious education, welfare assistance, family advice, including mediation services, as well as a busy calendar of social, cultural and sporting activities.

As part of efforts to revive the country's heritage, an environmental and handicrafts programme was instituted in 1978 at the Women's Federation in association with the United Nations Development Programme and ministries of health, labour and social affairs.

In April 1998, Sheikh Zayed inaugurated the new premises of the Women's Federation in Abu Dhabi. The three-storey building, designed in a traditional Islamic style, occupies an area of 8,000 square metres and was built at a total cost of Dh 22 million.

Social planning

The priority of the Women's Federation in the early days was to help women emerge out of seclusion, use their leisure time to become literate, and acquire knowledge about the modern world in order to enable them to raise their family's standard of living. But today's goals are linked to comprehensive social planning in the country with a view to increasing social cohesiveness.

The Federation is involved in the first demographic survey of women and in the implementation of the resolutions issued by the 1995 women's summit in Beijing. The Federation is also engaged in health, education and social campaigns to raise the standard of living of UAE families. Sheikha Fatima has stressed the need to make further efforts to upgrade the standard of humanitarian and social services. She also called for priority to be given to the aged and disabled as part of the Women's Federation strategy for 1999. The Federation is currently cooperating with the Marriage Fund's efforts to provide support for the family unit.

International women's movement

UAE women have played an active role in the international women's movement, always taking care to ensure that proper attention is paid to the recognition of the differences between religions, cultures and traditions. The UAE strongly believes that Islam offers guarantees for the position of women that can act as a useful example to the rest of the world. Inkeeping with this philosophy the UAE Women's Federation has participated in all of the major international women's conferences of the last couple of decades, beginning with that held in New Mexico, in 1975, followed by Copenhagen in 1980 and Nairobi in 1985, culminating in Beijing in 1995.

Seminars and conferences

In addition the Women's Federation has both participated in and organised numerous local and regional seminars on matters of particular importance to women and the family. The Federation is also a prominent member of the Abu Dhabi-based Gulf Coordination Committee, also chaired by Sheikha Fatima.

In line with the Federation's desire to spearhead the advancement of women, Technosphere '99, a three-day conference to study the impact of science and technology on Arab women, was held at the Women's Federation building in April 1999. Forty experts

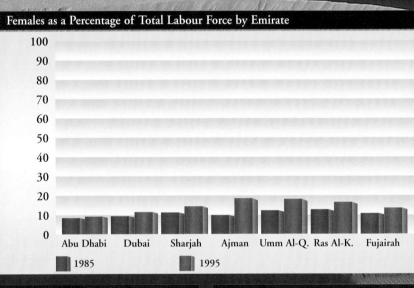

Females as a Percentage of Total Labour Force by Emirate

■ 1985   ■ 1995

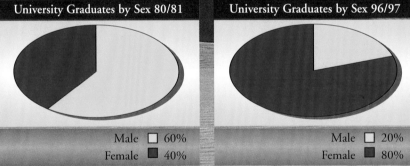

University Graduates by Sex 80/81

Male ☐ 60%
Female ■ 40%

University Graduates by Sex 96/97

Male ☐ 20%
Female ■ 80%

Source: *Development Indicators in the UAE 1999*, Crown Prince Court – Research and Studies Dept., Abu Dhabi.

from 20 Arab countries participated. Recommendations were made and a draft strategy formulated to expand technological and vocational education for women in the Arab world. This strategy is to be submitted to the UNESCO conference on science and technology in Romania late in 1999.

The UAE also hosted the Arab Women's Week, honouring the Arab family and the Refugee Women Week addressing the problems of refugee women. The latter was organised in collaboration with the UAE Red Crescent Society, of which Sheikha Fatima is honorary chairwoman, and the UNHCR.

MARRIAGE FUND

In the past social stability in the UAE has been threatened by the high rate of marriage between UAE nationals and foreign women, leaving many young UAE women unmarried and a significant number of UAE children being brought up by mothers without any cultural or religious affinity with the UAE. The high cost of marriage in the UAE, including lavish wedding receptions and expensive dowries, was a major contributing factor to this phenomenon. Over and above financial, religious and cultural issues, more marriages between national men and women end in divorce than those between national men and national women.

Recognising that a remedy was required Sheikh Zayed decreed the creation of a special Marriage Fund financed by the Government, which offers substantial long-term loans (up to Dh 70,000) to young UAE men wishing to marry UAE women, in order to defray the costs of getting started in life.

At the same time Sheikh Zayed has waged a vocal and successful campaign against the practice of high dowries and extravagant weddings. Upper limits of Dh 50,000 have been set for dowries and the prohibition on lavish weddings can now be enforced by legal sanctions: a prison sentence or a Dh 500,000 fine for the couples concerned. Special wedding halls have been built where celebrations can be held without the expenses that would be incurred in other venues. Group weddings are also becoming a popular way of avoiding these excesses.

The Marriage Fund, having succeeded in reducing the rate of foreign marriages by UAE nationals, has embarked on a strategy to become a comprehensive social organisation concerned with family well-being in all its aspects. Its main aim is to ensure the stability of the family which is the basic element in society.

WOMEN IN EDUCATION

Educational opportunities, the real stimulus for emancipation and development, are now open to women at all levels in the UAE. The number of female students registered at UAE schools has increased 14-fold: statistics show that approximately 270,000 female students were registered in the academic year 1996–97 compared with 19,000 in 1972–73. Of the 14,104 students attending local universities in the 1996–97 academic year, 11,125 were female and 2,979 were male. The 1975 census lists 3,005 females with a first university degree or equivalent. By the 1995 census that figure had risen to a staggering 61,496. During the same period 18,564 women graduated from illiteracy eradication centres. Female students are also achieving impressive results in their studies, outstripping their male counterparts at every level. Sheikha Fatima has said that women have no choice but to excel in education to compensate for the years that they had endured without the light of knowledge.

WOMEN IN EMPLOYMENT

This avid embrace of educational opportunities has given UAE women a chance to participate in the development of their society alongside men. Today UAE women are making their presence felt in society as civil servants, university professors, teachers, lawyers, engineers, doctors, under secretaries, business women, administrators, media and as members of the police force and the army.

Despite the major advances, however, more needs to be done. For example, there remains a need to increase the apparent unwillingness of some well-educated women to take up employment. In 1985 females constituted 9.6 per cent of the labour force, by 1995 this figure had risen only to 11.7 per cent. In part, studies have shown that this is due to custom and tradition while economic prosperity also means that employment is a matter of choice, rather than of necessity. There are also indications that the educational qualifications obtained by many of the UAE's women are not always those most in demand in the job market. A significant number of UAE women also cease working after marriage and bearing children, partly because of an insufficiency of child-care centres and partly because of the well-founded belief that maternal care is likely to be more beneficial for their children.

Another problem that has been identified is the need for women to take up employment in a wider range of professions. Although barriers have begun to crumble in recent years, there is still a strong emphasis on the health and education sector. Civil Service Commission figures show that in 1996 44.3 per cent of federal government employees were women. In the same period over 65 per cent of teachers were female.

Maternity leave

To address some of the issues discouraging women from working the Federal National Council approved a law governing maternity leave in February 1999. The FNC revised the text of Article 55 to give women entitlement to three months' maternity leave with full pay. On mothercare and childhood issues, the Council has said that a woman would be entitled to five separate periods of maternity leave during her employment. The law stipulates that a woman is also entitled to nine months' leave in total to look after her newborn child, comprising three months with full pay and six months at half pay.

WOMEN IN POLITICS

Sheikha Fatima has stressed that society as a whole will benefit enormously if the UAE enters the twenty-first century empowered by the participation of women in all walks of life, particularly the political arena. This, she considers, is a natural development, women having excelled in all other fields. Sheikha Fatima believes that women should not consider entry into political life as an honour but rather a duty. 'Women joining the FNC should

serve all of society and not only women's rights', she said. Sheikha Fatima added that UAE women enjoyed all their legal rights and freedom and have occupied some of the highest posts in the country thanks to the support of Sheikh Zayed. 'Despite this progress, UAE women maintain their traditional role as mothers, adhere to the teachings of Islam and are determined to reflect the true picture of their country'.

HUMANITARIAN AWARD

Sheikha Fatima received the Humanitarian Personality of the Year award for 1998 at a glittering function in Dubai. The award was presented by Sheikha Hind bint Maktoum bin Juma Al Maktoum, wife of General Sheikh Mohammed bin Rashid Al Maktoum, Crown Prince of Dubai and UAE Defence Minister, in the presence of a number of women leaders from the Arab world, including Queen Rania, wife of King Abdullah of Jordan Princess Sarah Al Saud from Saudi Arabia and Sheikha Latifa, wife of Kuwait's Crown Prince. Wives of Their Highnesses Members of the Supreme Council and Rulers of the Emirates were also present. The ceremony was organised by the Rashid Paediatric Therapy Centre (RPTC) under the patronage of Sheikha Hind to confer the award, instituted by the RPTC, on the UAE's First Lady.

Sheikha Fatima had already received the United Nations Shield in 1986 from the UN Population Fund and in December 1997, in recognition of her achievements, she had the unique honour of being presented with simultaneous accolades and awards of recognition by five organisations of the UN system.

The ceremony publicly acknowledged Sheikha Fatima's leadership of the women's movement for over a quarter of a century and by so doing represented an expression of recognition and commendation from the UN system for the UAE Government and its people.

CULTURE AND HERITAGE

Cultural identity in the UAE is a rich blend of traditional Arab, Islamic and contemporary elements. Following the foundation of the state and the increased availability of educational opportunities private and public cultural centres and libraries began to spring up around the country, helping to promote cultural awareness and assisting in the preservation of the country's rich heritage.

The main objective of the Ministry of Information and Culture is to promote and support the country's cultural activities at home and abroad. The Ministry has under its administration 11 public libraries throughout the state's seven emirates. This is in addition to 30 cultural groups, which perform dance, drama and music during festivals, exhibitions and ceremonies in the UAE or held outside the country. The Ministry's Cultural Department also plays an important role, publishing books related to heritage, culture art and theatre, organising lectures, seminars and other cultural activities and participating in international book fairs. The Ministry's Exhibitions Department participates in international exhibitions which serve to introduce the UAE's rich heritage to a global audience.

CULTURAL ORGANISATIONS

Prominent cultural centres and organisations are: the Cultural Foundation in Abu Dhabi, the Cultural and Scientific Forum in Dubai, the Department of Culture and Information in Sharjah, the Fujairah Cultural Organisation, the Studies and Archives Centre in Ras al-Khaimah, and the Juma Al Majid Centre. Significant too in the promotion of cultural activities are annual awards such as the Sultan Al Owais Award, the Sheikha Latifa bint Mohammed bin Rashid Award and the Sheikha Fatima bint Hazza Award. Other institutions which continue to make meaningful contributions to cultural awareness include the National Heritage Revival Organisation and the Marriage Fund.

The Cultural Foundation in Abu Dhabi is made up of three major institutions, the Arts and Culture Establishment, the National Library and the National Archives. Recently, the Centre for Documentation and Research, which was originally part of the Cultural Foundation, has transferred to the President's Office. The National Library contains a large collection of books known as the Gulf and Arabian Peninsula Library, a significant collection of manuscripts and an online database. Its publishing section has in recent times been very active, issuing a wide selection of books on science, art, heritage and historical subjects. There is also a section for the production of compact discs, audio and videocassettes of selected programmes and publications.

In Dubai the Culture and Scientific Forum has organised a number of cultural activities, including the annual Rashid Award which honours UAE graduates with distinctions in various subjects. Sharjah has a wide range of cultural institutions. Notable among them is the Department of Culture and Information which organises the annual book fair in November. It also organises annual cultural and technical festivals for children and the Sharjah Arts Biennial, an international event which attracts artists from all over the world. Other cultural events include the Sharjah Award for Arab Creativity. In recognition of Sharjah's outstanding role in promoting Arab and Islamic culture the emirate was chosen by the Arab League as the Arab City of Culture in 1998.

In Fujairah an active cultural role is being played by the Fujairah Cultural Organisation with the assistance of lectures and seminars. The Ras al-Khaimah Studies and Archives Centre is another institution whose cultural role in the country cannot be over emphasised. The centre aims to present to the world the true picture of the Arabian Gulf and its history, a target also set for the Abu Dhabi-based Emirates Centre for Strategic Studies and Research (ECSSR) which specialises in the analysis of local and international issues.

To consolidate the drive for cultural awareness among the country's youth a number of sports and cultural clubs were set up in addition to newspapers, magazines, radio and TV channels which enriched the artistic and cultural life of the community. Substantial capital investment has also been made in establishing state-of-the art museums, as well as renovating and conserving historic monuments and sites.

EMIRATES CENTRE FOR STRATEGIC STUDIES AND RESEARCH

The ECSSR, founded in 1994, has the biggest specialist library in the country and has produced a large number of books on subjects such as politics, economics, defence, science and environment. In particular, the ECSSR's efforts in conducting dialogue and analysing political, economic and social issues pertinent to the UAE, the Gulf and the Arab world, were highlighted in the centre's annual book released in December 1998.

The centre attracts a wide range of specialists who are assigned to study and analyse issues of vital importance to the state and to propose possible strategies to manage such issues. The ECSSR's aim is to promote global exchange of ideas and it welcomes association with like-minded institutions around the world. The centre also aims to develop the analytical and research skills of UAE nationals so that they will be equipped to manage the ever increasing complexities of the future. To achieve its goals the ECSSR has held conferences, hosted academic gatherings and encouraged scholarly research in the four years since its inception.

The first major annual conference was held in January 1995 on the subject of: 'Iran and the Gulf – a search for stability'. Since then, the ECSSR has had a busy calendar of conferences, symposia and specialised workshops. Security issues and energy resources in the Gulf, the impact of the communications revolution, privatisation programmes in the Gulf region, the Middle East peace process and a host of other issues pertaining to the

region have been discussed at the conferences. The ECSSR publishes four journals: *Strategic Studies, International Studies, The Emirates Occasional Papers* and *The Emirates Lecture Series*. The centre is also establishing an electronic database that will serve as a comprehensive source of information on issues of importance to the Gulf region.

MUSEUMS AND HERITAGE VILLAGES

The UAE has a wide range of museums and heritage villages which provide a fascinating introduction to its traditional lifestyle, offering a host of authentic experiences, such as an evening sitting around a campfire drinking *gahwah* (Arabic coffee) while a camp guide describes bedouin crafts and customs. Other experiences capture the ancient techniques and traditional culture associated with village life, boating and pearl diving through reconstructions of dhows, old souqs (marketplaces), winter settlements and date gardens.

Several of the emirates' magnificent old forts house museums full of items of archaeo-logical, natural history and ethnographic interest. Here too, one can find vivid reconstructions of town and country life. Other purpose-built museums use the latest interactive media to tell the story of the country's ancient past or illustrate the wonders of nature. Audio-visual displays, computer games and scaled models of ancient settlements have all been utilised to interpret the past and the present.

In Dubai and Sharjah, whole streets have been restored to their former glory. Particularly interesting in terms of vernacular architecture are windtowers which are designed to catch even the slightest breeze and funnel the cooler air down to the courtyard houses, providing the visitor with first-hand experience of this early form of air-conditioning. Narrow streets wind between white-washed walls, with copper-studded wooden doors giving access to shaded courtyards and traditionally-furnished houses.

ZAYED PRIZE FOR HERITAGE AND HISTORY

A recent development in the move to preserve the country's heritage is the creation of the Zayed Prize for Heritage and History. This is to be awarded for outstanding research conducted by individuals or establishments on the heritage and history of the country. The award has an important role to play in highlighting local and Islamic heritage and researchers are urged to pay attention to the documentation of heritage through seminars and conferences.

THEATRE INSTITUTE

The Sharjah Higher Institute for Theatrical Arts (SHITA) was officially opened in March 1999 by HH Dr Sheikh Sultan bin Mohammed Al Qasimi, Ruler of Sharjah. The first of its kind in the UAE, SHITA was set up by Dr Sheikh Sultan during the 'Eight Sharjah Theatre Days 1998' in an initiative to enhance the local theatrical movement. Located at the Arts Square in Old Sharjah, the new building includes two theatres seating 280 and 250 people respectively and also comprises a library, an administrative section and other services.

SHEIKH MOHAMMED CENTRE

The Sheikh Mohammed Centre for Cultural Understanding, an institution for the introduction and presentation of Arab culture, was formally inaugurated in March 1999. The unique project, under the patronage of Dubai Crown Prince and Defence Minister General Sheikh Mohammed bin Rashid Al Maktoum, aims to familiarise expatriates with various facets of local culture. The Centre will conduct familiarisation and Arabic language courses as well as lectures on Islam, in addition to guided tours to local homes and places of worship. It will also house a comprehensive library, gift and book shops, a café and a large meeting room.

EXPO 2000 AT HANNOVER

The Exhibitions Department of the Ministry of Information and Culture had hardly recovered from an exhausting but highly successful participation in EXPO 1998 in Lisbon before it became deeply involved in preparations for EXPO 2000 at Hannover. The success of its participation at Lisbon is confirmed by the fact that the UAE pavilion was officially ranked as the third most popular pavilion for the whole exhibition. This was a remarkable performance against all the world's major countries.

The theme of EXPO 2000, due to open on 1 June 2000, is 'Humankind, Technology and Nature'. The UAE pavilion design is based upon Al Jahili fort, built approximately 100 years ago, which has a characteristic large round tower and a series of interconnected buildings protecting a large courtyard. The pavilion will house a series of exhibits, beginning with a 'walk through time' that takes the visitor through the different periods of the UAE's past. Guests will be guided from there to a traditional village complete with local craftsmen and women. A traditional coffee shop will contrast with a modern cybercafé, bringing visitors to the present era. Gardens will reflect the UAE's culture and a unique film will be shown in the round tower. A key feature of the UAE's participation at Hannover will be displays by its folklore team which performs local dances and songs, reflecting on the modern UAE's strong links with its traditional past.

MEDIA AND INFORMATION

It is UAE policy to encourage a free press, subject only to normal constraints underpinning the spiritual, moral and political integrity of the country and its people. As a result, the country's mass media enjoys substantial freedom. This has been emphasised by the recent call made by the Minister of Information and Culture, Sheikh Abdullah bin Zayed Al Nahyan, to those working in the media, specially journalists, to discharge their duties without fear or favour, reminding them that journalism is about seeking the truth, while at the same time correcting mistakes, or helping to avoid them.

RADIO, TV AND NEWSPAPERS

The UAE now boasts six satellite TV stations in addition to a number of other non-satellite TV stations. There are also more than seven radio stations throughout the seven emirates. The Emirates News Agency, WAM, provides news items and features related to daily events in the country for these radio and TV stations as well as local newspapers. This news is also broadcast to the outside world according to agreements signed with other international news agencies. In the field of publications, there are five Arabic and three English dailies in circulation in the country in addition to more than 160 magazines and journals published by local and national establishments, cultural centres, clubs, chambers of commerce and industry, municipalities and educational institutions.

EMIRATES MEDIA INCORPORATED

Sheikh Zayed issued a federal decree in January 1999 establishing Emirates Media Incorporated (EMI), an independent body attached to the Ministry of Information and Culture. The new Corporation, which will be managed in keeping with the spirit and framework of the private sector, will make a significant contribution to the progress of the country's media. The 34-article law, which has been endorsed by the Federal Supreme Council, sets out the objectives of EMI. The law stipulates that the Corporation is to be run by a board of directors, headed by the Minister of Information and Culture and comprising nine national members. The aim of the Corporation is to promote information and culture in the country, focusing on national culture and its Arab and Islamic aspects. It will also seek to encourage the development of radio and television services and to give nationals media training and encourage them to take up careers within the Corporation.

Revenue will come from printing, production, distribution, advertisement, marketing and publishing services as well as grants from other sources and revenues from investment and the sale of property.

The law annuls the 1995 federal decree which set up the Emirates Broadcasting Corporation (EBC) and the 1977 federal decree which established the Al Ittihad Press and Publishing Corp, both of which have been subsumed into the new organisation.

NATIONAL TRAINING SCHEMES

Stressing the importance of the media's role in national development, Sheikh Abdullah called upon national students studying in the field of information to take up employment in the national media. 'The percentage of national students working in the media at present is below our aspirations', he said. 'We are working hard to raise this to satisfactory levels in accordance with the directives of President His Highness Sheikh Zayed bin Sultan Al Nahyan, whose constant concern is the interests of the nation and its citizens.'

In a move to attract more UAE nationals into the field of broadcasting, Sheikh Abdullah announced that Emirates Media Incorporated had formulated a new sponsorship and training programme for national students in this field.

The media training scheme applies only to UAE nationals who are registered with universities in the country. They will be eligible for training in specialisations required by EMI. Trainee students who have completed their studies will be employed according to their qualifications and the needs of the broadcasting station.

The Ministry of Information and Culture is also reviewing a move that would make it obligatory for local mass media to employ a certain percentage of nationals as is the case in the banking sector. This percentage would gradually rise to reach over 50 per cent within a short period. Sheikh Abdullah pointed out that Emirates Media Incorporated is the only non-military institution that gives incentives to school-going UAE nationals in order to encourage them to work in the mass media sector.

NEW PUBLICATIONS

During the last year the Ministry of Information and Culture has continued an active programme of producing high quality informative publications on the UAE, of which the annual Yearbook is an important part. Special books included a magnificent new pictorial study of the Emirates: *UAE in Focus*, which is a large format book of 304 pages with a unique collection of stunning photographs. The text is in English, Arabic, French, Spanish and German. Focusing the camera on the UAE of today it provides a wonderful visual record of the country at the dawn of the third millennium.

Other recent books published with the involvement and support of the Ministry of Information and Culture include *Waves of Time: The Marine Heritage of the United Arab Emirates; Perspectives on the United Arab Emirates*; and the *Abu Dhabi Islands Archaeological Survey*. More recent books in its list include *Ancient Magan: The Secrets of Tell Abraq; The Gulf Cooperation Council;* and two new books on Sîr Banî Yâs island together with the present Yearbook.

In addition to its involvement in book publishing the Ministry of Information and Culture is also active in producing posters and brochures on the UAE in a variety of languages. It has also created two unique CD-ROMs that provide a large amount of information on the Emirates. It is involved with two major Internet web sites: the recently launched site for Emirates News Agency, WAM (www.wam-uae.gov.ae) and the long-running UAEINTERACT web site (www.uaeinteract.com). The latter has attracted over three million hits and is a standard reference source for people worldwide who have an interest in the UAE.

ENVIRONMENT AND WILDLIFE

The last year has been a phenomenal one for progress in the fields of environmental protection and wildlife management in the UAE. While much of the progress has taken place without fanfare or publicity it is clear that government commitment, corporate support and greatly enhanced awareness of the general public – all factors that have received sustained attention over previous years – have borne considerable fruit. The evidence for this progress is to be seen almost everywhere one looks in the Emirates, from the widespread improvements in environmental controls to the impressive wildlife breeding, conservation and public display projects. The fact that, after 10 years of careful study and habitat development, the greater flamingo finally bred successfully in Abu Dhabi during the winter of 1998–99, the first confirmed breeding of this species in the UAE and the first confirmed breeding anywhere on the mainland of the Arabian Peninsula, is much more than an ornithological triumph. It is also a reassuring confirmation that UAE policy on environment and species protection is actually working.

As is well known in the UAE and among the world's leading conservationists, the role of Sheikh Zayed in protecting and rescuing Arabian wildlife has been crucial. He grew up close to nature and with a deep respect for the plants and animals that he encountered in the mountains, deserts, oases and coastal waters. While seeking to provide his people with the benefits of the modern world, he has never lost sight of the vital need to protect the natural one. Sheikh Zayed's government and the people have both been led by and, perhaps more importantly inspired by, his own appreciation for the environment and wildlife.

Over the years a number of government organisations have been established with the role of studying and protecting wildlife. Abu Dhabi's Environmental Research and Wildlife Development Agency (ERWDA) has a major national role in this regard. In addition there are other regional departments which have their own programmes for environment protection, wildlife protection and, most importantly for increasing public awareness.

ENVIRONMENT DAY

The UAE's National Environment Day is by now a well established event that serves to focus the attention of government, the corporate sector and the general public on matters of environmental concern. On the occasion of the 1999 National Environment Day, Sheikh Zayed once again commented on the importance of the environment, calling it

'a dear part of our heritage, civilisation and future'. This year's event focused on the particular needs of the marine environment, with the slogan: 'Together for the protection of our marine environment'. The President also announced that he had ordered the relevant authorities to issue any new regulations they deemed necessary to ensure protection of the environment.

ENVIRONMENT AWARDS

Sheikh Zayed's lifetime concern with the environment has been honoured over the years in a variety of ways, including major awards such as the WWF Gold Panda Award (for which he was the first sitting Head of State to be so honoured). It is particularly fitting that the country's major award for environmental work should be named after him. Carrying a purse of US $1 million the first prize in the Zayed International Prize for Environment is scheduled to be awarded in the year 2001 for the 'best environmental project submitted by individuals, companies or research centres from around the world, which serves to save the environment'. Eligible projects include marine and land protection, water safety, agriculture and improving human hygiene. The prize has been sponsored by General Sheikh Mohammed bin Rashid Al Maktoum, the Crown Prince of Dubai and UAE Minister of Defence, in honour of Sheikh Zayed.

The Dubai International Award for Best Practices to Improve the Living Environment for the year 2000 was also announced. The deadline for applications is 31 March 2000 and guidelines are available at the following web site at: http://www.bestpractices.org/bp2000.

ENVIRONMENT CONFERENCE

Given the sharp focus on the environment, it is appropriate that the capital city Abu Dhabi should be selected as host for a major international conference and exhibition on the environment scheduled to take place from 4 to 8 February 2001. The 'Environment 2001 Conference and Exhibition' will be co-sponsored by the UAE government, the UN Environment Programme (UNEP), UN Development Programme (UNDP) and other international institutions. The goal of the event is to continue international global dialogue on environmental and sustainable development issues, present working solutions that can be applied in both developed and developing worlds and to identify further areas for technical improvement. Commenting at the formal announcement of the conference, UN Deputy-Secretary General and Executive Director of UNEP, Dr Klaus Topfer, stated that many of the world's top scientists and professionals working in the field of environmental conservation would speak at the conference and the exhibition will provide industry and other organisations with an opportunity to display their capabilities in solving environmental issues.

WILDLIFE FILMS

While such conferences will no doubt focus considerable media attention on the UAE's impressive strides in the field of environment affairs, there has already been an increase in media attention with both national and international broadcasting bodies turning to the UAE for wildlife and environmental content. The BBC filming team for David

Attenborough's hugely successful *Life of Birds* series visited the UAE in order to film crab plovers. Meanwhile CNN included several programmes in its *Earth Matters* series on UAE topics. The programmes, excerpts of a major film made for ERWDA, entitled 'Environmental Oasis', included a review of environmental research, incorporating studies of the botany of the desert and of breeding colonies of seabirds on Qarnein, as well as examples of the positive aspects of man's relationship with wildlife and the environment, such as the captive breeding programme for endangered wildlife on the island of Sîr Banî Yâs and the utilisation of surplus recycled sewage for the creation of a wildlife reserve and bird sanctuary at the Al Wathba lakes near Abu Dhabi, site of the flamingo breeding colony.

One programme screened in September 1998 in CNN's *Solution Seekers* segment dealt with ERWDA's satellite tracking programme for marine turtles. As the television film so beautifully illustrated, small satellite transmitters are fixed on the backs of green turtles in order to monitor their movements from the coastal waters of the UAE as they swim out into the southern Arabian Gulf and the Gulf of Oman and further into the Indian Ocean.

The turtle tagging programme, like the houbara and falcon tagging programmes also managed by ERWDA, break new ground in researching precise requirements for habitat protection as part of conservation programmes aimed at individual species. As a consequence of this and associated research work, protection of the nesting beaches of the two species of turtle that are known to breed in the Emirates – the green turtle and the hawksbill – has been accorded a high priority by ERWDA. Meanwhile, ERWDA's Deputy Chairman, Sheikh Hamdan bin Zayed Al Nahyan, has personally enforced a tough protection programme on the offshore island of Qarnein, northwest of Abu Dhabi. Mainland breeding sites include the coastline at Jazirat al-Hamra, in Ras al-Khaimah.

A second CNN programme in the *Earth Matters* slot comprised a short feature on the work of the Sharjah Breeding Centre for Endangered Arabian Wildlife. It included exclusive film of the young leopard cub born at the centre last year. It is believed that there are only approximately 100 Arabian leopards left in the wild, making it one of the rarest animals in the world.

The third programme in the CNN series, screened in April 1999, reviewed the campaign inspired and implemented by Sheikh Zayed to protect the environment through a major afforestation programme and proactive wildlife conservation policy. The short programme drew attention worldwide to the country's successful efforts at protecting the Arabian oryx, the Arabian leopard and the satellite tagging and tracking programmes of houbara bustard, the saker falcon and the green turtle. The Al Wathba bird reserve and flamingo sanctuary near the capital was also featured.

LEOPARD BREEDING

The Arabian leopard breeding project, like that for houbara bustard, has drawn on technologies that have been employed in other areas of broodstock management, such as with race horses and camels. Animals that may not otherwise be successful in raising young have had sperm frozen to be used later in test-tube fertilisations of eggs removed from females. Embryos have then been implanted into females where they have grown normally. Given the very small number of surviving Arabian leopards such techniques

have become necessary to ensure that every avenue is followed to maximise breeding success. However, the young Arabian leopards that can now be seen at the Sharjah Breeding Centre have been raised from natural matings and normal births. Nevertheless, the centre has successfully retrieved sperm from two male leopards who underwent surgery at the breeding centre. This vital genetic material has been frozen in liquid nitrogen. In a parallel operation, some of this sperm was used to fertilise two ova removed from a female Arabian leopard which was treated with hormones and darted with tranquillisers to allow the procedure to take place. At the time of writing the resultant embryos are being stored in liquid nitrogen, awaiting future implantation.

The Sharjah Breeding Centre contains a virtually complete collection of Arabian fauna, with the exception of insects, some of the smaller invertebrates, and birds. The centre, situated 30 kilometres in the desert south of Sharjah city, was opened in 1997 by HH Dr Sheikh Sultan bin Mohammed Al Qasimi, Ruler of Sharjah, and is managed by the Environment and Protected Areas Authority of Sharjah. In addition to successful breeding of the Arabian leopard, the centre has also raised sandcats, Gordon's wildcat and a large number of other species.

INTERNATIONAL COOPERATION

As highlighted in the CNN programmes, excerted from 'Environmental Oasis', one of the most significant features of the UAE's captive wildlife breeding programme is its work on the houbara bustard, most of which is concentrated at ERWDA's National Avian Research Centre (NARC) situated at Sweihan in Abu Dhabi. The project has had a number of key successes and celebrated its tenth year in operation by hatching of chicks from eggs fertilised by previously frozen and stored semen – a technology that will be put to good use in the ongoing breeding of these endangered birds. Another aspect of the houbara work epitomises the international cooperation that is increasingly becoming a feature of wildlife conservation. In the latest example of regional cooperation a new agreement was signed by both the UAE and Saudi Arabia for exchange of captive bred birds in order to strengthen the gene pool without recourse to wild birds.

Meanwhile, the oryx programme continues to provide examples of regional and international cooperation. In late 1999, a number of scimitar horned oryx, successfully reared on Sîr Banî Yâs, were transferred to their native habitats in north Africa.

WILDLIFE MANAGEMENT PROGRAMME

During the period under review the Private Department of the President's Office has carried out a major restructuring of its own wildlife management programme under the direction of its Environment and Wildlife Management Department (EWM). The department is responsible for management of wildlife on Sîr Banî Yâs island as well as reserves or sanctuaries at the Sea Palace, Rawdat al-Reef, Al Jarf area (Hizam Al Ghabat), Bida Khalifa and Ghantoot area. It is particularly concerned with conservation of the houbara bustard and breeding programmes on Arabian oryx, sand gazelle, mountain gazelle, Arabian tahr and other threatened wildlife species.

SÎR BANÎ YÂS

The Environment and Wildlife Management Department's major project is Sîr Banî Yâs island where wildlife numbers have reached impressive figures (see table below).

Wildlife species on Sîr Banî Yâs and percentage change in numbers

ANIMAL	SCIENTIFIC NAME	1997	1998	% Change
Arabian oryx	*Oryx leucoryx*	231	311	34.6%
Scimitar horned oryx	*Oryx dammah*	475	672	41.5%
Beisa oryx	*Oryx gazella beisa*	162	211	30.2%
Gemsbok	*Oryx gazella gemsbok*	111	130	17.1%
Addax	*Addax nasomaculatus*	7	8	14.3%
Common eland	*Taurotragus oryx*	241	301	24.9%
Defassa waterbuck	*Kobus defassa*	4	4	(All female)
Fallow deer	*Dama dama*	22	32	45.5%
Red deer	*Cervus elaphus*	15	24	60%
Axis deer	*Axis axis*	283	371	31.1%
Hog deer	*Cervus porcinus*	4	3	-33%
Barbary sheep	*Amnotragus lervia*	4	4	—
Wild sheep	*Ovis ammon*	421	620	47.3%
Blackbuck	*Antilope cervicapra*	622	827	33%
Grant's gazelle	*Gazella granti*	148	191	29.1%
Giraffe (reticulated)	*Giraffa camelopardalis*	15	19	26.7%
Sand gazelle	*Gazella subgutturosa*	12,424	16,636	33.9%
Dorcas gazelle	*Gazella dorcas*	215	300	39.5%
Arabian gazelle	*Gazella gazella cora*	217	311	37%
Llama	*Lama glama*	9	8	-12%
Arabian tahr	*Hemitragus jayakari*	4	7	75%
Rock hyrax	*Procavia capensis*	21	30	42.9%
Brandt's hedgehog	*Paraechinus hypomelas*	many	many	?
Ethiopian hedgehog	*Paraechinus aethiopicus*	many	many	?

Source: EWM *First Annual Report, 1997-1998*; issued by The Private Department for HH Sheikh Zayed bin Sultan Al Nahyan.

Antelope such as the gazelle are fed on rhodes grass and irrigated pastures are available where the free-ranging animals can graze at will, as well as some fenced pastures where separated stock can feed. The grass feed is supplemented with beef pellet concentrate and a mineral lick to ensure that deficiencies in minerals and vitamins do not occur. Feed is placed inside wooden troughs which are widely distributed in order to avoid overcrowding and extra boxes are installed each year to cater for increased numbers of animals.

Animals are either free-ranging or held in large enclosures with particular emphasis placed on separation to prevent cross-breeding and hybridisation. Fresh water is provided in continuously replenished drinking troughs and feed containers are regularly cleaned and maintained by a team of 30 workers. Some stock, such as the giraffes, require special feed in the form of alfalfa hay which is brought over from the mainland. Birds are fed on an assortment of seeds or specially formulated diets.

Meticulous records are the basis for the high level of wildlife management on Sir Ban Yas. When the numbers of a particular species reach optimum figures surplus animals enter a programme for re-stocking mainland areas or for special exchanges with other breeding centres. Interbreeding is reduced by techniques such as reduction of yearlings, exchanges and importation of males from other countries. One of the relocation programmes during 1998–99 included moving 170 sand gazelle and 40 wild sheep to into a forested area in the Western Region of Abu Dhabi. Monitoring takes place after such releases in order to assess how the animals are coping in their new surroundings.

Three veterinary doctors are based on the island and are responsible for close surveillance of the condition of the animals with the aim of reducing any threats from disease. Inevitably, with such large numbers of animals on the island, some die from causes other than natural old age. Main causes of mortality include intraspecific aggression in the form of fighting between males, especially in the breeding season; snakebites; ingestion of foreign material such as plastic; certain reproductive difficulties such as torsion of the uterus or malposition of the foetus during birth; and finally traumatic injuries sustained by animals fleeing from vehicles and accidentally running into fences, leading to broken necks, horns and other pathological conditions.

The EWM is also responsible for a wide variety of wildlife and environment related projects. Apart from those already mentioned it also runs the Abu Dhabi Falcon Research Hospital, Balghelam Island rabbit fish farm, Al Ajban fish farm, Al Ajban sheep, goat and poultry farm, Rawdat al-Reef animal farm, Shawamekh dairy farm and a mangrove plantation section.

WILDLIFE RESERVES

Environmental regulations, public awareness and wildlife breeding programmes form only part of the measures undertaken in wildlife conservation. Of equal or even greater importance is the protection of natural habitats in the form of reserves. Sîr Banî Yâs is a prime example of such a reserve. There are however a number of other reserves are already established in the UAE, and more are under consideration.

Al Sammaliah island, situated 4 kilometres miles northeast of Abu Dhabi city, and its surrounding waters were recently declared a protected zone and operational base for the Commission for Environmental Research (CER), part of the Emirates Heritage Club which has begun a series of initiatives, most notably to help preserve marine turtles. The Commission is also developing a huge mangrove plantation as part of a research project in association with the EU. The oldest part of the island, which has been formed by joining several smaller islands together by dredged sand, is thought to predate Islamic times. In addition to Al Sammaliah, the CER operates in three other areas of Abu Dhabi: at Masnoaa island, close to Futaisi island, on the mainland coast at Qarn al-Aysh and a desert site at Al Ajban.

The UAE's conservation work with turtles received unexpected encouragement as a result of recent commercial development projects in which beaches that had been smoothed off for cosmetic reasons attracted nesting turtles. The observation indicated the possibility that availability of suitable nesting beaches could act as a controlling factor in the region's turtle population.

ENVIRONMENTAL ISSUES

In March 1999 a new law was passed aimed at reducing air pollution. Developed in consultation with the different municipalities the new regulations limit excessive use of harmful gases. New regulations were also under discussion for controlling the use of leaded fuel which produces harmful emissions.

The UAE enforces strict laws governing the use of chemical insecticides in agriculture to protect public health and reduce negative impacts on the environment. It has banned the importation of 57 chemical insecticides, permitting only the importation of those products which are already licensed for use in agriculture in the US, Canada, Japan and EU. It has also refused to license the manufacture of chemical insecticides in the UAE.

Wherever possible natural control methods are employed. In Dubai, for example, chemical pesticides were recently replaced in favour of a common local plant called *Al Neem* which has the properties of a natural pesticide. Seeds of the plant are powdered and mixed with water so that the active ingredient can be sprayed in parks and other landscaped areas. The plant also has other uses in herbal medicine, a field of research that has received increased attention in the UAE.

The sixth meeting of AGCC ministers in charge of environmental affairs was held in Doha during the period under review. Attended by a strong UAE delegation, the meeting discussed a number of environmental issues of concern in AGCC countries, such as hazardous chemicals management, unified AGCC standards and specifications, and coordination of positions with regard to regional and international agreements including the Vienna Ozone Protection Agreement, Montreal Protocol, United Nations Anti-desertification Agreement and the Draft Law on Wildlife Conservation. AGCC-EU cooperation in environmental issues and the Regional Organisation for the Protection of the Marine Environment (ROPME) programme were also discussed. The Regional Strategy for the Protection of the Environment, a long-term action programme prepared by the AGCC General Secretariat in cooperation with the member states, aimed at implementing Agenda 21, also received attention.

The UAE's participation in an important new international initiative concerned with the environment was sealed by its signature to the GLOBE agreement on 7 June 1999. The acronym stands for Global Learning and Observation to Benefit the Environment, and was signed by Health Minister and Chairman of the Federal Environmental Agency (FEA) Hamad Abdul Rahman Al Midfa and US Ambassador Theodore Kattouf. GLOBE is a hands-on environmental science and education programme that unites students, educators and scientists from around the world in studying the global environment. It is aimed at enhancing the environmental awareness of individuals worldwide, increasing scientific understanding of

the earth and improving students' achievement in science and mathematics. The Minister pointed out that the education ministry had nominated a number of government schools from various educational zones to join the first stage of the programme. Private schools will also be involved and the FEA will provide all necessary equipment.

In line with international concerns about global warming and destruction of the ozone layer the UAE took positive steps to ban the importation of ozone depleting chemicals. At the present time any company wishing to import ozone-unfriendly material must obtain prior permission from the FEA. By the year 2005 it will be illegal to deal in any ozone depleting substances. Although the UAE's consumption of ozone-unfriendly substances does not exceed the rate prescribed in the Montreal Protocol the Government is also concerned about controlling the re-export of harmful substances.

DOMESTIC WASTE

The UAE has one of the world's highest levels of domestic waste. Per capita household waste has reached an average annual 730 kilos in Abu Dhabi and 725 kilos in Dubai. In the US the average is 710 kilos, in Australia 690 kilos and in the UK 300 kilos. Additional refuse comes from street litter, gardens and from the waste dumped in the sea and on beaches. This has imposed a heavy burden on the municipalities. The problem is only partly solved by converting organic waste into agricultural fertiliser. Some waste such as paper, glass and tin cans can be recycled, and special incinerators have been set up to dispose of medical waste.

In Abu Dhabi waste is at present being stored and disposed of in Al Dhafra, some 70 kilometres away from the capital. The municipality has a large plant in the area for disposing of non-organic and hazardous wastes. A new modern landfill is under construction at Mussafah. Meanwhile the disposal of radioactive waste has also attracted attention. A new law will ensure supervision and inspection of all activities involving the use of radioactive elements or equipment. It will ban import, export, transport, storage, manufacture or sale of any radioactive elements without official permission from a special department for radiation control to be established at the Ministry of Health. The law was under discussion with representatives from the ministries of Electricity and Water, Interior and Justice in addition to the Federal Environment Agency. Representatives from all municipalities, the UAE University, the WHO and the IAEA also attended the discussions.

After chemical and radioactive pollution, the polluting effects of noise are also of serious concern to the UAE authorities. Local by-laws state that noise caused by construction or demolition works at construction sites should not disturb people living in the neighbourhood. Dubai's regulations state that noise average should not exceed 55 decibels from 7 a.m. to 8 p.m. and should not exceed 45 decibels in the period from 8 p.m to 7 a.m.

SETTING STANDARDS

Recognition of the high standards being achieved in a number of sectors within the general field of environment is important to the UAE in its strategy to become a leader in this field and in setting standards that will ensure a healthy environment for its

citizens. The fact that Abu Dhabi Municipality's Food and Environment Control Centre (FECC) became the first government institution in the Middle East and Africa to obtain the ISO 9002 international quality certificate, issued in December 1998 by Bureau Veritas Quality International (BVQI), was a source of great satisfaction to the UAE Government. The presentation ceremony was attended by Adel Mahfouz Khalifa, the United Nations Resident Coordinator and United Nations Development Programme (UNDP) Resident Representative. He said the UNDP had been working with the FECC and the UN International Trade Centre to introduce the ISO 9002 quality management system in food inspection and testing, veterinary control and environmental inspection and monitoring.

SPORTS AND LEISURE

One of the priorities emphasised by Sheikh Zayed is the building of sports facilities for the youth of the UAE. Sports clubs have been formed with government support, stadiums built and football has become the national game. First-class government and private sports and leisure centres have been established throughout the country. As a result, UAE citizens now participate eagerly at home and abroad in a wide range of modern sports and leisure activities, from basketball and bowling, to golf, cricket and ice hockey.

Despite the eagerness with which the UAE has embraced these contemporary activities, heritage sports continue to have a strong following: camel-racing and traditional boat-racing are subjects of a major heritage revival movement. Traditional skills honed in the past have also been developed in sports in which the UAE competes with considerable success internationally, such as powerboat-racing and various forms of equestrianism.

International recognition has also been forthcoming for the staging of spectacular events and invitation tournaments in the UAE, especially in sports such as golf, tennis and snooker. These events attract world-class international sportsmen, increasing awareness of such competitive sports in the UAE, thereby encouraging wider participation, as well as assisting in the drive to promote tourism.

FOOTBALL

Football remains the most popular sport in the UAE. Promotion of the sport through football clubs at schools and colleges, as well as at local, regional and national levels, has paid dividends in terms of raising the standard of the game in the country. Twenty-six football clubs, each with approximately 150 players, are currently affiliated with the UAE Football Association (UAE FA), which was established in 1971. The UAE FA joined FIFA in 1972, followed by both the Arab Football and Asian Soccer federations in 1974.

In 1999 Al Ain Football Club reached the semi-finals of the Asian Club League Winners Championships. The national team, however, had a disappointing year and is now preparing for the year 2000 Asian Cup in Lebanon.

CAMEL-RACING

Camel-racing, a traditional sport, is extremely popular in the Emirates. It was originally staged in an informal setting, at weddings or special festivals, but now customised tracks

have been built throughout the country where race meetings are held in the winter months from October to April, culminating in the annual camel race festival at Al Wathba which attracts entrants from all over the world.

Sheikh Zayed's sponsorship of the Zayed Grand Prize camel races, also held at Al Wathba racetrack to celebrate UAE National Day, is an indication of the special focus and encouragement given to the revival of heritage sports and camel-racing festivals as an occasion for the gathering of UAE citizens.

The necessity to formulate rules and regulations for the sport has required the establishment of the Camel-Racing Federation which is now responsible for guiding and controlling camel-racing events in the Emirates and promoting events abroad.

One such international event, the Sheikh Zayed's President's Cup, held in Sydney, Australia in September 1999 for the second consecutive year, has proved to be a popular event which also raises considerable funds for the Australian Research Institute for Child Cancer. A heritage festival held at the same time around a tent erected between the Modern Arts Museum and the Sydney Opera Theatre attracted large crowds.

Camel-breeding

As a result of the growth in the popularity of camel-racing, greater attention has been paid to the challenges of breeding, including application of the latest technology. The Al Ain-based Embryo Transfer Research Centre for Racing Camels, established in 1989, has pioneered artificial insemination and embryo transfer in camels. Associated with the scientific research programme a well-equipped veterinary hospital has been built, which is engaged not only in treating sick camels but also in advising owners on the best possible care for their animals.

The Camel Reproduction Centre in Dubai has also pioneered breeding methods and is the instigator of a cross-breeding programme which produced Rama the 'cama', the world's first hybrid between a camel and llama. The centre's focus is on artificial insemination and embryo transfer and the same techniques apply in both the 'cama' and camel breeding programmes. The centre is working on ways to produce better racing camels, not necessarily faster racing camels, but animals of better genetic stock, in addition to improving the freezing of embryos and semen.

HORSE-RACING

The horse has always been an essential part of Arab life. Until recently, however, the relationship took the form of an enduring partnership based upon survival in one of the world's toughest environments. With the arrival of prosperity, the Emirati's relationship with the horse made a crucial shift from survival to recreation. Today, all forms of equestrian sport are enormously popular in the UAE, with the pure-bred Arabian horse still having pride of place.

In 1985 the UAE joined the Federation Equestre International (FEI) and the UAE Equestrian and Racing Federation was formed in 1992 with the clear mission to promote and sponsor equestrian sport in the UAE. Since the Federation's inception, equestrian

sport has become focused and highly successful. Racing has already taken its place on the world stage and showjumping and endurance riding are now poised to follow its lead.

The Federation, implementing Sheikh Zayed's directives, hosts an auction of Arab thoroughbreds each December to provide opportunities for citizens to own race horses and participate in the revival of sports associated with the country's heritage. A number of horses trained for racing, endurance races, polo and jumping are sold at the auction.

Endurance riding

Endurance riding involves long-distance racing over a gruelling course under strictly-controlled conditions for horse and rider. Pure-bred Arab horses, bred for stamina in inhospitable terrain over thousands of years, are particularly suited to this demanding sport and, consequently, it has become immensely popular in the UAE.

Riders of international stature frequently compete in the country: 1998 was particularly eventful since a very successful 160-kilometre FEI World Endurance Championship was held in the UAE in December.

Most of the top riders and horses from the world endurance riding circuit were once again back in the UAE the following March, four days before the Dubai World Cup, to race in a 'champion of champions' endurance ride. The 130-kilometre FEI World's Most Preferred Endurance Ride, organised by the Equestrian and Racing Federation, featured winners of the world's top Endurance Rides over the previous three years. Heading the list of riders was 1998 world endurance champion Valery Kanavy, 1997 champion Danielle Kanavy, Fausto Fiorucci of Italy (WEC '98 second place), Daisuke Yasunaga of Japan (WEC '98 third place) and other top champions. Sheikh Rashid bin Mohammed Al Maktoum was victorious in this tough contest, confirming the UAE as a force to be reckoned with in the sport of endurance riding. UAE riders also took second and third places, with three other UAE riders finishing in the top ten.

The UAE team regularly travels abroad to compete on the international circuit, with much success. In fact, Sheikh Rashid was rated fifth best in the world in 1998 by the Endurance and Long Distance Rides International Committee (ELDRIC) based on his performance in Europe.

In 1999 the UAE Equestrian and Racing Federation again sent a strong team abroad to competitions, including Syria, Landivisiau, France, Lenzburg, Switzerland, Wicklow, Ireland and the European Open Championship in Spain and Portugal.

Eight of the nine UAE riders who completed the FEI CEI-B 120-kilometre event in Syria finished in the top 10 with Sheikh Hamdan bin Mohammed Al Maktoum gaining the overall prize. The team also scored a thrilling win in the FEI Open Under-21 European Endurance Riding Championship in Donaueschingen-Germany in August, having already performed well in Compiegne in France and Tattersalls in Newmarket, England, in their first two events on the European circuit.

At the end of August the UAE's Mubarak Shafya capped a momentous season when, against considerable odds, he won the 206-kilometre Wicklow Hills Endurance Ride Maktoum Cup. Also in August, Sheikh Ahmed bin Humaid Al Nuaimi, representing his

country and the sole Middle East competitor, won the prestigious Queensland State Championship Endurance Ride, the first non-Australian ever to do so.

Track-racing

Professional racing as it is now practised in the UAE did not begin until the season of 1991–92. During the 1990s the sport enjoyed phenomenal growth throughout the UAE, and the country now boasts a number of prestigious racing venues and hosts the world's richest horse race, the Dubai World Cup.

A recent innovation but already one of the most talked about races in the sport's history, the 1999 Emirates-sponsored Dubai World Cup, held at Nad al-Sheba race course in March, had a total guaranteed purse of US $5 million – an increase of US $1 million over 1998. Other increases in sponsorship brought the total prize money on the night to a staggering US $6.25 million.

The 1999 event provided the Dubai-based Godolphin stable with their greatest sporting triumph, when unfancied Almutawakel, owned by Sheikh Hamdan bin Rashid Al Maktoum, trained by Saeed bin Suroor and ridden by Richard Hills, won in record-breaking time. Under the guidance of the Emirates Racing Association, horse-racing has achieved full international status and the Dubai World Cup has been awarded the sport's coveted Group One status, which places the race on a level with the Derby, Oaks and Arc de Triomphe classics.

The UAE has also gained a well-earned reputation in international horse-racing. In August the Godolphin-owned Dubai Millennium won the Prix Jacques le Marois – the syndicate's eleventh Group One prize in a season which included wins with Diktat in the Prix Maurice de Gheest, Daylami in the King George VI and Queen Elizabeth Diamond Stakes, Aljabr in the Sussex Stakes and Zahrat Dubai in the Nassau Stakes.

MARINE SPORTS

It is not surprising that marine sports are pursued with great vigour in the UAE considering its location and history. Marine facilities too have been radically improved in recent years. For example, the new Abu Dhabi International Marine Sports Club (ADIMSC) building was officially opened at the Breakwater in November 1998. The Club is a gift from Sheikh Zayed to the youth of the UAE to ensure that suitable training facilities are available for marine sports.

Traditional boat-racing

In the traditional arena, long-boat races, although the boats are not quite as long as in the past, create an impressive picture as their tightly-packed crews labour at their oars, propelling their svelte boats through calm inshore waters under the appreciative gaze of spectators.

Traditional sailing races are held at regular intervals during the period October – April. Majestic wooden dhows assemble at the start line, evoking the customs and traditions of a bygone era. Competition is intense and great attention is paid to the preparation of the boats and their massive rigs.

One major sailing event is the Mubarraz Island marine sports festival, held in December and organised under the auspices of Sheikh Zayed and Sheikh Maktoum as part of their efforts to promote the country's marine sports heritage. Eighty 60-foot boats from all over the country participated in the Dh 6 million 1998 race held over a 55-nautical mile course. It was decided that as from 1998 the number of nationals in each boat would be 50 per cent, to be increased gradually to 100 per cent by 2001.

In May 1999, 157 43-foot boats manned by 1,500 crew took part in the Al Dabb'iyya sailing race, finishing at the Abu Dhabi Corniche breakwater. In accordance with the traditional nature of the event, the race was preceded by the national anthem followed by folk dance and songs presented by local heritage troupes. Al Sarab owned by Dr Sheikh Sultan bin Khalifa Al Nahyan came in first , winning a cash prize, a gold model of a boat and a vehicle.

Modern racing

Modern sailboat races are also staged throughout the country, both at a local and international level. Races are held in dinghies such as Lasers, Optimists, Toppers and Kestrels, together with their faster and more exciting multi-hulled counterparts, the Hobie Cats. Larger sailing vessels are also catered for with a number of offshore races.

In October 1998 the UAE national sailing team competing abroad for the first time, won the Laser Class championship at the Alexandria Sailing Regatta. The UAE team was Robert Carver, Aqil Ismail, Ali Essa, Sultan Hareb and Abdulla Mubarak.

Powerboat-racing

Powerboat-racing has an extremely strong following in the UAE, especially since national teams, competing both at home and abroad have achieved world-prominence in this sport.

As is usual each year the final round of the Formula One World Championship was held at the Corniche breakwater on 2 and 3 December, along the sidelines of the Abu Dhabi Water Festival 'Gulf Aqua '98'. Over 26 participants from 13 countries competed for the coveted 1998 World Champion title. However, following the retirement of Humaid Bakhit in 1997, the UAE were unable to field a team. This was remedied in 1999 when ADIMSC recruited the American Scott Gillman, the 1997 World Champion. Gillman, who also trains the UAE's Formula Two and Four teams, had a number of wins during the season on the international circuit.

The UAE's Dubai-based, world-famous Victory Team, including Khalfan Harib and Mohamed Al Ghaith, Saeed Al Tayer and Felix Seralles, and Ali Nasser and Randy Scism, also had many successes in the heats leading up to the UIM Class One World Offshore Championship which is held each December in Dubai. Harib was Class One World Champion in 1993 and twice winner of the Class Two title. The only two-man team to have won more Class One titles are fellow Victory Team stars Saeed Al Tayer and Felix Serralles who have won 11 races.

In September Nasser and Scism were confirmed as the 1999 UIM Class One European Champions and were well ahead in the World Championships.

Jetskiing

Jetskiing, a relatively new sport, is another marine activity at which the UAE excels internationally. The UAE's Nader bin Hindi performed extremely well in the 1999 UIM Pro Class European Open 1,200 cc Championship. Bin Hindi was first crowned the runabout world champion in December 1995. The following year he repeated his success by taking the world title in the 785cc Jet Class.

Diving and snorkelling

Today the same UAE waters that attracted the pearl divers of old continue to draw large numbers of residents and tourists beneath their surface, but for very different reasons: sport-diving is extremely popular in the UAE and there are numerous clubs and dive centres throughout the country, many specialising in PADI courses.

GOLF

Less than three decades ago golfers were restricted to playing on oiled sand, putting on 'browns' rather than greens. Today proponents of the fastest growing sport in the UAE can take their pick of a number of world-class golf courses throughout the country, complete with distinctive clubhouses, immaculate greens and lush fairways. Some of the courses are of such a high standard that they have been selected to host major international golfing tournaments.

The Emirates Golf Club hosted the annual Dubai Desert Classic tournament each year until 1999, when the tournament was held at the Dubai Creek Golf and Yacht Club. The Desert Classic, which attracts all the top international players, is part of the ATP European Tour.

The resounding success of the Toyota Golf Pro-Am since its inception in 1994 is another indication of the UAE's capacity to host an array of events of international calibre.

Golf in the UAE is organised and promoted through the UAE Golf Association (UGA) which particularly proud of its junior development programme to encourage young nationals to excel in the sport. A junior national team participated in prestigious tournaments in Malaysia and Lebanon in 1999. The tournament in Beirut tied in with the launch of the 1999-2000 Junior Development Programme in September.

TENNIS

Assisted by the splendid facilities on offer throughout the country and heavily-promoted by the UAE Tennis Association, tennis is a much favoured sport in the UAE, both at amateur and professional levels.

Nine of the world's top 14 players competed in the 1999 Dubai Tennis Open (February 8–14), a US $1 million ATP Tour World Series event organised by Dubai Duty Free Aviation Club Tennis Centre. In 1998 the Dubai Tennis Open was presented with the 'Tournament of the Year' award in the 54-event 1998 ATP Tour World Series.

The Dubai Tennis Open is a week of serious competition for the world's top stars as well as a time of entertainment for families in the UAE. Surrounding events help to

promote tennis and to show through fun games and competitions how easy and accessible the game can be for all ages and levels of competence.

SNOOKER

The Dubai Classic is a major date in the snooker event calendar with international stars competing for big prizes. The sport has much local support and the UAE snooker team underlined its regional dominance by capturing the AGCC championship for the eighth successive time in Riyadh.

The UAE Billiards and Snooker Association is continuing to foster young talent with a special schools programme. Under this scheme the most talented players are selected for further coaching with the aim of giving the sport and the national team a broader base in the UAE.

MOTOR SPORTS

The Dubai International Rally (1–2 December 1998), comprising the final round of the 1998 FIA Middle East Rally Championship, was won for the tenth time in 14 years by Mohammed bin Sulayem, while fellow UAE driver Sheikh Abdullah Al Qasimi clinched his first Middle East success – the Middle East Group N title for production cars. Mohammed bin Sulayem had an amazing six wins in six rallies in 1998.

Bin Sulayem also had a momentous start to the 1999 season when he won the UAE Automobile and Touring Club ADNOC-FOD UAE International Rally which launches the FIA Middle East Championship each year. Mohammed went on to repeat this fine performance at events in Jordan, Cyprus, Lebanon and Qatar.

Another UAE driver Khalifa Al Mutaywi, won the Drakkar Noir 1,000 Dunes Rally series for the third time in 1999, successfully defending his title and winning the Golden Sword perpetual trophy outright. The 700-kilometre rally, the third in the series, was part of the motoring activities of the 1999 Dubai Shopping Festival and was organised by Emirates Motor Sports Federation (EMSF). The rally also constituted Round Three of the UAE National Rally Championship.

BOWLING

The UAE Bowling Federation organises competitive bowling in the UAE, a sport that has become even more popular in recent years as bigger and better bowling alleys are opened across the country.

This year the Khalifa International Bowling Centre at Zayed Sports City, which has 40 lanes, hosted the UAE International Annual Bowling Championship from 1–16 April 1999 and the FIQ World Bowling Championships in November 1999. The latter event featured participants from over 80 countries each fielding two teams.

CHESS

The UAE has a very active Chess Federation that organises domestic tournaments, as well as the successful participation of the UAE team in international championships.

البدايه START

DUTCO
Scaffoldin

August 1999 was a hectic month for the Abu Dhabi Chess and Culture Club with an international tournament played against Azerbaijan and the holding of the Ninth Abu Dhabi Chess Festival at the Abu Dhabi Cultural Foundation from August 21 to 31 with nearly 300 participants from various countries competing.

ATHLETICS

The International Law Enforcement Games track and field events were held at the Dubai Police stadium in November 1998. UAE-Dubai Police emerged champions on the final day after topping the medal table with 261 medals: 102 gold, 104 silver and 55 bronze. The USA were in second place with a total of 90 medals. Australia were third with 25 gold, 11 silver and seven bronze and UAE-Military Police were fourth with 22 gold, 13 silver and six bronze.

PAN-ARAB GAMES

The UAE were highly-successful participants in the pan-Arab Games held in Jordan in August 1999. UAE teams participated in nine sports including shooting, football, swimming, cycling, weightlifting and bodybuilding, chess, equestrian, athletics and karate and came away with eight gold, nine silver and 17 bronze medals.

The UAE cycling team won the first medal of the games for their country, a silver medal in the 84-kilometre race, while Khuwaiter Saeed won the first ever swimming medal for the UAE in the country's 23-year-old record in the biennial games. Subsequent races saw Ayub Salem winning a gold medal while Khuwaiter took a second medal, this time a bronze.

The shooting team also had considerable success bringing home gold, silver and bronze medals at team and individual levels. Immediately prior to the games Sheikh Saeed bin Maktoum Al Maktoum had won fourth place in the World Marksmanship Championship in Finland, confirming the UAE's prowess in this field.

Meanwhile, men and women from the UAE chess teams, produced impeccable performances, adding to the UAE's impressive collection of gold medals.

ASIAN GAMES

The UAE will participate in the Thirteenth Asian Games held in Bangkok from 6 to 20 December with the biggest delegation ever sent. The UAE is taking part in nine events: football, handball, basketball, shooting, bowling, cycling, karate, swimming and snooker. The UAE has fielded teams in every Asian Games since the Bangkok Games in 1978.

CRICKET

The UAE's relatively large expatriate population has meant that cricket has become a firm favourite in the country with well-established cricket grounds in Abu Dhabi and Sharjah.

The national team won the plate final of the Youth Asia Cup played in Singapore in July 1999 when they defeated Hong Kong by four wickets at the Singapore Cricket Club ground.

283

ICE HOCKEY

The UAE Transitional Committee for Ice Hockey selected the first national team to represent the country in the International Ice Hockey Championship held in Hong Kong in March. The team included 14 players selected from different clubs in Abu Dhabi, Dubai and Al Ain

WRESTLING

Some of the world's top wrestling champions competed for honours in a unique championship organised by the Abu Dhabi Combat Club at the end of March 1999. The Second World Submission Wrestling Championship along with the First Arabian Submission Wrestling Championship featured over 100 wrestlers from around the world in the three-day championships.

PHYSICALLY CHALLENGED ACHIEVERS

As part of the Dubai Summer Surprises festival, the Dubai Department of Economic Development honoured the physically challenged on their sporting achievements at a ceremony organised at the Town Centre shopping mall in Dubai. One of those honoured from the Dubai Handicapped Club was Khamis Masood Mubarak, a gold medallist in the shot-put competition in the World Championship in Birmingham in 1997, who has qualified to compete in the year 2000 Olympics in Sydney. Also honoured was Mohammad Humaid Al Muhairi who received a silver medal in the same championship. Ahmed Saif Zaal Al Muhairi from the Trust Club (Nadi Al Theqa) was honoured for his success in many international sport competitions. From the Abu Dhabi Medical Centre, Salem Hamad Naseeb an artist and painter with a considerable number of successes behind him in many sporting activities, was also honoured as was Ahmed Rashid Al Shamsi from the Al Ain Handicapped Club who won gold and silver medals in the International Open Championships in Germany in 1999.

EXHIBITIONS AND EVENTS

The UAE is a major world centre for an increasingly wide range of exhibitions and conferences that cater for virtually all major interest groups, from farmers to military advisers and from commercial trades to medical specialists. Well-equipped exhibition centres and conference facilities are present in each of the major cities. In addition to the big shows such as IDEX, TRIDEX and the Dubai Air Show, there are many other annual shows that attract thousands of visitors to the UAE, not all of which are for members of particular trades or professions: the Dubai Shopping Festival, for example, brings large numbers of ordinary shoppers to the Emirates and it is a great boos to local commerce.

Information on forthcoming events is now readily available on the key web sites of each region: Abu Dhabi Chamber of Commerce and Industry at http://www.adcci-uae.com/events/events.htm; Dubai World Trade Centre at http://www.dwtcuae.com/events/exh1999.htm; Sharjah Exhibition Centre at http://www.expo-centre.co.ae. In addition the web site sponsored by the UAE Ministry of Information and Culture, http://www.uaeinteract.com, has links to these and other sites and carries regular news items concerning exhibitions, together with a stored database of exhibition related information.

Organisation of major exhibitions is being undertaken by specialised bodies and considerable efforts are being made to maximise coordination between the various interested parties. In Abu Dhabi the General Exhibitions Corporation (GEC) was recently established to supervise all exhibitions and conferences held in the emirate, defence related or otherwise. GEC aims to create a framework for all event management companies in the various sectors, in order to maintain a unified international standard for all events held in Abu Dhabi. Forthcoming major events to be organised by GEC are the second session of the Triple International Defence Exhibition and Conference, TRIDEX 2000, followed by Environment 2001 Exhibition and Conference scheduled for February 2001. Meanwhile many exhibition centres are undergoing upgrading, expansion or new construction. The UAE Offsets Group (UOG) secured licenses for setting up World Trade Centres in each of the UAE's major cities. The licensing body is The World Trade Centres Association which has 330 centres in 101 countries. The landmark Dubai World Trade Centre was established in 1982 and a new Abu Dhabi World Trade Centre is now at the planning stage. At the time of writing four sites were under assessment and the actual site was expected to be finalised by late 1999.

ADIPEC

The Eighth Abu Dhabi International Petroleum Exhibition and Conference (ADIPEC) had as its theme: 'Oil and Gas Industry in the 21st Century – Technical and Environmental Challenges'. The four-day event was organised by the Abu Dhabi Chamber of Commerce and Industry and the Abu Dhabi National Oil Company. Over 800 companies from 34 countries participated. The largest oil and gas exhibition and conference in the Middle East, it is also rated among the top 10 oil and gas events in the world. The UAE pavilion was the largest with around 250 companies participating. Overseas participating national pavilions included those of the UK, Austria and Canada. Over 80 technical papers were presented on state-of-the-art technologies, scientific methods implemented in exploration and extraction of oil and gas, information technology and manpower planning. Over 8,000 visitors attended the exhibition and more than 90 per cent of the exhibitors confirmed their participation for the next event in the year 2000.

MILCON 1999

The International Defence Conference MILCON 1999 was opened by Sheikh Nahyan bin Mubarak Al Nahyan, Minister of Higher Education and Scientific Research and Chancellor of the Higher Colleges of Technology. 'What happens in the region affects the economy, security and stability of the world. We live in a world that is largely at peace, yet it is a world of many danger spots and full of uncertainty,' the Minister acknowledged in his opening speech. The conference theme, 'Defence Solutions for the 21st Century', addressed these issues and featured discussions on future defence and military training needs in the Gulf.

IDEX '99

The Fourth International Defence Exhibition and Conference IDEX '99 was officially inaugurated by Crown Prince of Abu Dhabi and Deputy Supreme Commander of the UAE Armed Forces Sheikh Khalifa bin Zayed Al Nahyan who commented that 'the UAE's policy, designed and cemented by President HH Sheikh Zayed bin Sultan Al Nahyan, is based on a strong belief that peace and stability are the cornerstones of development, progress and security'. He stressed that the UAE did not intend to take part in an arms race in the Gulf and that the country's concern over military issues would not overshadow its interest in development and progress.

In an interview with *Gulf Defence* magazine on the occasion of the IDEX opening, General Sheikh Mohammed bin Rashid Al Maktoum, Minister of Defence and Crown Prince of Dubai said that the UAE has put all its power and financial capabilities at the service of regional and international peace: 'We follow wise and balanced policies under the leadership of our President HH Sheikh Zayed bin Sultan Al Nahyan. These are based on openness and a close relationship with the outside world. We believe in peaceful dialogue to resolve our differences and disputes with others. It is not our policy to resort to the language or threats of war and we adhere to the principle of non-interference in the internal affairs of others,' the General added.

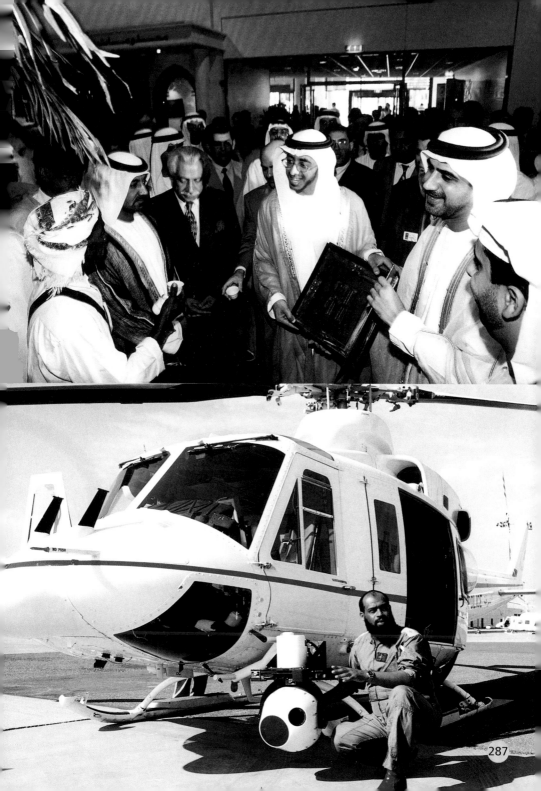

287

IDEX '99 featured the wares of 848 companies from 41 countries. From missiles and electronic control equipment to warships and aircraft, the five-day exhibition showcased the latest that the armament industry has to offer. By the conclusion of the event new contracts worth in excess of Dh 645 million (US $175 million) had been announced and talks on various other projects concerning the UAE's military equipment were continuing.

JEWELLERY EXHIBITION

The annual jewellery exhibition, now a major event in the UAE's calendar, was held during April 1999 at the Dubai World Trade Centre. International Jewellery Dubai '99, as it was known, was the biggest jewellery exhibition in the Middle East and attracted some of the most famous names, both regional and worldwide, in the jewellery industry.

BOAT SHOW

The Middle East International Boat Show MEIBS '99 took place at the Dubai International Marine Club from 17 to 20 March, focusing attention once more on the region's marine companies. In addition to the strong local presence, international participation included members of the marine industry from Italy, UK, Holland, Australia, Korea, Turkey and India.

CABSAT '99

The Fifth Middle East International Cable, Satellite and Broadcast Exhibition CABSAT '99, took place during March 1999 at the Dubai World Trade Centre. It featured the latest in antennae, cable installation equipment, connectors, decoders, digital audio equipment, down converters, feedhorns, LNBs, receivers, signal generators, telecom and test equipment, Pay-TV billing systems, digital compression systems and satellite service providers.

ENVIRONMENT 2001

The Environment 2001 Exhibition and Conference is scheduled to take place between 4–8 February 2001 in Abu Dhabi, coinciding with the fourth UAE National Environment Day. The event will provide a fitting opportunity for announcement of the winner of the Zayed Environment Prize and to highlight the UAE's leading role in environmental protection. The conference is being sponsored by the United Nations Environment Programme (UNEP), the United Nations Development Programme (UNDP) and the International Maritime Organisation (IMO).

ADIF '99

Abu Dhabi's largest general trade event, the Abu Dhabi International Fair ADIF '99, attracted over 600 companies from 30 countries. The exhibit profile was varied and comprehensive, spreading over an area of 16,000 square metres and offering visitors everything from toys, cosmetics, jewellery, electronics and home appliances, to foodstuff, automobiles and real estate. In the industrial sector products and services were featured relating to oil field supplies, storage tanks, construction equipment and tools.

DUBAI SHOPPING FESTIVAL

Justifying its claim as the UAE's biggest tourist attraction, the Dubai Shopping Festival attracted a record 2.4 million visitors and recorded sales of Dh 4.15 billion. The average daily spend in the retail sector during the 28-day-long Dubai Shopping Festival was Dh 141 million – a 14 per cent increase over the previous year. In addition a total of Dh 200 million was spent by shoppers on eating out and local transport. An independent study commissioned by the Government of Dubai showed that during the festival, from 18 March to 14 April, the daily visitor count went up by 18 per cent to 86,000 as compared with 73,000 in the previous year. The study recorded a dramatic increase in the number of foreign guests staying at hotels and furnished apartments in Dubai. The daily average number of foreign visitors from outside the UAE was 21,800. The average group size of foreign visitors increased from a little over three in 1998 to more than five in 1999; an indication that this year's festival attracted more families than single travellers and reflected the festival's family theme.

   Dubai Shopping Festival 2000, which will take place during the entire month of March, is likely to be an even greater success. The Dubai Shopping Festival, first launched in February 1996, is an emirate-wide shopping, entertainment, sporting and cultural extravaganza and is a joint effort by the public and private sectors.

DUBAI SUMMER SURPRISES

The 85-day Dubai Summer Surprises (DSS) provided a series of attractions for visitors to the emirate during the hot summer months. The DSS theme slogan 'Big Fun For Little Ones', was reflected by many of the events held to mark the 12-week period. The main function of DSS is to promote Dubai as an ideal holiday destination for families in the AGCC and the Middle East region. It is geared towards revitalising the trade and tourism sectors during summer, drawing visitors to hotels, shopping malls, entertainment centres and other climate-controlled facilities which offer families a fun-filled and cost-effective summer getaway.

ARABIAN TRAVEL MARKET

The Seventh Arabian Travel Market ATM '99 travel and tourism exhibition was held at the Dubai World Trade Centre. Attended by exhibitors from over 42 countries. The 1999 show was the biggest so far, with over 1,700 travel buyers pre-registered for the show, marking a rise of 40 per cent over 1998.

DUBAI 2000 AIRSHOW

The Dubai 2000 Airshow and Aerospace Exhibition held from 14 to 18 November 1999, took place at a Dh 300 million new purpose-built site occupying an area of 52,000 square metres, making it the world's second largest venue for such events. The show had previously been ranked the third most important in the world after Farnborough in the UK and Le Bourget in France, but has now surpassed the French exhibition. It is also the only air show with its own purpose-built site and exhibition halls. The total area, including an apron, was 30 per cent larger than the area devoted to the 1997 show.

The exhibition centre is interlinked with the main Dubai International Airport runway by a dedicated taxiway, providing exhibitors with the opportunity to transport their products directly off the plane and into the halls, saving both time and money. When not in use for the biennial airshow the exhibition centre will host the Dubai International Aerospace Exhibition, airport and aviation-related shows and other major trade exhibitions.

ABU DHABI BOOK FAIR

The opening of the Ninth Abu Dhabi International Book Fair by Sheikh Nahyan bin Mubarak Al Nahyan, Minister of Higher Education and Scientific Research, was transmitted on the Internet. Over 155,000 Arabic and foreign titles were on display with 523 Arabic and foreign publishers taking part. In his opening speech Sheikh Nahyan said: 'Despite the invasion of the computer in our lives, books still remain a very special and unique educational and recreational tool.'

ABU DHABI SALES FESTIVAL

The capital's first shopping festival, staged by Abu Dhabi Chamber of Commerce and Industry to mark its thirtieth anniversary, was opened by Saeed bin Jabr Al Suweidi, First Vice-President of the Chamber. The festival hoped to invigorate trade and tourism by offering significant discounts on all products. Discounts were on items related to a specific theme each week, beginning with gold, textiles and clothing, followed by food and beverages and electronics and household items. International artistes, musicians, jugglers, dancers and clowns entertained shoppers. Major attractions included a Dh 1 million raffle, draws for luxury cars and a 14-kilo gold raffle.

PEDIGREE DOG SHOW

A 19-month-old female white standard poodle, owned by Sheikha Hassa bint Mohammed Al Maktoum won the prize for Best in Show at the Dubai Pedigree Dog Show, an event that attracted 13,000 visitors. Other classes included pedigree puppies, won by a giant schnauzer, special yearling (border collie), hound (saluki), gun dog (American cocker-spaniel), working dog (rough collie), toy (bichan freise), terrier (West Highland white) and utility (standard poodle).

NATIONS IN BLOOM

Nations in Bloom '98, hosted by Al Ain city, attracted 18 communities, counties and cities from around the world in competition for the prestigious environmental awards. Sponsored by the United Nations Environment Programme (UNEP), the competition bestows awards to the top two cities in each of four categories, ranging from communities with populations of 10,000 people to those with more than 1 million. In 1997 Al Ain, known as the 'Garden City of the UAE', finished runner-up in the below-300,000 population category, narrowly losing out to Westminster, England. This year Al Ain did not compete since it was hosting the event, but Westminster again took a top prize. The award ceremony was held in a bedouin tent at the Al Ain Hilton Hotel.

GULF FOOD '99

The Seventh Gulf Food '99, Hotel and Equipment Exhibition, billed as the biggest show of its kind with more than 400 exhibitors from 37 countries, was held at the Dubai World Trade Centre. The event attracted some of the top names in the industry. A wide variety of environmentally-friendly products, a range of state-of-the-art catering products, the latest advances in hotel and catering equipment, a comprehensive range of bakery products, as well as food and beverages were on show. Dubai's growth as a centre for tourism in the region has also increased the importance of the exhibition for the booming hotel and restaurant industry.

ADITEX '99

At least 200 companies participated in the Abu Dhabi Information Technology Exhibition, ADITEX '99. Exhibitors included regional and overseas companies displaying a wide range of IT and telecommunications products. The show, which was held at the Cultural Foundation, comprised a number of elements including Abu Dhabi Information Technology '99, Abu Dhabi Computer Shopper '99 and Abu Dhabi Mobile Phone '99.

GITEX

What is now undoubtedly the largest IT exhibition in the Middle East, GITEX '99, which was held at the Dubai World Trade Centre, set new records in the number of visitors, new business partnerships, product launches and the number and quality of conferences and seminars. More than 60,000 visitors attended from 92 countries and more than 76,000 visited the adjacent Computer Shopper exhibition. The 450 exhibitors from 32 countries enjoyed an exceptional increase in business during the show.

GULF EDUCATION AND TRAINING EXHIBITION

More than 200 institutions from some 25 countries in Europe, North America, Asia, Africa and Australia as well as the Gulf exhibited at the Eleventh Gulf Education and Training Exhibition held at the Dubai World Trade Centre from 13 to 16 April 1999. In addition to schools and universities a wide selection of language tuition, distance learning, technical training and specialised courses for specific industries were represented. This exhibition is a useful forum for the exchange of educational information, not just in the UAE, but throughout the entire Gulf region. It brings together a wide range of specialists and enables individuals and organisations to obtain the necessary information required to make informed choices.

WORLD BANK CONFERENCE

The UAE has been chosen by the World Bank to host the annual conference in 2003 of the Bank and the International Monetary Fund (IMF). The high profile international conference will be attended by 180 member countries of the World Bank and the IMF. The role being played by the UAE at the international level, and the country's efforts to bring relief to the people of Kosovo, in addition to its generous assistance to poor countries of the world were reported to have contributed to the selection of the UAE as the venue for the 2003 conference.

EXHIBITIONS CALENDAR

DUBAI
1999

January 31–February 3
7th GULF FOOD, HOTEL AND EQUIPMENT
Food and beverage, hotel and catering equipment.
Dubai World Trade Centre (LLC)

February 7–10
PRINTING AND PACKING TECHNOLOGY
Goods and services in the printing and packaging industries.
Fairs and Exhibitions

February 8–10
SIGNS AND BANNERS Middle East
Products and services for the sign and banner industry.
International Expo-Consults (ME)

February 8–10
INTERSEC
The International Commercial Security, Fire and Safety Exhibition.
Channels

February 11–14
DUBAI DESERT CLASSIC
Dubai Creek Golf and Yacht Club

February 15–18
ARABLAB
Laboratory technology instrumentation equipment and services.
International Conferences and Exhibitions

February 22–25
ASIAN TIGERS
Products and services from seven Asian nations.
Intergulf Fairs and Exhibitions

February 28–March 5
ALGERIAN PRODUCTS FAIR
An exhibition of Algerian products and services.
Societe Algerienne des Foires et Exportations

March 2–4
Middle East International CABLE, SATELLITE AND BROADCAST
Cable, satellite, broadcasting and communication equipment.
Dubai World Trade Centre (LLC)

March 2–4
MIDDLE EAST TELECOMS
Communications, Internet, Satellite and Mobile Telecommunications.
Dubai World Trade Centre (LLC)

March 9–11
MIDDLE EAST INTER-NATIONAL LEISURE EXPO (MILE)
International exhibition on sporting goods, sportswear, fitness equipment, nutrition and leisure products and services, including garden furniture and camping, saunas, spas and pools, etc.
Infocenter International

March 9–11
THE MIDDLE EAST TOY FAIR incorporating CHILDREN'S FESTIVAL
Toys, games, hobbies, Books, gifts, stationery, apparel, licensing.
Infocenter International

March 14–18
INTERNATIONAL SPRING TRADE FAIR
General trade fair.
Al Fajer Information and Services

March 17–20
MIDDLE INTERNATIONAL BOAT SHOW
Watersports equipment and boats.
Venue : Dubai International Marine Club
Dubai Rai

March 21–23
WATER CONSERVATION EXHIBITION '99
An exhibition of products, services and achievements related to water conservation.
Dubai Electricity and Water Authority

March 23–25
THEME PARKS and FUN CENTRES SHOW
International exhibition on technology, products and services for theme/leisure parks, family fun centres, electronic games, etc.
International Expo-Consults (ME)

April 11–13
HOUSE OF TALENTS
Women's handicrafts exhibition.
Dubai Shopping Festival

April 6–10
INTERNATIONAL JEWELLERY
Jewellery, luxury gifts, watches and gems.
Dubai World Trade Centre

April 13–16
GULF EDUCATION AND
TRAINING
International student
recruitment show.
International Conferences and
Exhibitions

April 20–23
AGRI BUSINESS and
GARDENS
Goods and services related to
the agricultural industry.
Mediac Communications and
Promotion

April 21–24
MOTEXHA/CHILDEXPO/
LEATHER SHOW
Trade fair for fashion and
accessories, children's wear and
care.
IIR Exhibitions
ARABIAN TRAVEL
MARKET
Inbound and outbound travel
and tourism for the Middle
East region.
Reed Exhibitions

June 26–September 9
SUMMER CAMP
Polar Sports Event
Management

June 28–29
JOB FAIR
Career opportunities for
nationals within the emirates
industry.
Emirates Airlines

July 1–7
CUISINE OF THE WORLD
Dubai Shopping Festival

September 20–23
INTERNATIONAL
PREMIUM EXHIBITION
Corporate gifts, premiums,
incentives and stationery.
Channels

September 22–25
MOTEXHA
Trade fair for fashion, textiles,
clothing and footwear.
IIR Exhibitions

September 22–25
AMBIENTE ARABIA
Gift items and luxury goods in
the Arab world.
IIR Exhibitions

September 22–25
THE LEATHER SHOW
Leather fashion wear,
accessories and gift items.
IIR Exhibitions

September 22–25
GULF TEX-STYLES
Equipment, raw materials,
processes, accessories for
textile/clothing manufacturing.
IIR Exhibitions

September 28–30
GULF BEAUTY
The 4th International Trade
Fair for perfumes, cosmetics
and body care.
Channels

**September 28–October
1**
ARAB HUNTING
Hunting equipment and
accessories.
Mediac Communications and
Promotion

October 6–10
INDEX
The 9th Middle East
International. Furniture and
Interior Design Exhibition.
DMG Index Exhibitions Ltd

October 6–10
ARABSHOP
The 6th International
Shopfitting, Retail and Display
Exhibition.
DMG Index Exhibitions Ltd

October 16–19
ARAB OIL AND GAS
The showpiece for the oil and
gas industry in the Arab world.
International Conferences and
Exhibitions

October 17–21
BIG 5
Water, building, refrigeration
and air conditioning, glass and
metal, cleaning and
maintenance and construction.
International Conferences and
Exhibitions

October 30–November 3
GITEX
For suppliers and users of
computers, communications,
electronic office systems and
services.
Dubai World Trade Centre
(LLC)

October 30–November 3
COMPUTER SHOPPER
Retail showcase for GITEX
specialising in home computer
equipment.
Dubai World Trade Centre
(LLC)

November 10–14
ME INTERNATIONAL
MOTOR SHOW
Exhibition for the motor trade
in the Arabian Gulf.
Dubai World Trade Centre
(CLLC)

November 21–25
INTERNATIONAL
AUTUMN TRADE FAIR
General trade fair.
Al Fajer Information and
Services

November 23–26
PHOTOVISION
Photographic, audio-visual and
imaging industries.
Dubai Rai

November 24–28
WOMAN
Exhibition for women
consumers.
Channels

**November
30–December 3**
ARAB INTERNATIONAL
EQUINE EXHIBITION (AL
FARES)
Exhibition of equine related
services and products.
Al Fajer Information and
Services

DUBAI
2000

Although the information in this exhibition calendar is correct at the time of going to press, details may be altered at any time without liability on the part of Dubai World Trade Centre (LLC) or the publishers. You are advised to check details of the exhibition with the relevant organiser.

January 24–26
INTERSEC
The International Commercial Security, Fire and Safety Exhibition.
Channels

January 25–27
SIGNS AND BANNERS
Middle East
International exhibition of equipment, products and services for the visual communication market, external long terms, large format, fixed communications and screen printing.
International Expo-Consults (ME)

February 1–4
TURKISH EXHIBITION
An exhibition of Turkish products, services and technology.
Ladin

February 6–9
HARDWARE, TOOLS and HOUSEWARES
An exhibition of hardware, tools, DIY products and household goods.
EPOC International

February 6–9
MIDDLE EAST ELECTRICITY
The 25th Middle East Premier Power Generation and Electrotechnical

Exhibition
IIR Exhibitions

February 10–13
OPTICAL
Ophthalmic and optical equipment.
Dubai World Trade Centre (LLC)

February 20–23
FREEZEX
World of Free Zone Exhibition and Conference.
Al Fajer Information and Services

February 20–23
MIDDLE EAST COATINGS
Incorporating industrial and marine coatings protection, raw materials, chemicals and equipment for paint and printing ink manufacture.
FMJ International

February 22–24
ASIAN TIGERS
Products and services from 10 Asian nations.
Intergulf Fairs and Exhibitions

February 29–March 2
MIDDLE EAST TELECOMS
Communications, Internet, satellite and mobile tele-communication,
Dubai World Trade Centre (LLC)

February 29–March 2
ME INTERNATIONAL CABLE, SATELLITE and BROADCAST
Cable, satellite, broadcasting and communication equipment
Dubai World Trade Centre (LLC)

March 5–9
INTERNATIONAL SPRING TRADE FAIR
A general trade fair.
Al Fajer Information and Services

March 7–9
MIDDLE EAST TOY FAIR
Toys, games, hobbies, books, gifts, stationery, apparel, licensing.
Infocenter International

March 26–28
REHAB 2000
International exhibition and congress on rehabilitation of the Disabled.
Al Fajer Information and Services

March 28–30
MIDDLE EAST INTER-NATIONAL LEISURE EXPO (M.I.L.E.)
International exhibition on sporting goods, sportswear, fitness equipment, nutrition and leisure products and services, including garden furniture and camping, saunas, spas and pools, etc.
International Expo-Consults (ME)

March 28–30
THEME PARKS and FUN CENTRES
International exhibition on technology, products and services for theme/leisure parks, family fun centres, electronic games, etc.
International Expo-Consults (ME)

April 5–8
MOTEXHA SPRING
The 36th Leading Middle East International Fashion, Accessories and Leather Products Exhibition.
IIR Exhibitions

April 5–8
GULF TEX-STYLES
The 2nd Middle East Exhibition for the Garment and Textile Manufacturing Industry.
IIR Exhibitions

April 11–14
BRITAIN AND THE GULF
An exhibition of products and
services from Britain.
International Conferences and
Exhibitions

April 11–14
GULF EDUCATION and
TRAINING
International student
recruitment show.
International Conferences and
Exhibitions

April 25–28
ARAB AGRIBUSINESS
EXPO MIDDLE EAST 2000
Goods and services relating to
the agricultural and gardening
industry.
Mediac Communication and
Promotion

April 25–28
MIDDLE EAST BAKING and
CONFECTIONERY
TECHNOLOGY
EXHIBITION
Goods and services relating to
the baking industry.
Mediac Communication and
Promotion

May 2–5
ARABIAN TRAVEL
MARKET
Inbound and outbound travel
and tourism for the Middle
East region.
Reed Exhibitions

May 14–18
MILLENNIUM HOME
The consumer exhibition for
the home.
Channels

May 14–18
KITCHENS, BATHROOMS
and LIGHTING
The 3rd International Trade
Fair for the kitchens,
bathrooms and lighting
industries.
Channels

May 16–20
INTERNATIONAL
JEWELLERY
Jewellery, luxury gifts, watches
and gems.
Dubai World Trade Centre

September 17–20
TEKNO 7
An exhibition of industrial
machinery and machine tools.
Al Fajer Information and
Services

September 19–21
INTERNATIONAL
PREMIUM EXHIBITION
Corporate gifts, premiums,
incentives and stationery.
Channels

September 26–28
GULF BEAUTY
The 5th International Trade
Fair for perfumes, cosmetics
and body care.
Channels

September 26–28
TAX-FREE EXHIBITION
An exhibition of tax free
products and services.
Channels

September 26–29
MOTEXHA AUTUMN
incorporating MOTEXHA
SHOPPER,
MEN'S LIFESTYLE and
FASHION SHOWS
The 37th Leading Middle East
International Fashion,
Accessories and
Leather Products Exhibition.
IIR Exhibitions

September 26–29
AMBIENTE ARABIA
The 6th Middle East
International Gift Fair.
IIR Exhibitions

September 26–29
THE LEATHER SHOW
Leather fashion wear,
accessories and gift items.
IIR Exhibitions

September 26–29
ARAB HUNTING
An exhibition of hunting
equipment and accessories.
Mediac Communication and
Promotion

October 4–8
INDEX
The 10th Middle East
International Furniture and
Interior Design Exhibition.
DMG Index Exhibitions Ltd

October 4–8
ARABSHOP
The 7th International
Shopfitting, Retail and Display
Exhibition.
DMG Index Exhibitions Ltd

October 15–19
BIG 5
Water, building, refrigeration
and air conditioning, glass and
metal, cleaning and
maintenance and construction.
DMG Index Exhibitions Ltd

October 15–18
ITALY IN THE GULF
An exhibition of Italian
products and services.
IIR Exhibitions

October 16–19
MIDDLE EAST ELEVATORS
and ESCALATORS
TECHNOLOGY
EXHIBITION
Mediac Communication and
Promotion

October 28–November 1
GITEX
For suppliers and users of
computers and
communications.
Dubai World Trade Centre
(LLC)

October 28–November 1
COMPUTER SHOPPER
Retail showcase for GITEX
specialising in home computer
equipment.
Dubai World Trade Centre

November 7–9
PROPERTY and
INVESTMENT
An exhibition of investment,
property and insurance
Channels
November 15–19
WOMAN
The 9th international
exhibition for women
consumers.
Channels
November 19–22
AUTOSTOP
The 3rd Middle East dedicated
Garage Equipment, Refinishing
and Autoparts Exhibition.
IIR Exhibitions
November 19–23
INTERNATIONAL
AUTUMN TRADE FAIR
General trade fair
Al Fajer Information and
Services

ABU DHABI
1999–2000

Although the information in
this exhibition calendar is
correct at the time of going to
press, details may be altered at
any time without liability on
the part of exhibition organisers
or the publishers. You are
advised to check details of the
exhibition with the relevant
organiser.

March 4–18
INTERNATIONAL
DEFENCE EXHIBITION and
CONFERENCE (IDEX)
Abu Dhabi Chamber of
Commerce and Industry
April 6–11
CHINESE WEEK
Cultural Foundation

April 12–19
ADIF 99
The 5th Abu Dhabi
International Fair.
Abu Dhabi Chamber of
Commerce and Industry
April 13–20
The Painter Sadd Al Tai'.
Cultural Foundation
April 24–30
Exhibition of Seychelles Island.
Cultural Foundation
May 31–June 8
Exhibition of Venice
Renovation.
Cultural Foundation
June 15–August 10
SUMMER FESTIVAL '99
Al Ain Exhibitions
August 1–20
ACCESSION DAY
EXHIBITION
Cultural Foundation
September 25–30
ALGERIAN WEEK
Cultural Foundation
October 6–15
EGYPTIAN PRODUCTS
Abu Dhabi International
Exhibitions
November 1–7
MOROCCAN PRODUCTS
Abu Dhabi Chamber of
Commerce and Industry
November 1–5
ARAB JEWELLERY and
WATCH '99
Emirates Exhibition Services
**November
24–December 12**
SYRIAN PRODUCTS '99
Abu Dhabi Chamber Of
Commerce And Industry
December 1–5
Accomplishments Of HH
Sheikh Zayed Al Nahyan.
Abu Dhabi Chamber of
Commerce and Industry
March 5–9, 2000
TRIDEX 2000
Gen. Exhib.Corp.

Sharjah
1999–2000

May 12–16
GULF INTERIORS FAIR
Expo Centre Sharjah
September 1–7
KID EXPO
Expo Centre Sharjah
September 11–14
IMAGE-EXPO
Expo Centre Sharjah
September 18–21
SHOES and HANDBAGS
Expo Centre Sharjah
September 25–28
THAILAND
Expo Centre Sharjah
October 3–8
INTERNATIONAL FOOD
FAIR
Expo Centre Sharjah
October 2–24
MIDEAST WATCH and
JEWELLERY
Expo Centre Sharjah
November 2–13
SHARJAH WORLD BOOK
FAIR
Expo Centre Sharjah

Ras al-Khaimah
1999

May 27–June 11
SALE FAIR '99
Ras al-Khaimah Exhibition
Centre
October 7–17
AL SHAM PRODUCTS
EXHIBITION '99
Ras al-Khaimah Exhibition
Centre
November 2–October 3
RAK FAIR
Ras al-Khaimah Exhibition
Centre

FUJAIRAH
1999

February 25–March 6
SPRING FAIR
Fujairah Exhibition Centre
April 29–May 8
CONSUMER FAIR '99
Fujairah Exhibition Centre
October 7–12
AUTUMN FAIR '99
Fujairah Exhibition Centre
December 1–10
FUJAIRAH EXHIBITION
Fujairah Exhibition Centre

Exhibition Organisers:

DUBAI WORLD TRADE CENTRE (LLC)
Tel: 971 4 308 6043
Fax: 971 4 318 034

FAIRS AND EXHIBITIONS.
Tel: 00 44 171 935 8537
Fax: 00 44 171 935 8161
Dubai Tel: 9714 822 855
Fax: 9714 822 866

INTERNATIONAL EXPO-CONSULTS (ME)
Tel: 971 4 354 960
Fax: 971 4 354 964

CHANNELS
Tel: 971 4 824 737
Fax: 971 4 825 757

INTERNATIONAL CONFERENCES AND EXHIBITIONS
Tel: 44 1442 878 222
Fax: 44 1442 879 998
Dubai Tel: 971 4 460 503
Dubai Fax: 971 4 460 498

INTERGULF FAIRS AND EXHIBITIONS
Tel: 971 4 282 355
Fax: 971 4 228 311

SOCIETE ALGERIENNE DES FOIRES ET EXPORTATIONS
Tel: +231 2 210 123/30
Fax: +231 2 210 630

INFOCENTER INTERNATIONAL
Tel: 971 4 310 551
Fax: 971 4 310 096

AL FAJER INFORMATION AND SERVICES
Tel: 971 4 377 727
Fax: 971 4 378 788

Dubai Rai
Tel: 971 4 362 900
Fax: 971 4 362 988

DUBAI ELECTRICITY AND WATER AUTHORITY
Tel: 971 4 324 8299
Fax: 971 4 324 4922

DUBAI SHOPPING FESTIVAL
Tel: 9714 235 444
Fax: 9714 234 888

MEDIAC COMMUNICATIONS AND PROMOTION
Tel: 971 4 692 004
Fax: 971 4 691 296

IIR EXHIBITIONS
Tel: 9714 365 161
Fax: 9714 364 006

REED EXHIBITIONS
Tel: 44 181 910 7958
Fax: 44 181 910 7733

POLAR SPORTS EVENT MANAGEMENT
Tel: 9714 3439693
Fax: 9714 3435792

EMIRATES AIRLINES
Tel: 971 4 295 1111
Fax: 971 4 295 0669

DMG INDEX EXHIBITIONS LTD
Tel: 971 4 319 688
Fax: 971 4 319 480

LADIN
Tel: +90 312 479 79 20
Fax: +90 312 479 79 25

EPOC INTERNATIONAL
Tel: +971 4 380 1021
Fax: +971 4 380 041

FMJ INTERNATIONAL
Tel: +44 1737 768 611
Fax: +44 1737 760 510

INDEX

PHOTO ACKNOWLEDGEMENTS

The following list indicates page numbers on which pictures occur, photographer and copyright.

4: Al Maqta Bridge. (J & H. Eriksen; Trident Press)

6: HH Sheikh Zayed. (UAE Government)

24-25: City of Abu Dhabi. (R.Westphal; Trident Press)

27: Oasis in the Liwa area. (R.Westphal; Trident Press)

28-29: City of Dubai. (R.Westphal; Trident Press)

34: Hili tomb. (A. Smailes; Trident Press)

35: Greyware pot. (A. Woolfitt; Trident Press)

37: Gold pendant, 1800-1500BC, from Qattarah. (A. Woolfitt; Trident Press)

39: Pearling dhow. (Ronald Codrai)

42: Archaeologists dig at Tell Abraq. (Jens & Hanne Eriksen; Trident Press)

45: Stone pendant found at Tell Abraq. (Jens & Hanne Eriksen; Trident Press)

49: Sir Wilfred Thesiger with Bin Kabina, one of his companions during desert travels half a century ago, at an exhibition of his historic photographs. (Gulf News)

50: Camel (A. Woolfitt; Trident Press)

53: A large collection of natural pearls. (A. Smailes; Trident Press)

55: Falconer with falcon.(Editiones Gaia)

56: Traditional building in Bur Dubai(A. Woolfitt; Trident Press)

60: Sheikh Zayed chairs a Supreme Council meeting (WAM, UAE Government)

71 upper: Arab leaders with President Nelson Mandela and Kofi Annan at the AGCC Summit Meeting held in December 1998. (WAM, UAE Government)

71 lower: Sheikh Zayed with Egyptian President Hosni Mubarak
and Jordan's King Abdullah.   (WAM, UAE Government)

78: UAE Aid to Kosovo. (WAM, UAE Government)

83: UAE Mission visits Kukes Refugee Camp. (WAM, UAE Government)

84: At the field hospital in Kukes Refugee Camp.   (WAM, UAE Government)

90–91: City of Abu Dhabi from the new corniche. (R.Westphal; Trident Press)

98–99: City of Sharjah. (R.Westphal; Trident Press)

102-103: City of Umm al-Qaiwain. (R.Westphal; Trident Press)

106: Illegal videotapes confiscated by the Ministry of Information and Culture. (Gulf News)

108–109: City of Ajman. (R.Westphal; Trident Press)

112–113: City of Ras al-Khaimah. (R.Westphal; Trident Press)

115: Commercial banking. (R. Westphal; Central Bank)

118: On an offshore oil rig. (Jens & Hanne Eriksen; Trident Press)

120-121: Part of the Umm Shaif offshore complex. (Jens & Hanne Eriksen; Trident Press)

125: Scene at offshore oil and gas platform. (Jens & Hanne Eriksen; Trident Press)

129: Recording aluminium ingots at DUBAL. (A. Woolfitt; Trident Press)

132–133: Construction work in the UAE (Gulf News)

140–141: City of Fujairah. (R.Westphal; Trident Press)

146–147: Desert agriculture in Abu Dhabi. (R.Westphal; Trident Press)

149: Date palm tissue culture. (WAM, UAE Government)

153: East coast fishing village. (P.Vine, Trident Press)

157: Emirates Golf Club in Dubai. (A. Woolfitt; Trident Press)

159 upper: Beach-like swimming area at Wild Wadi. (Gulf News)

159 lower: Regatta race off Dubai International Marina Club. (Gulf News)

160–161: Khor Fakkan city and coastline. (R.Westphal; Trident Press)

165: Recent housing scheme in the Liwa area. (R.Westphal; Trident Press)

166–167: City of Al Ain. (R.Westphal; Trident Press)

169: Abu Dhabi main street. (R.Westphal; Trident Press)

171: Abu Dhabi corniche area, seen from the sea. (R.Westphal; Trident Press)

175: Sunset scene at Abu Dhabi International Airport. (A. Smailes, Trident Press)

179: Mina Zayed quay and warehouses from the air. (R.Westphal; Trident Press)

182-183: Khor Fakkan and bay. (R.Westphal; Trident Press)

189: Wadi leading to UAE town in eastern mountains. (P. Vine, Trident Press)

193: Satellite communications dish. (A. Woolfitt; Trident Press)

198: UAE student with electron microscope. (A. Woolfitt; Trident Press)

201: Dubai Dry docks. (C. Crowell, Trident Press)

207: Back to school. (Gulf News)

209: upper: Pupil at Al Worood School, Abu Dhabi. (A. Woolfitt; Trident Press)

209: lower: Female students in class. (Gulf News)

213: Father with new born child at hospital in Al Ain. (A. Woolfitt; Trident Press)

217: Health care. (upper: A. Woolfitt; lower: A. Smailes; both Trident Press)

223: Mother and new baby. (Gulf News)

227: Women attending Abu Dhabi Womens Conference. (Gulf News)

231: Fine books for preservation. (R.Westphal; Trident Press)

233: Museum conservation work. (A. Smailes; Trident Press)

234: Traditional sword dance. (A. Woolfitt; Trident Press)

237: Students in multimedia class-work. (Gulf News)

241: Arabian oryx on Sîr Banî Yâs. (Jens & Hanne Eriksen; Trident Press)

242-243: Flamingos at Sîr Banî Yâs. (Jens & Hanne Eriksen; Trident Press)

245: Arabian tahr on Sîr Banî Yâs. (Jens & Hanne Eriksen; Trident Press)

247: Scimitar-horned oryx on Sîr Banî Yâs. (Jens & Hanne Eriksen; Trident Press)

248: Desert sand fox at Arabian Peninsula Zoo, Sharjah. (Jens & Hanne Eriksen; Trident Press)

249 upper: Chameleon at Arabian Peninsula Zoo. (Jens & Hanne Eriksen; Trident Press)

249 lower: Hedgehog at Arabian Peninsula Zoo. (Jens & Hanne Eriksen; Trident Press)

251: Giraffe parents with young giraffe, at Sîr Banî Yâs. (Jens & Hanne Eriksen; Trident Press)

255: Arabian leopard at Arabian Peninsula Zoo, Sharjah. (Jens & Hanne Eriksen; Trident Press)

256–257: A popular feeding station on Sîr Banî Yâs. (Jens & Hanne Eriksen; Trident Press)

259: Young ibex at Arabian Peninsula Zoo, Sharjah. (Jens & Hanne Eriksen; Trident Press)

262-263: Al Ain won the President's Football Cup. (Gulf News)

265: Rama the Cama, half camel, half llama, celebrating his first birthday. (Gulf News)

266: Gen. Sheikh Rashid bin Mohammed Al Maktoum at an Endurance Race. (Gulf News)

268: Celebrating Almutawakel's victory at Dubai World Cup '99. (Gulf News)

269: Alanudd winning at Abu Dhabi Equestrian Club. (Gulf News)

271: Traditional sailing boat race. (Gulf News)

273 upper: Traditional rowing boat race. (Gulf News)

273 lower: A German team boat in the Dubai Regatta Match Race '99. (Gulf News)

274: Winner of the wooden powerboat race, at the Abu Dhabi Corniche. (Gulf News)

275: World-famous Victory Team members, Saeed Al Tayer and Felix Seralles. (Gulf News)

277 upper: Winner of the Dubai Desert Classic, David Howell, receives the trophy from Sheikh Ahmed bin Saeed Al Maktoum. (Gulf News)

277 lower: Mohammed bin Sulayem and co-driver Ronan Morgan, after winning the UAE International Rally in Abu Dhabi. (Gulf News)

279: Mohammed Khalifa Al Qubeisa, 1998 World Champion in ten-pin bowling. (Gulf News)

280: upper: Start of race in GCC Cross-Country Championship. (Gulf News)

280: lower: Terry Fox Run. (Gulf News)

281 upper: Yahya Saleh won the UAE Junior National Chess Championship. (Gulf News)

281 lower: Members of UAE's team for the 9th Arab Games return to a hero's welcome after winning 34 medals. (Gulf News)

283: Match between Scotland and a combined team formed by Dubai and Sharjah. (Gulf News)

287 upper: Sheikh Abdullah bin Zayed Al Nahyan, Minister of Information and Culture presents a plaque at the Arabian Travel Market

287 lower: Helicopter at Dubai airport. (Gulf News)

291 upper: Henna is applied at Dubai Shopping Festival. (A. Smailes; Trident Press)

291 lower: Festival time in Dubai. (Gulf News)